G.I. JOE

COBRA CIVIL WAR

COBRA

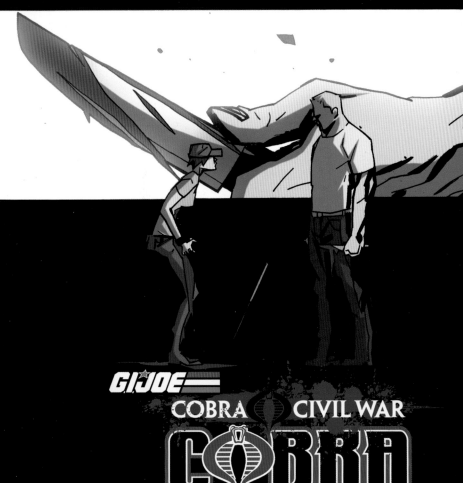

G.I.JOE

COBRA ⊙ CIVIL WAR

COBRA

Written by
Mike Costa

Art by
Werther Dell'Edera
and **Antonio Fuso**

Colors by
Arianna Florean
and **ScarletGothica**

Letters by
Shawn Lee
and **Neil Uyetake**

Original Series Edits by
Carlos Guzman
and **John Barber**

Cover by
David Williams

Cover Colors by
Kelsey Shannon

Collection Edits by
Justin Eisinger
and **Alonzo Simon**

Collection Design by
Neil Uyetake

Special thanks to Hasbro's Aaron Archer, Andy Schmidt, Derryl DePriest, Joe Del Regno, Ed Lane, Joe Furfaro, Jos Huxley, and Michael Kelly for their invaluable assistance.

IDW founded by Ted Adams, Alex Garner, Kris Oprisko, and Robbie Robbins | International Rights Representative, Christine Meyer: christine@gfloystudio.com

ISBN: 978-1-61377-179-2   15 14 13 12   1 2 3 4

Ted Adams, CEO & Publisher
Greg Goldstein, President & COO
Robbie Robbins, EVP/Sr. Graphic Artist
Chris Ryall, Chief Creative Officer/Editor-in-Chief
Matthew Ruzicka, CPA, Chief Financial Officer
Alan Payne, VP of Sales

Become our fan on Facebook **facebook.com/idwpublishing**
Follow us on Twitter **@idwpublishing**
Check us out on YouTube **youtube.com/idwpublishing**
www.IDWPUBLISHING.com

Originally published as G.I. JOE: COBRA: VOL. 2 Issues #5–8.

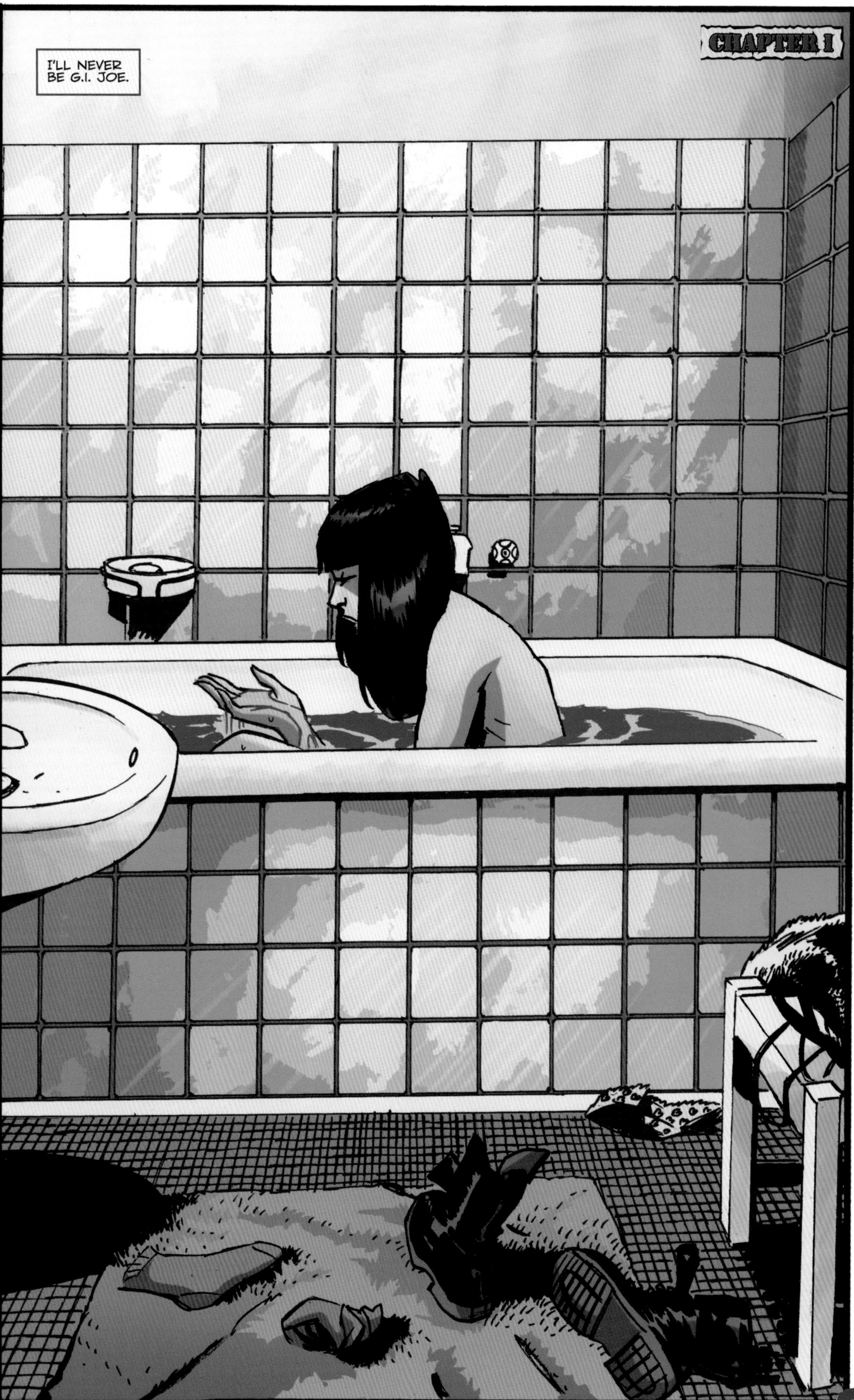
CHAPTER 1
I'LL NEVER BE G.I. JOE.

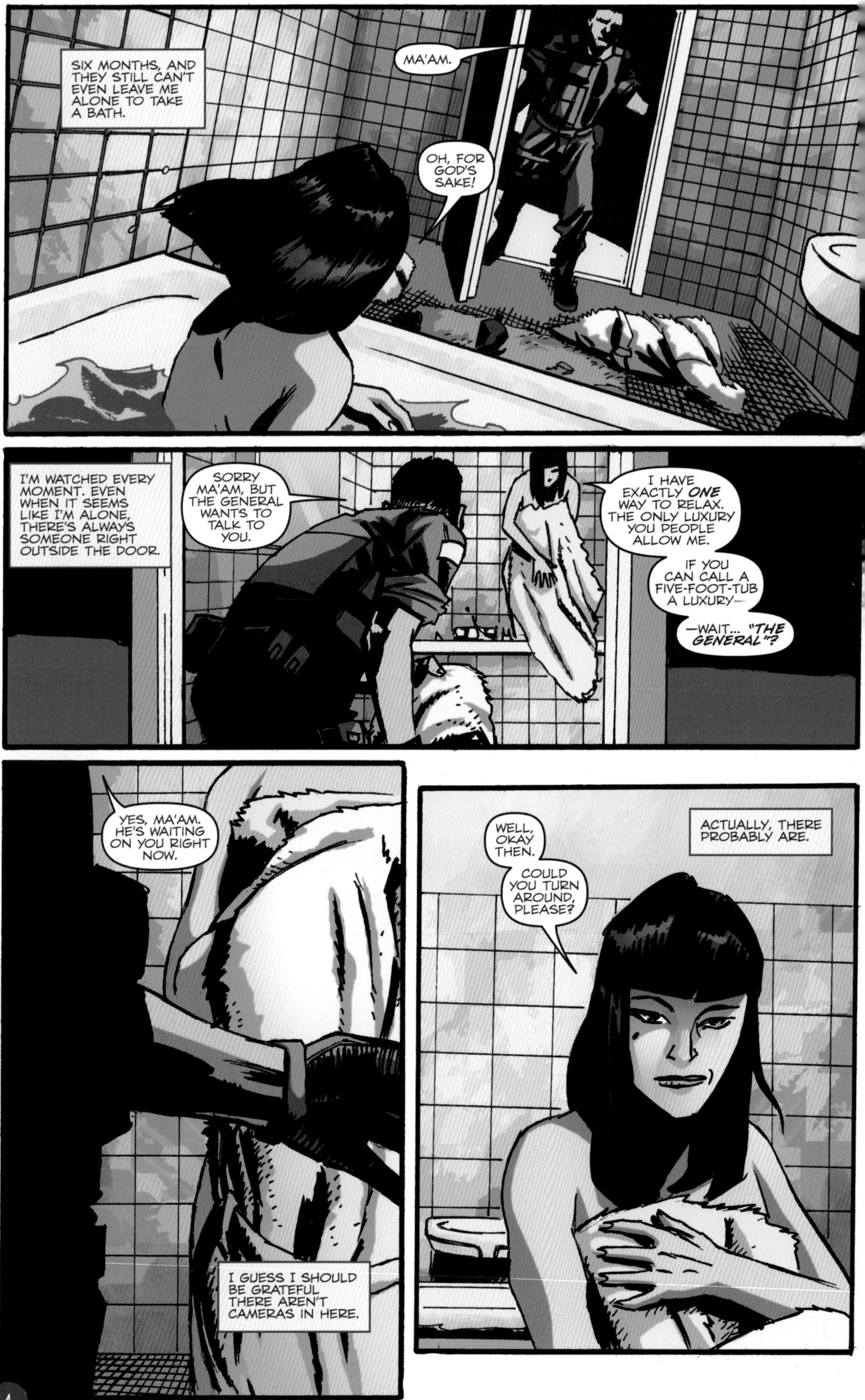
SIX MONTHS, AND THEY STILL CAN'T EVEN LEAVE ME ALONE TO TAKE A BATH.
MA'AM.
OH, FOR GOD'S SAKE!
I'M WATCHED EVERY MOMENT. EVEN WHEN IT SEEMS LIKE I'M ALONE, THERE'S ALWAYS SOMEONE RIGHT OUTSIDE THE DOOR.
SORRY MA'AM, BUT THE GENERAL WANTS TO TALK TO YOU.
I HAVE EXACTLY ONE WAY TO RELAX. THE ONLY LUXURY YOU PEOPLE ALLOW ME.
IF YOU CAN CALL A FIVE-FOOT-TUB A LUXURY—
—WAIT... "THE GENERAL"?
YES, MA'AM. HE'S WAITING ON YOU RIGHT NOW.
I GUESS I SHOULD BE GRATEFUL THERE AREN'T CAMERAS IN HERE.
WELL, OKAY THEN.
COULD YOU TURN AROUND, PLEASE?
ACTUALLY, THERE PROBABLY ARE.

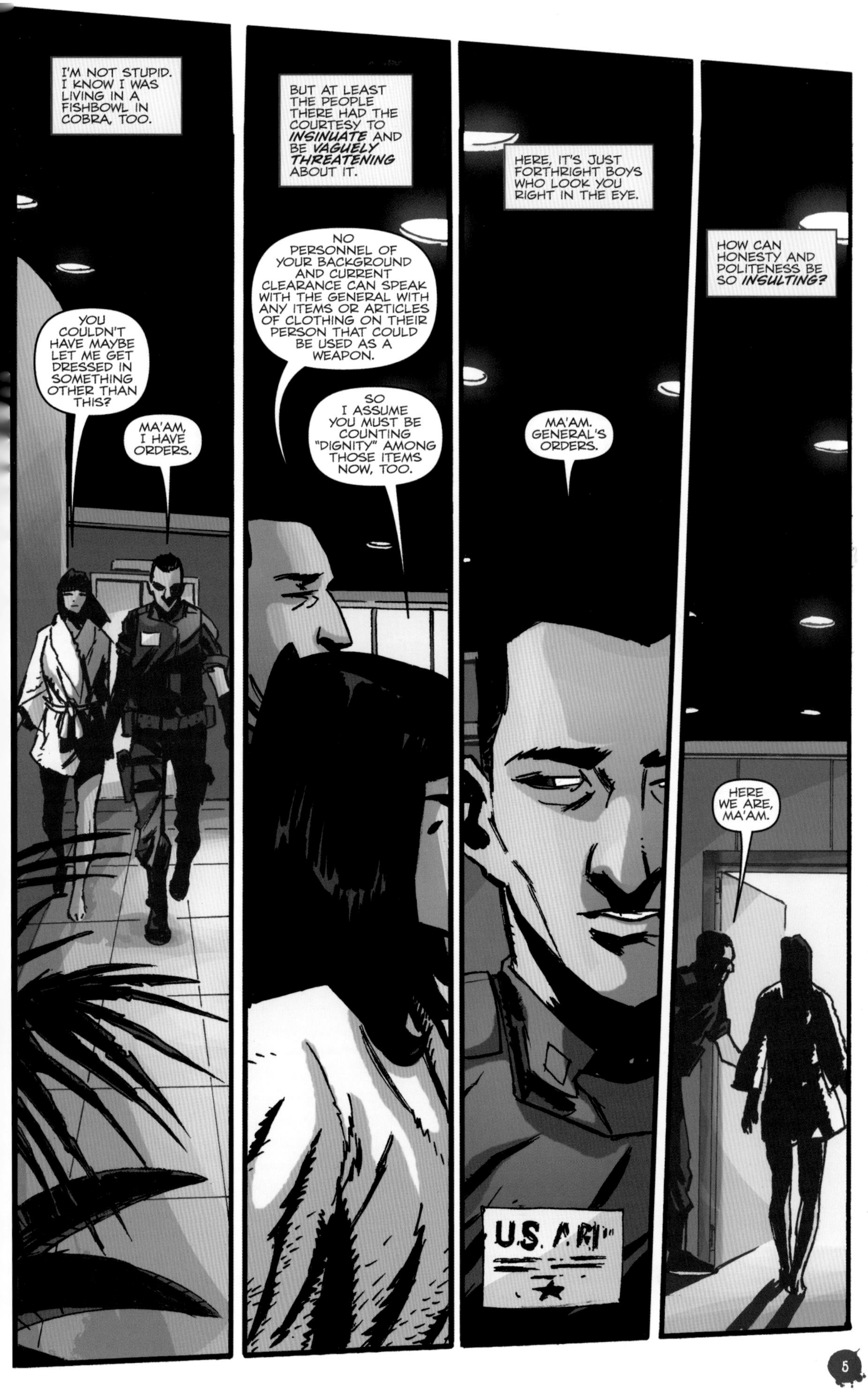
I'M NOT STUPID. I KNOW I WAS LIVING IN A FISHBOWL IN COBRA, TOO.
YOU COULDN'T HAVE MAYBE LET ME GET DRESSED IN SOMETHING OTHER THAN THIS?
MA'AM, I HAVE ORDERS.
BUT AT LEAST THE PEOPLE THERE HAD THE COURTESY TO INSINUATE AND BE VAGUELY THREATENING ABOUT IT.
NO PERSONNEL OF YOUR BACKGROUND AND CURRENT CLEARANCE CAN SPEAK WITH THE GENERAL WITH ANY ITEMS OR ARTICLES OF CLOTHING ON THEIR PERSON THAT COULD BE USED AS A WEAPON.
SO I ASSUME YOU MUST BE COUNTING "DIGNITY" AMONG THOSE ITEMS NOW, TOO.
HERE, IT'S JUST FORTHRIGHT BOYS WHO LOOK YOU RIGHT IN THE EYE.
MA'AM. GENERAL'S ORDERS.
HOW CAN HONESTY AND POLITENESS BE SO INSULTING?
HERE WE ARE, MA'AM.

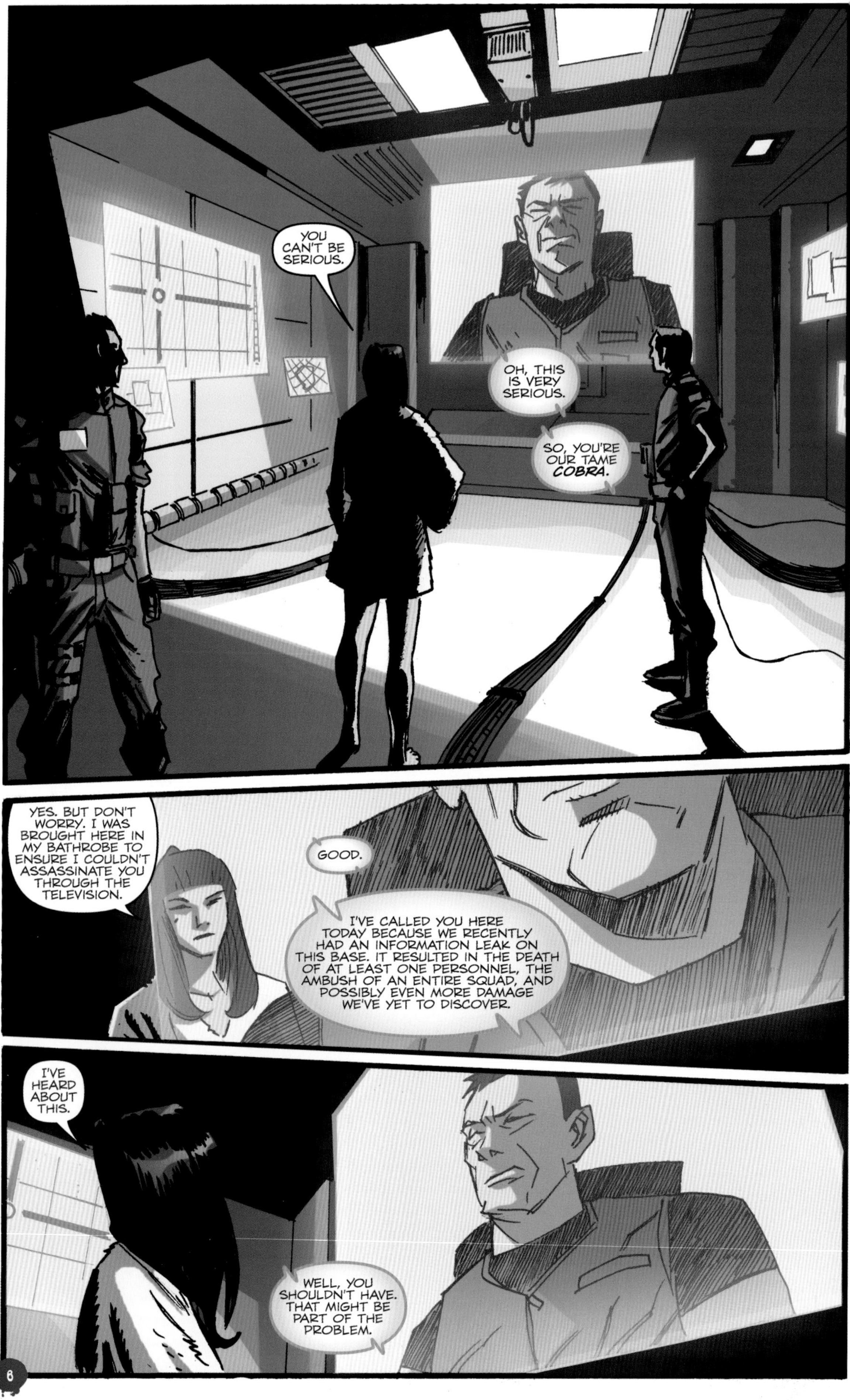

YOU CAN'T BE SERIOUS.
OH, THIS IS VERY SERIOUS.
SO, YOU'RE OUR TAME **COBRA**.
YES. BUT DON'T WORRY. I WAS BROUGHT HERE IN MY BATHROBE TO ENSURE I COULDN'T ASSASSINATE YOU THROUGH THE TELEVISION.
GOOD.
I'VE CALLED YOU HERE TODAY BECAUSE WE RECENTLY HAD AN INFORMATION LEAK ON THIS BASE. IT RESULTED IN THE DEATH OF AT LEAST ONE PERSONNEL, THE AMBUSH OF AN ENTIRE SQUAD, AND POSSIBLY EVEN MORE DAMAGE WE'VE YET TO DISCOVER.
I'VE HEARD ABOUT THIS.
WELL, YOU SHOULDN'T HAVE. THAT MIGHT BE PART OF THE PROBLEM.

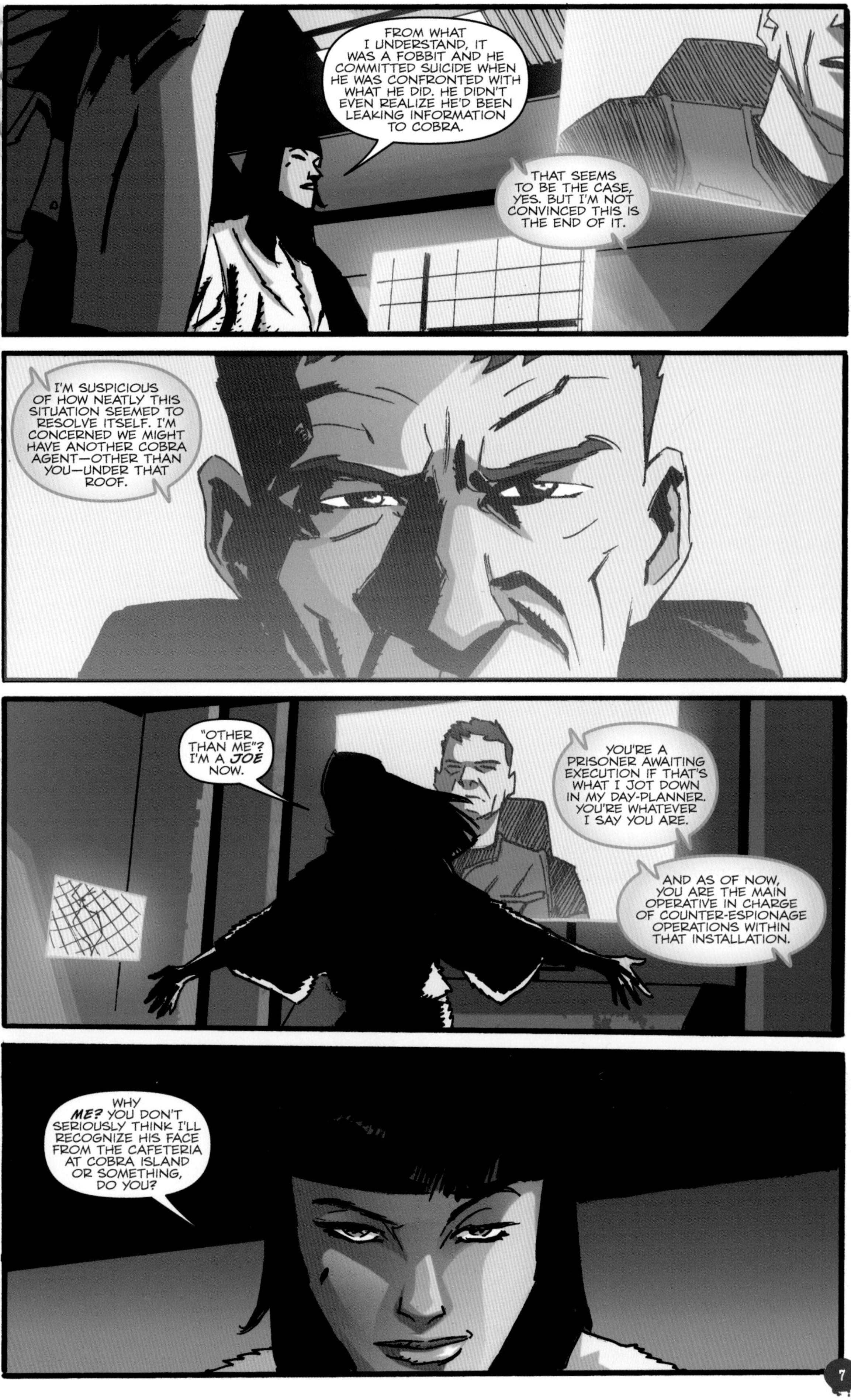
FROM WHAT I UNDERSTAND, IT WAS A FOBBIT AND HE COMMITTED SUICIDE WHEN HE WAS CONFRONTED WITH WHAT HE DID. HE DIDN'T EVEN REALIZE HE'D BEEN LEAKING INFORMATION TO COBRA.
THAT SEEMS TO BE THE CASE, YES. BUT I'M NOT CONVINCED THIS IS THE END OF IT.
I'M SUSPICIOUS OF HOW NEATLY THIS SITUATION SEEMED TO RESOLVE ITSELF. I'M CONCERNED WE MIGHT HAVE ANOTHER COBRA AGENT—OTHER THAN YOU—UNDER THAT ROOF.
"OTHER THAN ME"? I'M A *JOE* NOW.
YOU'RE A PRISONER AWAITING EXECUTION IF THAT'S WHAT I JOT DOWN IN MY DAY-PLANNER. YOU'RE WHATEVER I SAY YOU ARE.
AND AS OF NOW, YOU ARE THE MAIN OPERATIVE IN CHARGE OF COUNTER-ESPIONAGE OPERATIONS WITHIN THAT INSTALLATION.
WHY *ME?* YOU DON'T SERIOUSLY THINK I'LL RECOGNIZE HIS FACE FROM THE CAFETERIA AT COBRA ISLAND OR SOMETHING, DO YOU?

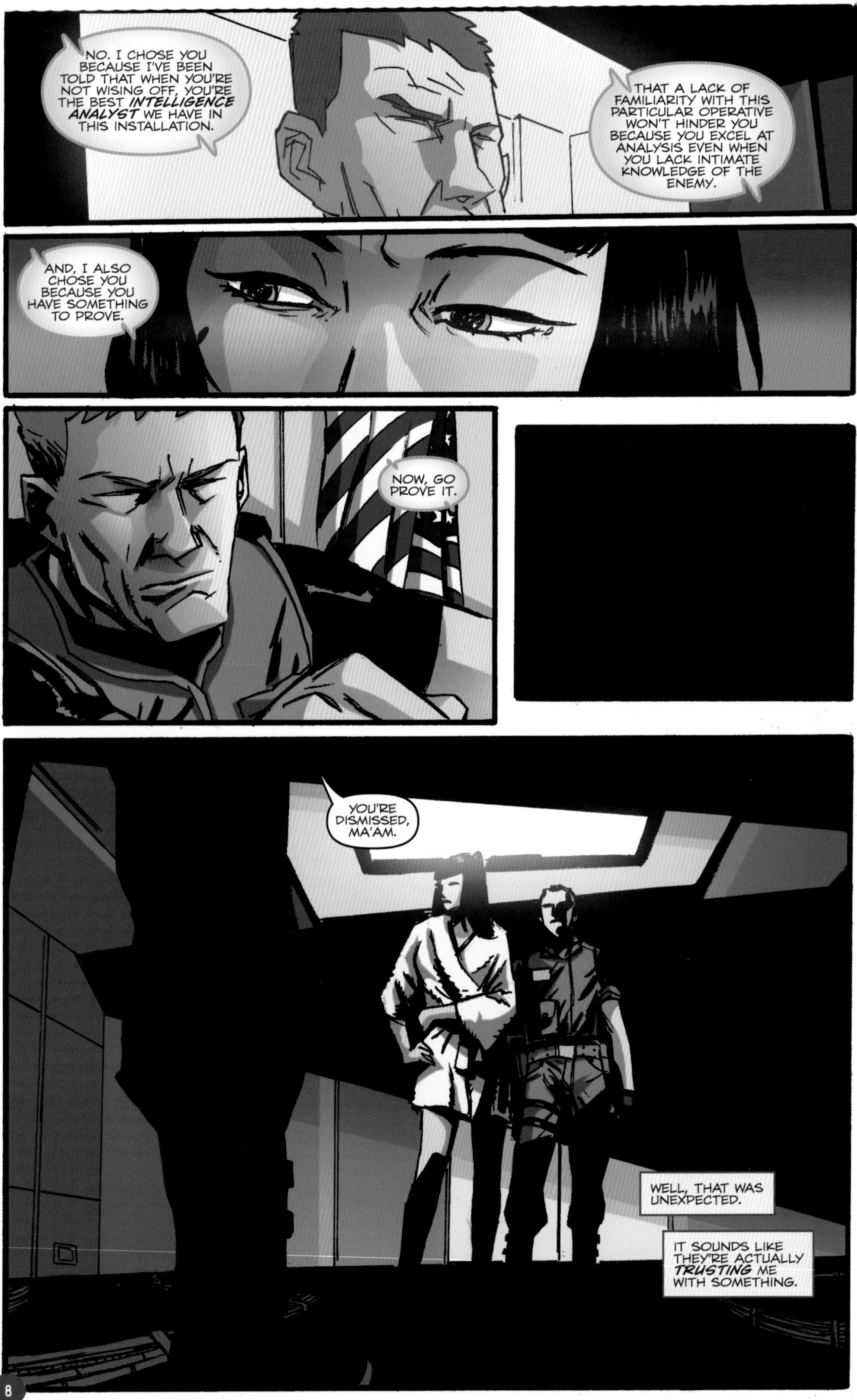
NO. I CHOSE YOU BECAUSE I'VE BEEN TOLD THAT WHEN YOU'RE NOT WISING OFF, YOU'RE THE BEST INTELLIGENCE ANALYST WE HAVE IN THIS INSTALLATION.
THAT A LACK OF FAMILIARITY WITH THIS PARTICULAR OPERATIVE WON'T HINDER YOU BECAUSE YOU EXCEL AT ANALYSIS EVEN WHEN YOU LACK INTIMATE KNOWLEDGE OF THE ENEMY.
AND, I ALSO CHOSE YOU BECAUSE YOU HAVE SOMETHING TO PROVE.
NOW, GO PROVE IT.
YOU'RE DISMISSED, MA'AM.
WELL, THAT WAS UNEXPECTED.
IT SOUNDS LIKE THEY'RE ACTUALLY TRUSTING ME WITH SOMETHING.

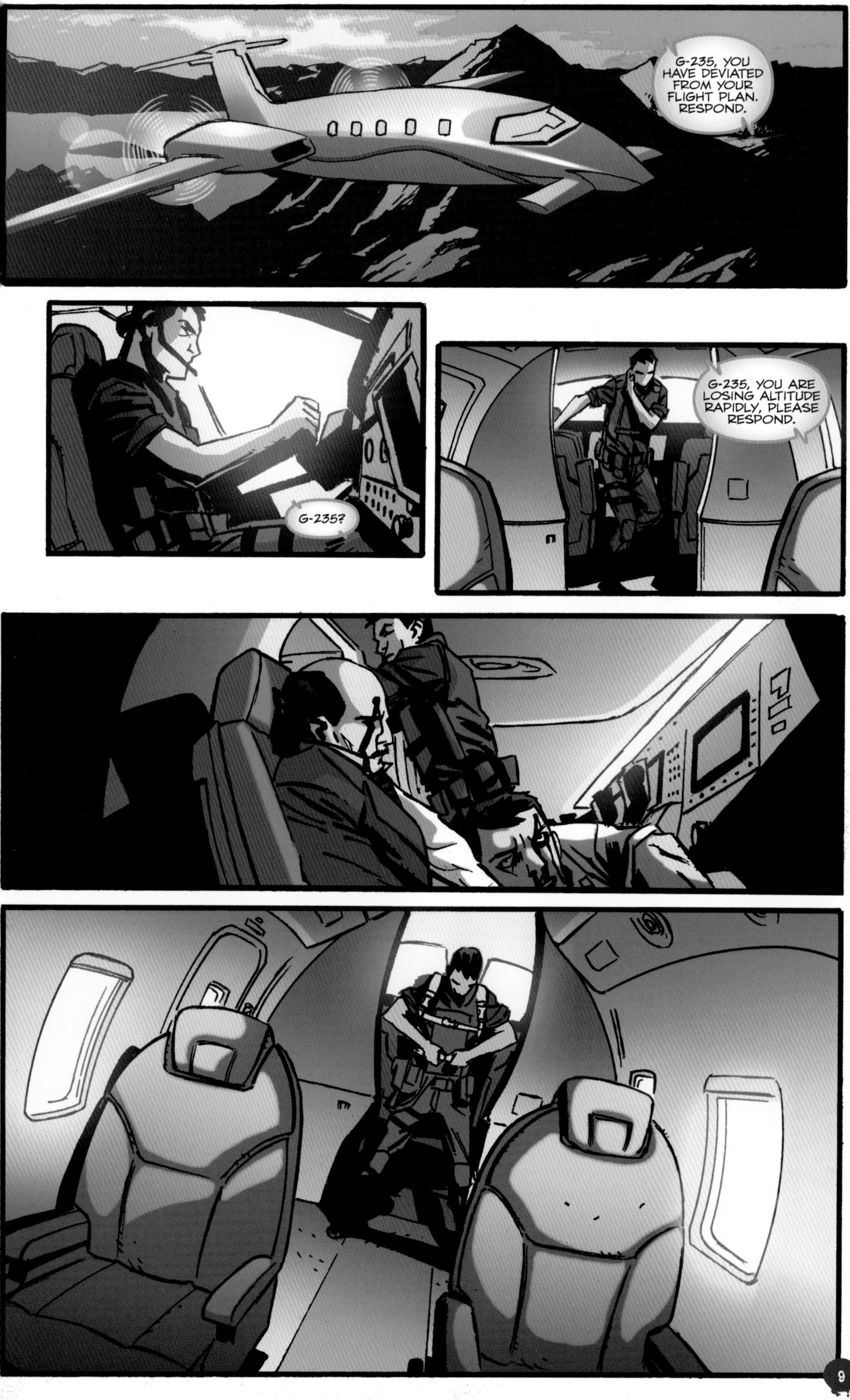
G-235, YOU HAVE DEVIATED FROM YOUR FLIGHT PLAN. RESPOND.
G-235?
G-235, YOU ARE LOSING ALTITUDE RAPIDLY, PLEASE RESPOND.

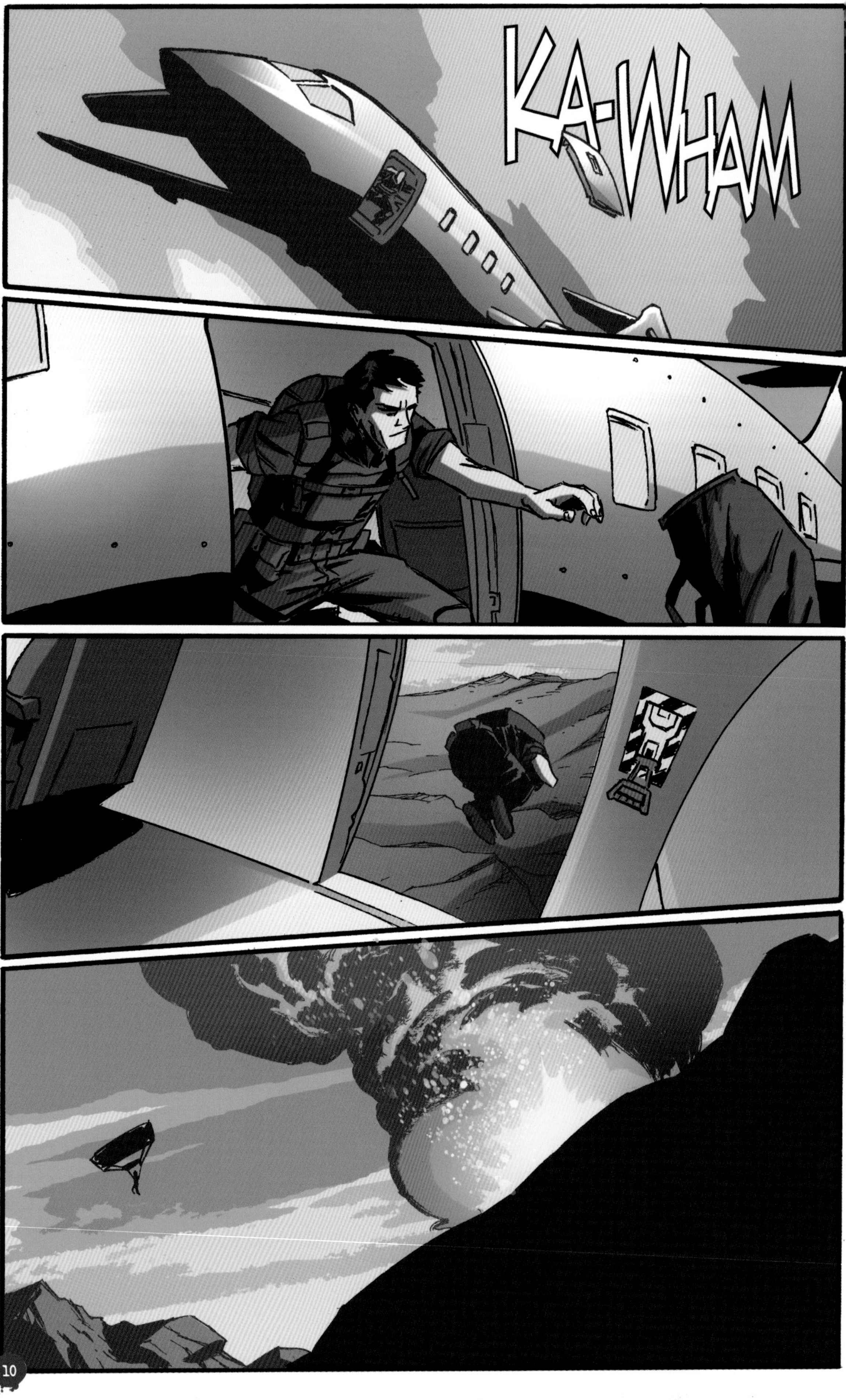
KA-WHAM

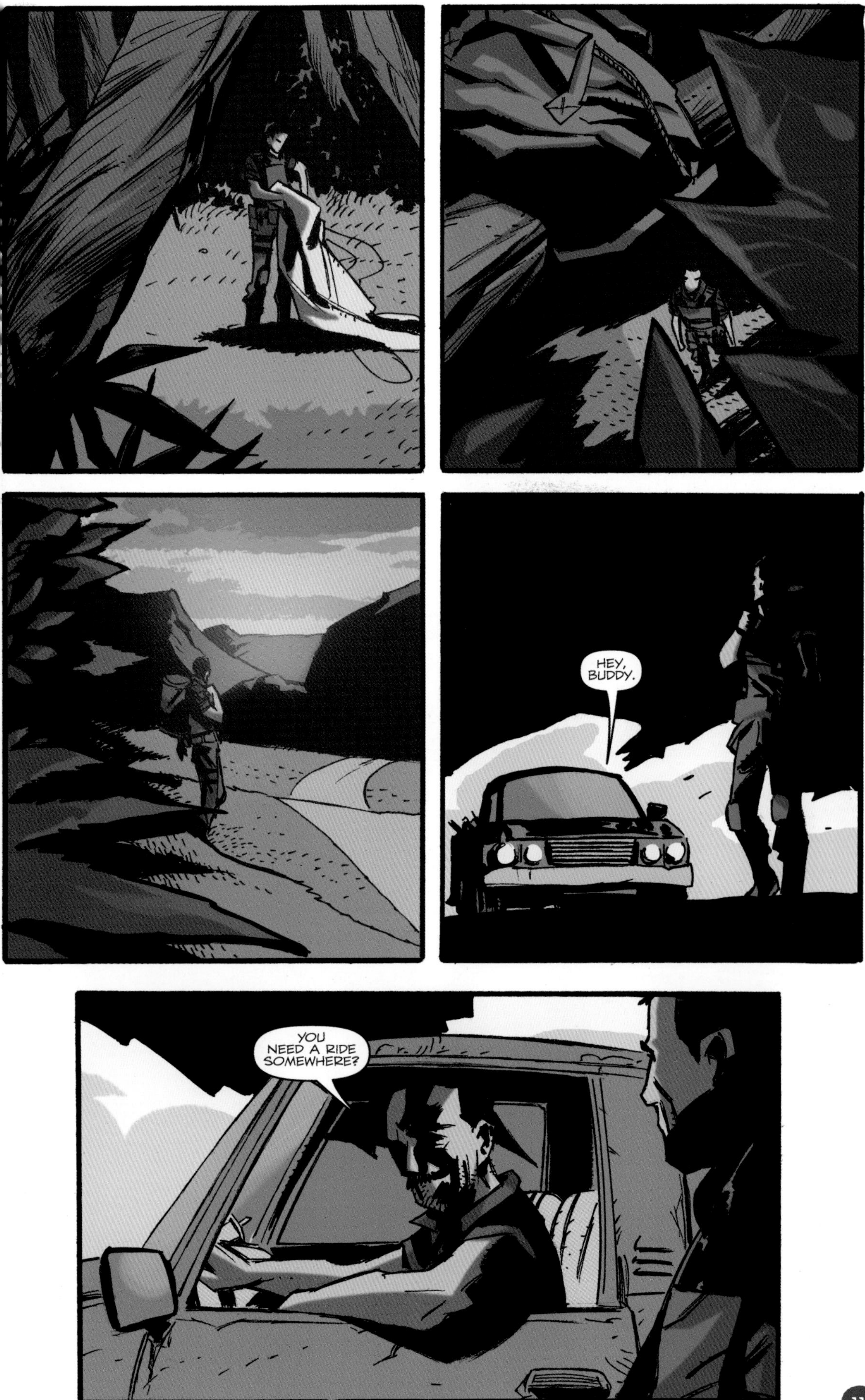
HEY, BUDDY.
YOU NEED A RIDE SOMEWHERE?

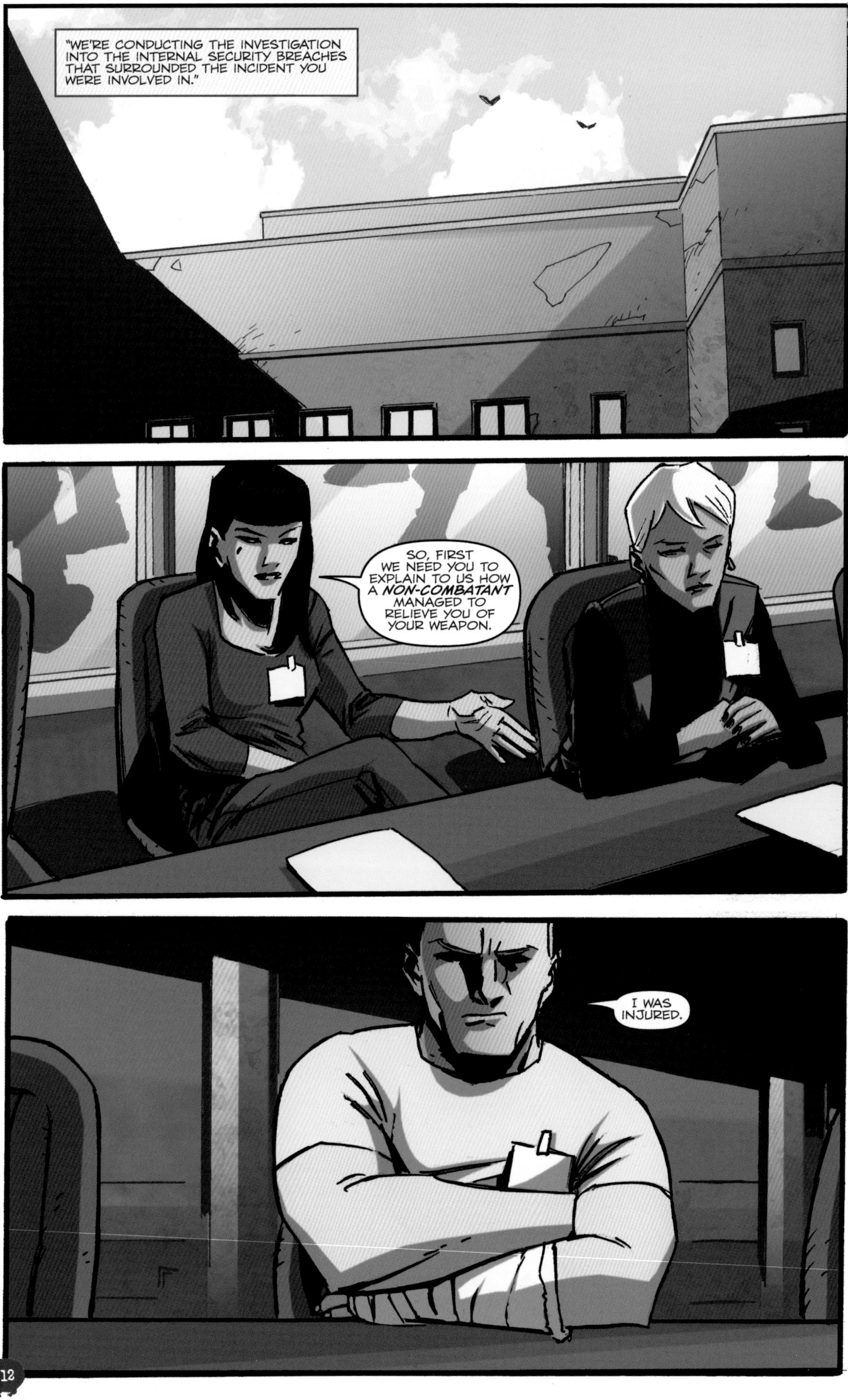
"WE'RE CONDUCTING THE INVESTIGATION INTO THE INTERNAL SECURITY BREACHES THAT SURROUNDED THE INCIDENT YOU WERE INVOLVED IN."
SO, FIRST WE NEED YOU TO EXPLAIN TO US HOW A NON-COMBATANT MANAGED TO RELIEVE YOU OF YOUR WEAPON.
I WAS INJURED.

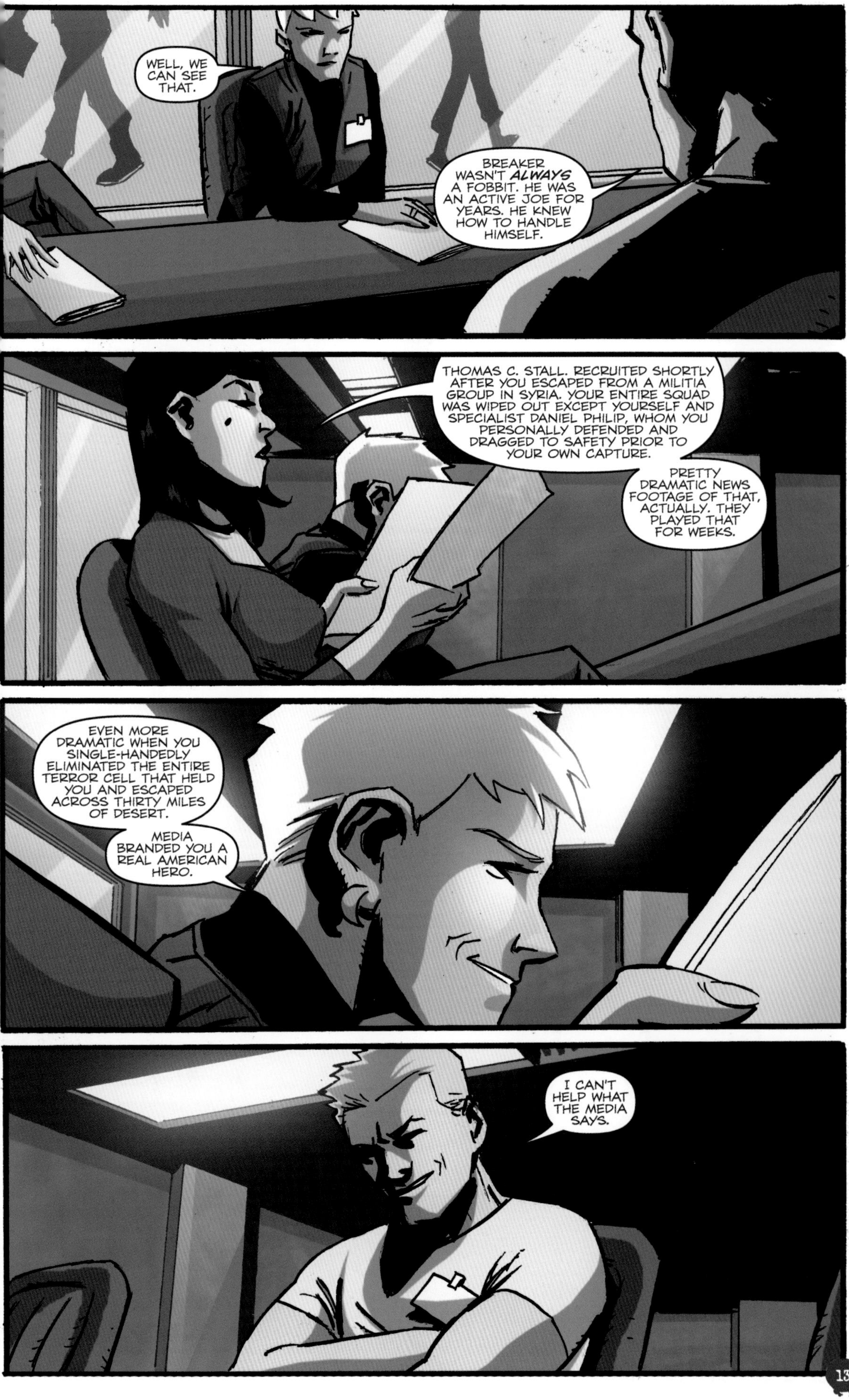

WELL, WE CAN SEE THAT.
BREAKER WASN'T ALWAYS A FOBBIT. HE WAS AN ACTIVE JOE FOR YEARS. HE KNEW HOW TO HANDLE HIMSELF.
THOMAS C. STALL. RECRUITED SHORTLY AFTER YOU ESCAPED FROM A MILITIA GROUP IN SYRIA. YOUR ENTIRE SQUAD WAS WIPED OUT EXCEPT YOURSELF AND SPECIALIST DANIEL PHILIP, WHOM YOU PERSONALLY DEFENDED AND DRAGGED TO SAFETY PRIOR TO YOUR OWN CAPTURE.
PRETTY DRAMATIC NEWS FOOTAGE OF THAT, ACTUALLY. THEY PLAYED THAT FOR WEEKS.
EVEN MORE DRAMATIC WHEN YOU SINGLE-HANDEDLY ELIMINATED THE ENTIRE TERROR CELL THAT HELD YOU AND ESCAPED ACROSS THIRTY MILES OF DESERT.
MEDIA BRANDED YOU A REAL AMERICAN HERO.
I CAN'T HELP WHAT THE MEDIA SAYS.

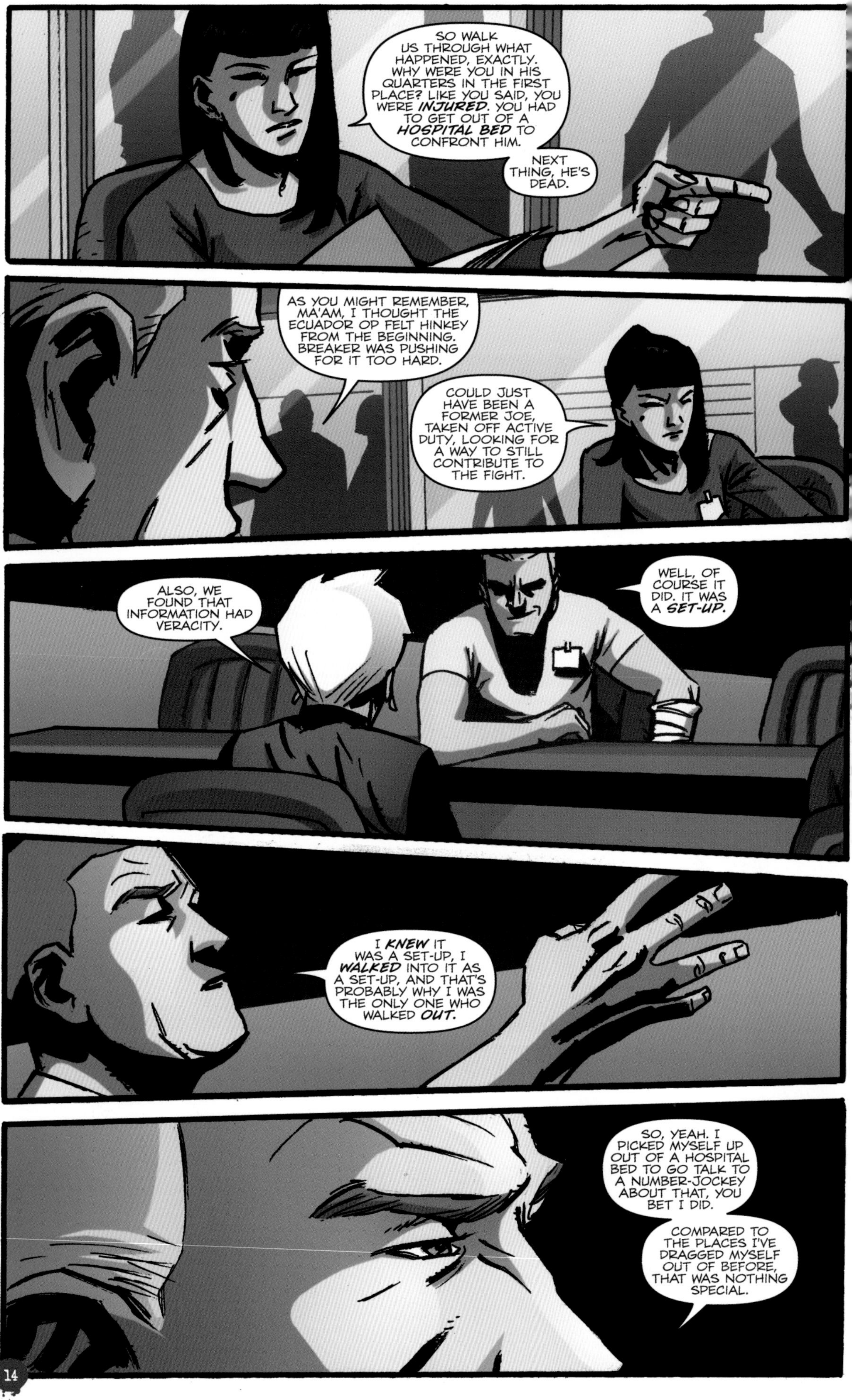

SO WALK US THROUGH WHAT HAPPENED, EXACTLY. WHY WERE YOU IN HIS QUARTERS IN THE FIRST PLACE? LIKE YOU SAID, YOU WERE *INJURED*. YOU HAD TO GET OUT OF A *HOSPITAL BED* TO CONFRONT HIM.
NEXT THING, HE'S DEAD.
AS YOU MIGHT REMEMBER, MA'AM, I THOUGHT THE ECUADOR OP FELT HINKEY FROM THE BEGINNING. BREAKER WAS PUSHING FOR IT TOO HARD.
COULD JUST HAVE BEEN A FORMER JOE, TAKEN OFF ACTIVE DUTY, LOOKING FOR A WAY TO STILL CONTRIBUTE TO THE FIGHT.
ALSO, WE FOUND THAT INFORMATION HAD VERACITY.
WELL, OF COURSE IT DID. IT WAS A *SET-UP*.
I *KNEW* IT WAS A SET-UP, I *WALKED* INTO IT AS A SET-UP, AND THAT'S PROBABLY WHY I WAS THE ONLY ONE WHO WALKED *OUT*.
SO, YEAH. I PICKED MYSELF UP OUT OF A HOSPITAL BED TO GO TALK TO A NUMBER-JOCKEY ABOUT THAT, YOU BET I DID.
COMPARED TO THE PLACES I'VE DRAGGED MYSELF OUT OF BEFORE, THAT WAS NOTHING SPECIAL.

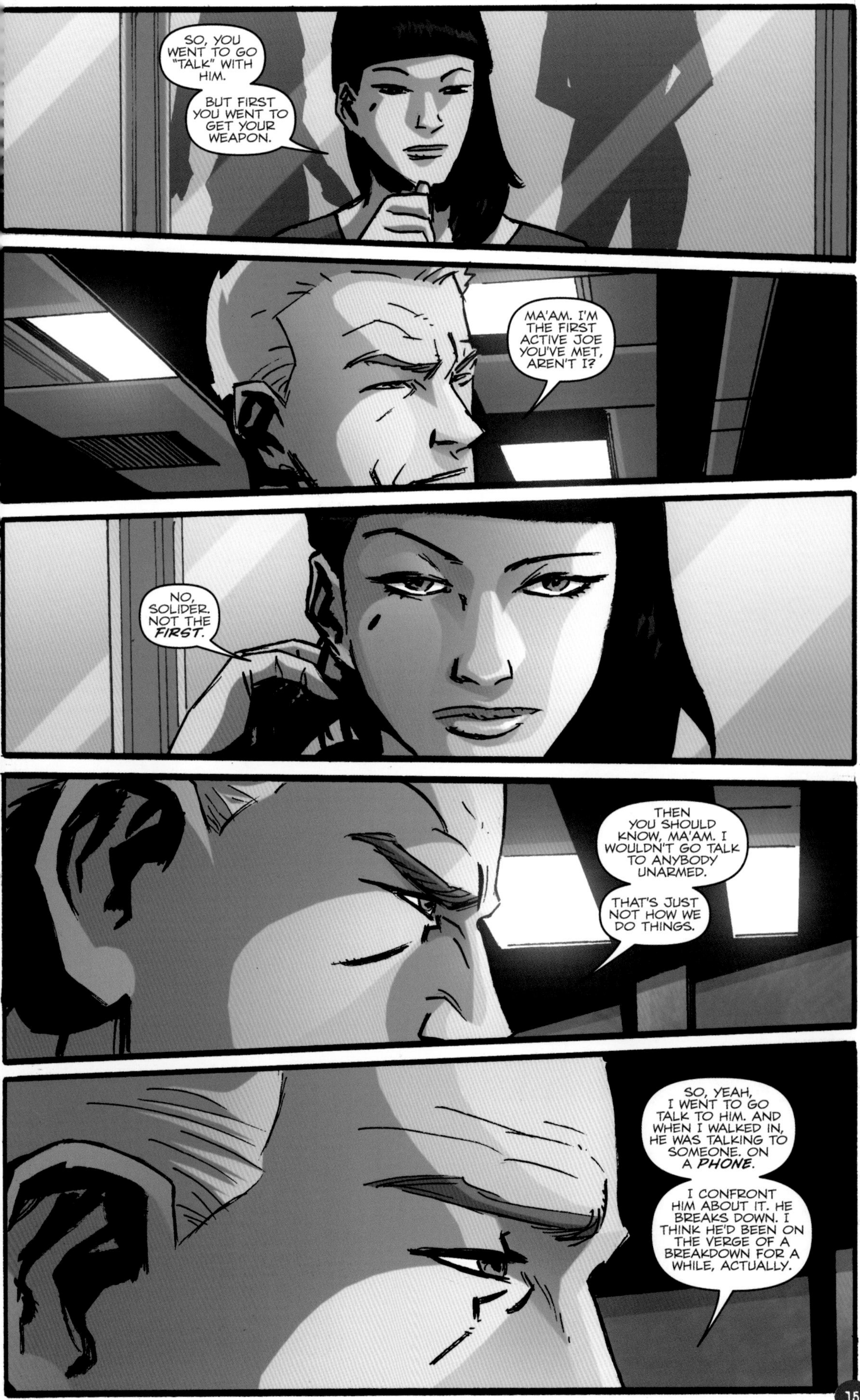
SO, YOU WENT TO GO "TALK" WITH HIM.
BUT FIRST YOU WENT TO GET YOUR WEAPON.
MA'AM. I'M THE FIRST ACTIVE JOE YOU'VE MET, AREN'T I?
NO, SOLIDER. NOT THE *FIRST*.
THEN YOU SHOULD KNOW, MA'AM. I WOULDN'T GO TALK TO ANYBODY UNARMED.
THAT'S JUST NOT HOW WE DO THINGS.
SO, YEAH, I WENT TO GO TALK TO HIM. AND WHEN I WALKED IN, HE WAS TALKING TO SOMEONE. ON A *PHONE*.
I CONFRONT HIM ABOUT IT. HE BREAKS DOWN. I THINK HE'D BEEN ON THE VERGE OF A BREAKDOWN FOR A WHILE, ACTUALLY.

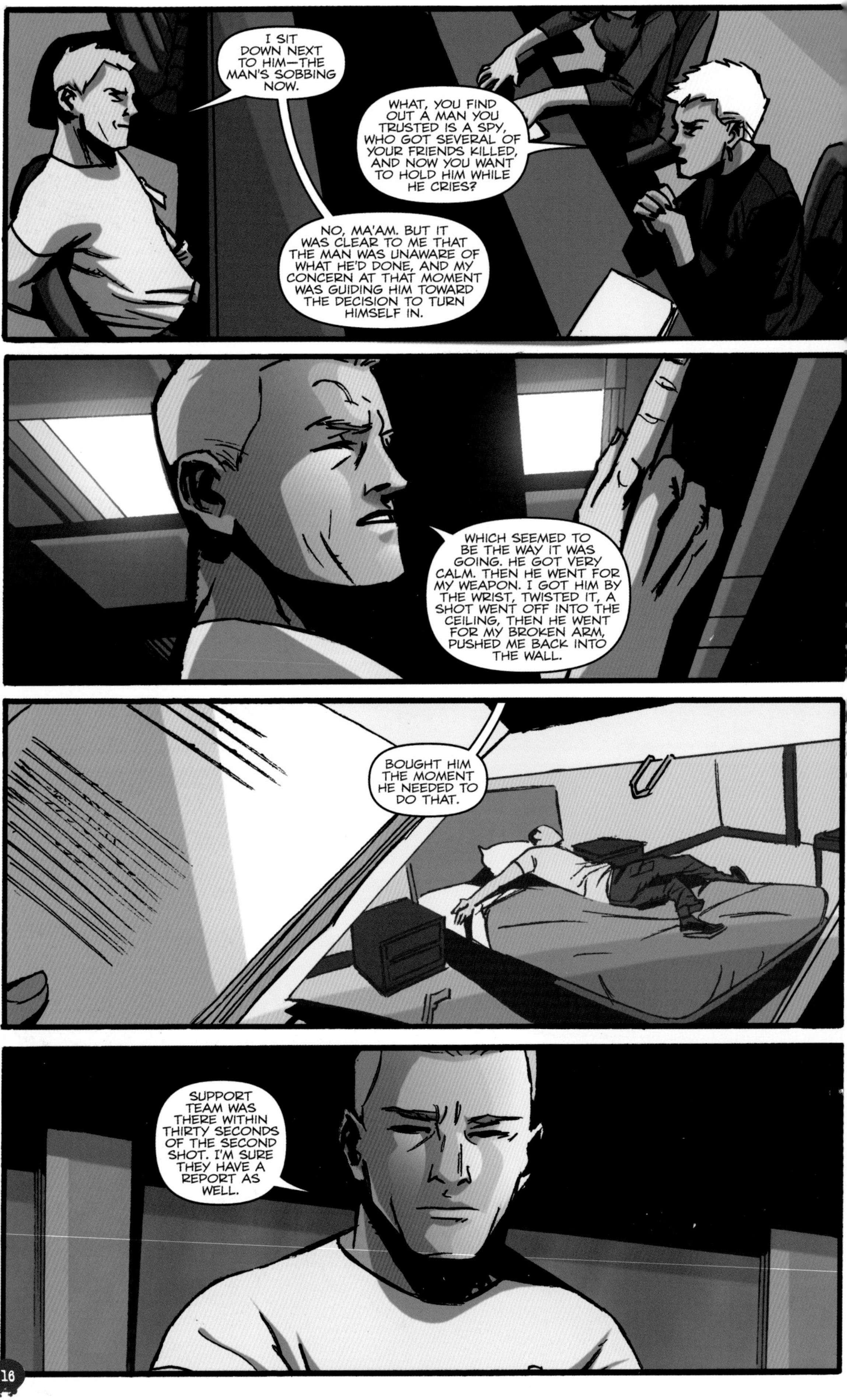
I SIT DOWN NEXT TO HIM—THE MAN'S SOBBING NOW.
WHAT, YOU FIND OUT A MAN YOU TRUSTED IS A SPY, WHO GOT SEVERAL OF YOUR FRIENDS KILLED, AND NOW YOU WANT TO HOLD HIM WHILE HE CRIES?
NO, MA'AM. BUT IT WAS CLEAR TO ME THAT THE MAN WAS UNAWARE OF WHAT HE'D DONE, AND MY CONCERN AT THAT MOMENT WAS GUIDING HIM TOWARD THE DECISION TO TURN HIMSELF IN.
WHICH SEEMED TO BE THE WAY IT WAS GOING. HE GOT VERY CALM. THEN HE WENT FOR MY WEAPON. I GOT HIM BY THE WRIST, TWISTED IT, A SHOT WENT OFF INTO THE CEILING, THEN HE WENT FOR MY BROKEN ARM, PUSHED ME BACK INTO THE WALL.
BOUGHT HIM THE MOMENT HE NEEDED TO DO THAT.
SUPPORT TEAM WAS THERE WITHIN THIRTY SECONDS OF THE SECOND SHOT. I'M SURE THEY HAVE A REPORT AS WELL.

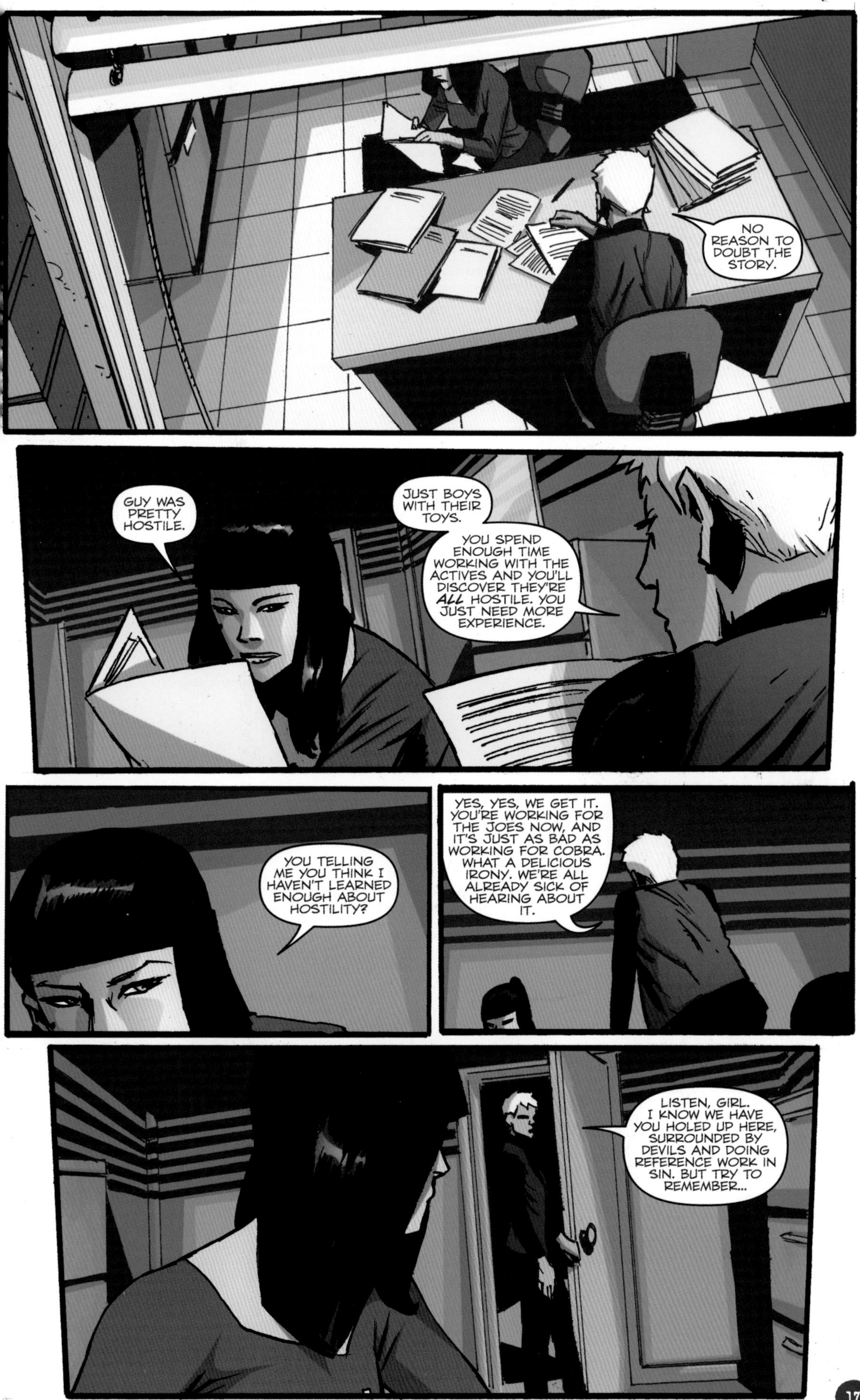
NO REASON TO DOUBT THE STORY.
GUY WAS PRETTY HOSTILE.
JUST BOYS WITH THEIR TOYS.
YOU SPEND ENOUGH TIME WORKING WITH THE ACTIVES AND YOU'LL DISCOVER THEY'RE *ALL* HOSTILE. YOU JUST NEED MORE EXPERIENCE.
YOU TELLING ME YOU THINK I HAVEN'T LEARNED ENOUGH ABOUT HOSTILITY?
YES, YES, WE GET IT. YOU'RE WORKING FOR THE JOES NOW, AND IT'S JUST AS BAD AS WORKING FOR COBRA. WHAT A DELICIOUS IRONY. WE'RE ALL ALREADY SICK OF HEARING ABOUT IT.
LISTEN, GIRL. I KNOW WE HAVE YOU HOLED UP HERE, SURROUNDED BY DEVILS AND DOING REFERENCE WORK IN SIN. BUT TRY TO REMEMBER...

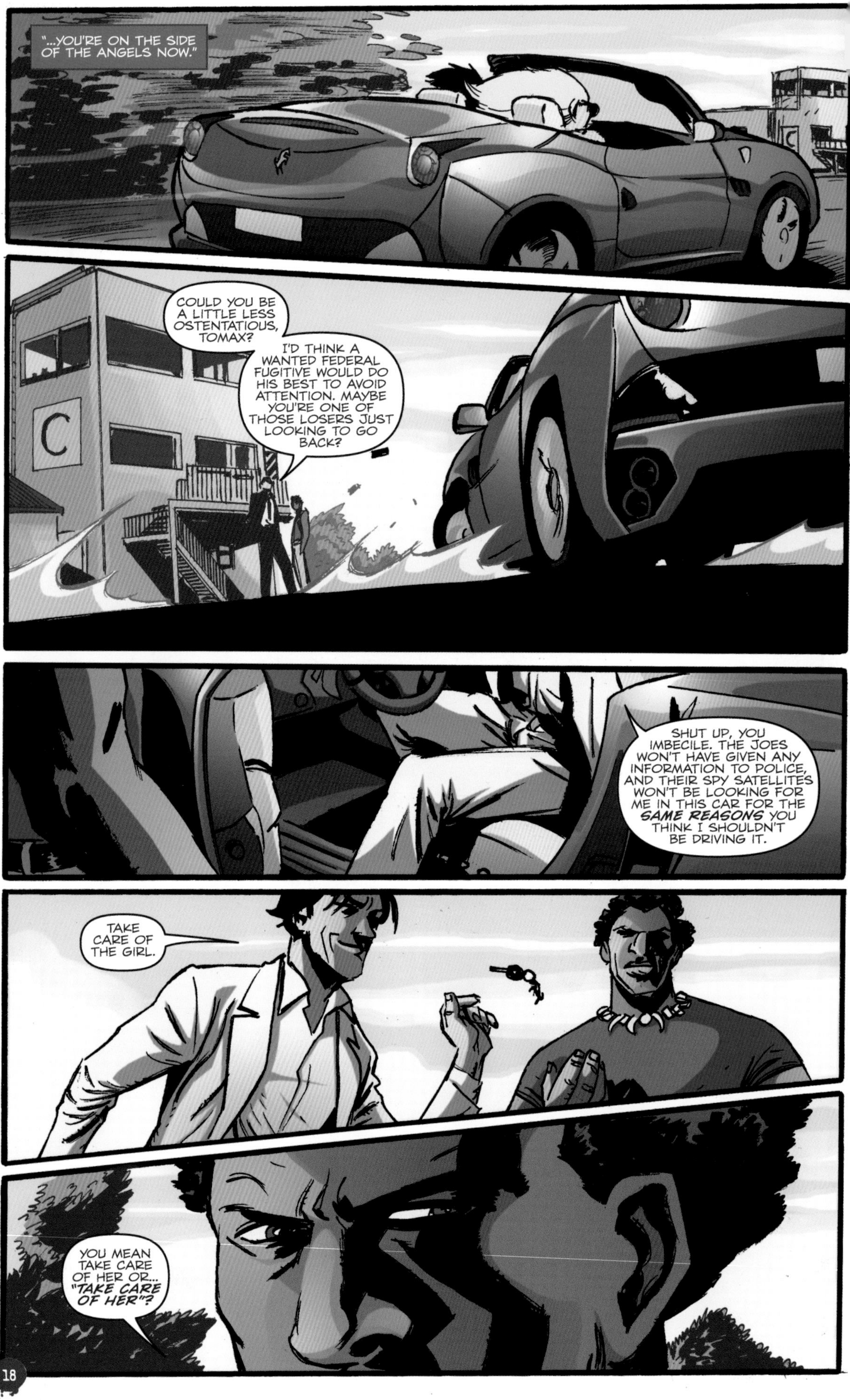
"...YOU'RE ON THE SIDE OF THE ANGELS NOW."
COULD YOU BE A LITTLE LESS OSTENTATIOUS, TOMAX?
I'D THINK A WANTED FEDERAL FUGITIVE WOULD DO HIS BEST TO AVOID ATTENTION. MAYBE YOU'RE ONE OF THOSE LOSERS JUST LOOKING TO GO BACK?
SHUT UP, YOU IMBECILE. THE JOES WON'T HAVE GIVEN ANY INFORMATION TO POLICE, AND THEIR SPY SATELLITES WON'T BE LOOKING FOR ME IN THIS CAR FOR THE SAME REASONS YOU THINK I SHOULDN'T BE DRIVING IT.
TAKE CARE OF THE GIRL.
YOU MEAN TAKE CARE OF HER OR... "TAKE CARE OF HER"?

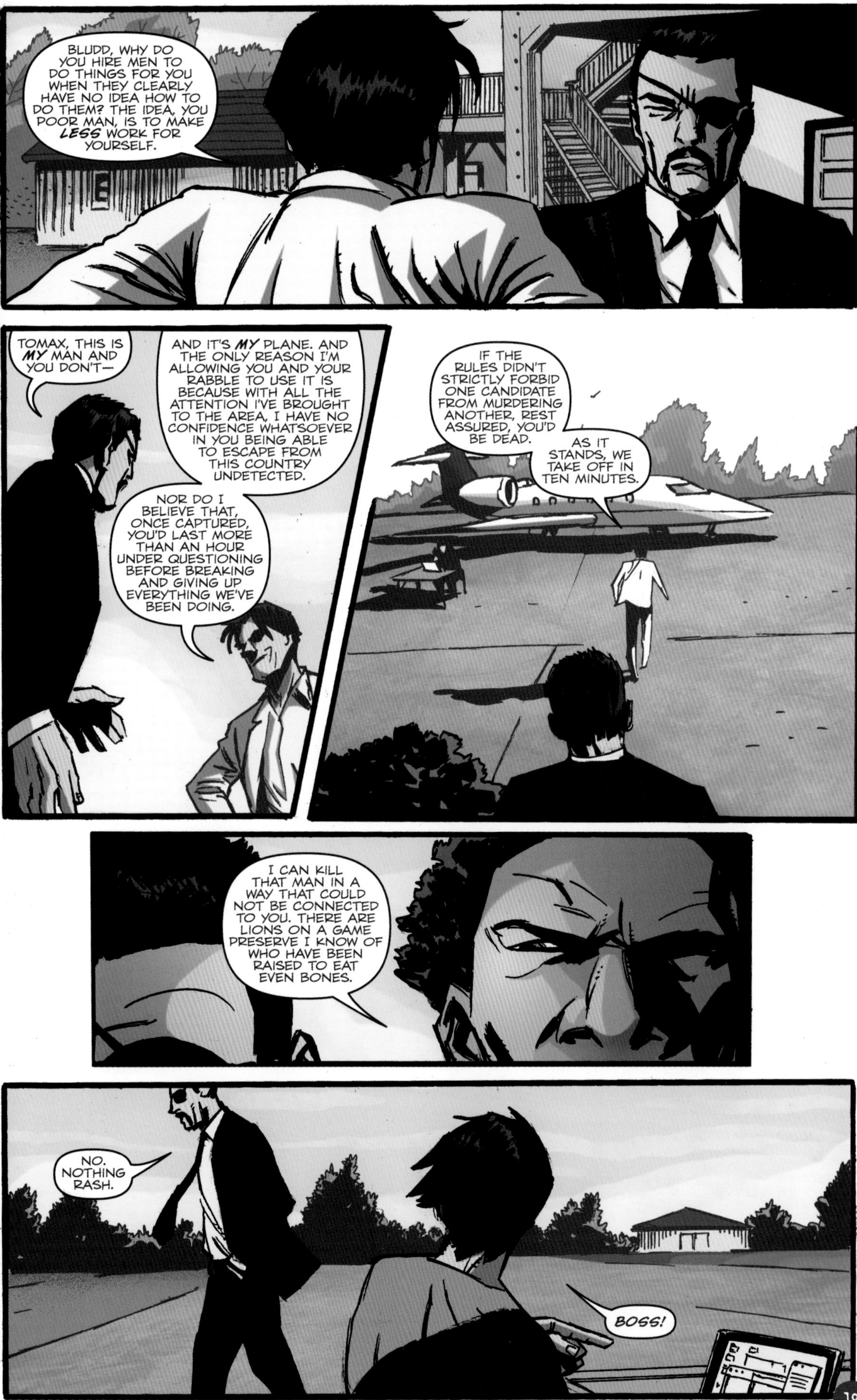
BLUDD, WHY DO YOU HIRE MEN TO DO THINGS FOR YOU WHEN THEY CLEARLY HAVE NO IDEA HOW TO DO THEM? THE IDEA, YOU POOR MAN, IS TO MAKE LESS WORK FOR YOURSELF.
TOMAX, THIS IS MY MAN AND YOU DON'T—
AND IT'S MY PLANE. AND THE ONLY REASON I'M ALLOWING YOU AND YOUR RABBLE TO USE IT IS BECAUSE WITH ALL THE ATTENTION I'VE BROUGHT TO THE AREA, I HAVE NO CONFIDENCE WHATSOEVER IN YOU BEING ABLE TO ESCAPE FROM THIS COUNTRY UNDETECTED.
NOR DO I BELIEVE THAT, ONCE CAPTURED, YOU'D LAST MORE THAN AN HOUR UNDER QUESTIONING BEFORE BREAKING AND GIVING UP EVERYTHING WE'VE BEEN DOING.
IF THE RULES DIDN'T STRICTLY FORBID ONE CANDIDATE FROM MURDERING ANOTHER, REST ASSURED, YOU'D BE DEAD.
AS IT STANDS, WE TAKE OFF IN TEN MINUTES.
I CAN KILL THAT MAN IN A WAY THAT COULD NOT BE CONNECTED TO YOU. THERE ARE LIONS ON A GAME PRESERVE I KNOW OF WHO HAVE BEEN RAISED TO EAT EVEN BONES.
NO. NOTHING RASH.
BOSS!

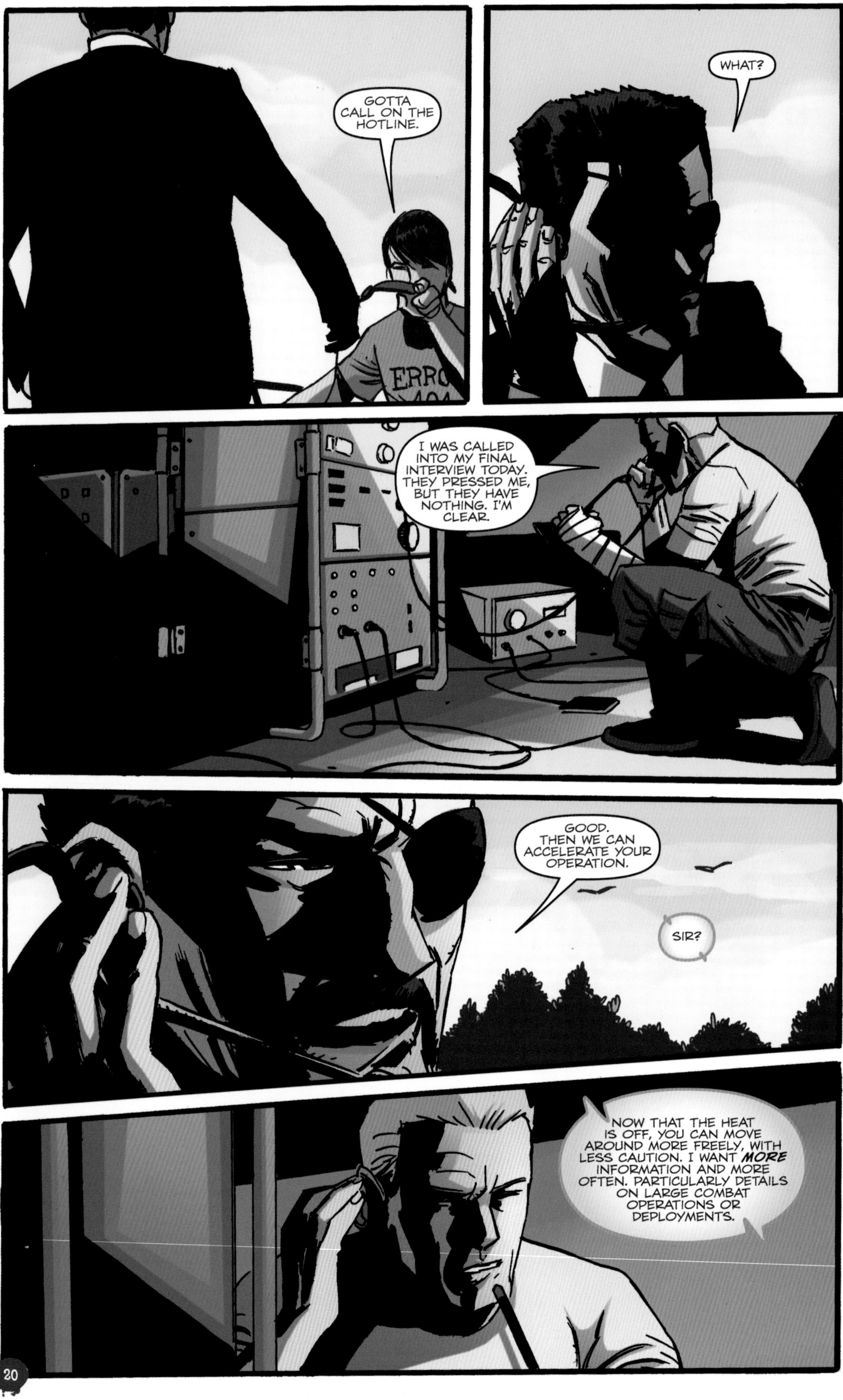
GOTTA CALL ON THE HOTLINE.
ERRO
WHAT?
I WAS CALLED INTO MY FINAL INTERVIEW TODAY. THEY PRESSED ME, BUT THEY HAVE NOTHING. I'M CLEAR.
GOOD. THEN WE CAN ACCELERATE YOUR OPERATION.
SIR?
NOW THAT THE HEAT IS OFF, YOU CAN MOVE AROUND MORE FREELY, WITH LESS CAUTION. I WANT ***MORE*** INFORMATION AND MORE OFTEN. PARTICULARLY DETAILS ON LARGE COMBAT OPERATIONS OR DEPLOYMENTS.

THAT'S A LOT MORE EXPOSURE THAN I NORMALLY RISK. IT WOULDN'T BE TOO SMART OF ME TO RAISE SUSPICION NOW AND BLOW—

THEN *DON'T* RAISE SUSPICION. JUST GET IT *DONE.*

IDIOT.

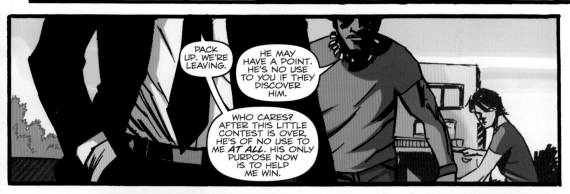

PACK UP. WE'RE LEAVING.

HE MAY HAVE A POINT. HE'S NO USE TO YOU IF THEY DISCOVER HIM.

WHO CARES? AFTER THIS LITTLE CONTEST IS OVER, HE'S OF NO USE TO ME *AT ALL.* HIS ONLY PURPOSE NOW IS TO HELP ME WIN.

YOU DON'T THINK IT WOULD BE ADVANTAGEOUS TO HAVE SOMEONE WITHIN *G.I. JOE?*

WHY?

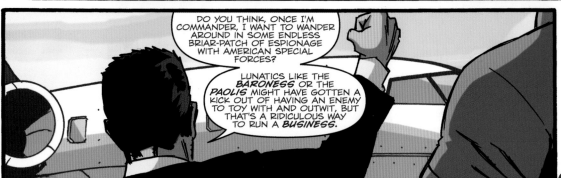

DO YOU THINK, ONCE I'M COMMANDER, I WANT TO WANDER AROUND IN SOME ENDLESS BRIAR-PATCH OF ESPIONAGE WITH AMERICAN SPECIAL FORCES?

LUNATICS LIKE THE *BARONESS* OR THE *PAOLIS* MIGHT HAVE GOTTEN A KICK OUT OF HAVING AN ENEMY TO TOY WITH AND OUTWIT, BUT THAT'S A RIDICULOUS WAY TO RUN A *BUSINESS.*

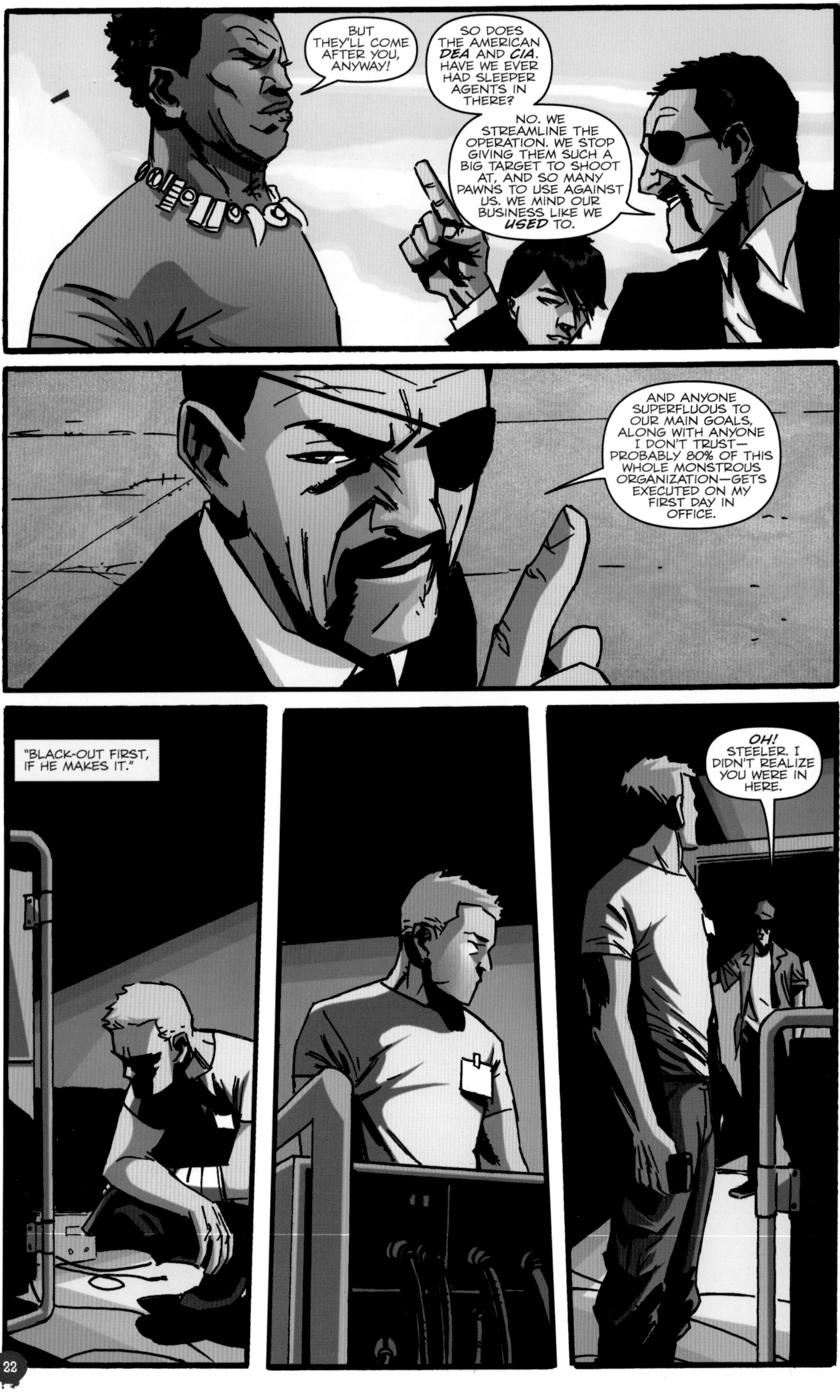
BUT THEY'LL COME AFTER YOU, ANYWAY!
SO DOES THE AMERICAN *DEA* AND *CIA*. HAVE WE EVER HAD SLEEPER AGENTS IN THERE?
NO. WE STREAMLINE THE OPERATION. WE STOP GIVING THEM SUCH A BIG TARGET TO SHOOT AT, AND SO MANY PAWNS TO USE AGAINST US. WE MIND OUR BUSINESS LIKE WE *USED* TO.
AND ANYONE SUPERFLUOUS TO OUR MAIN GOALS, ALONG WITH ANYONE I DON'T TRUST—PROBABLY 80% OF THIS WHOLE MONSTROUS ORGANIZATION—GETS EXECUTED ON MY FIRST DAY IN OFFICE.
"BLACK-OUT FIRST, IF HE MAKES IT."
OH! STEELER. I DIDN'T REALIZE YOU WERE IN HERE.

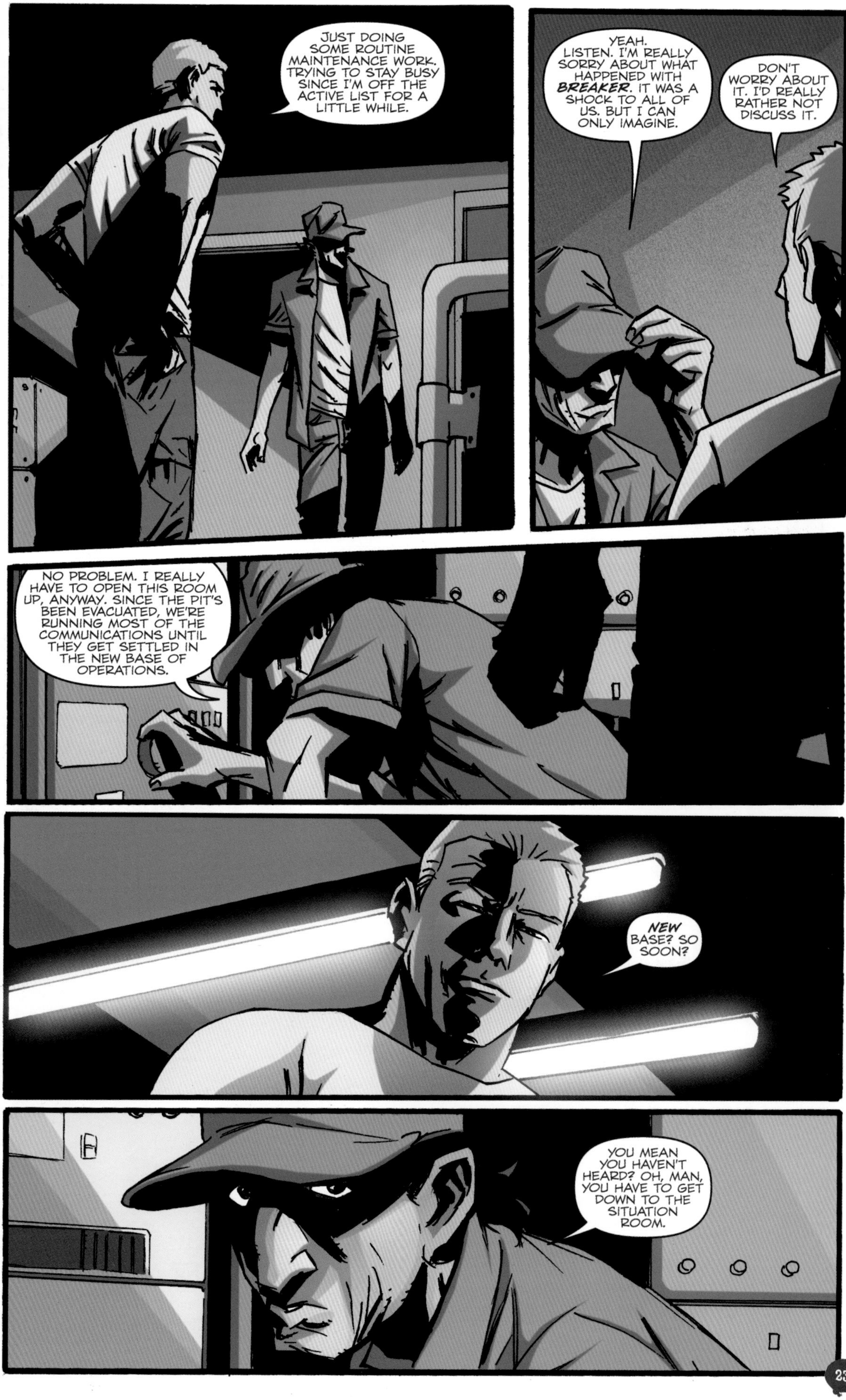
JUST DOING SOME ROUTINE MAINTENANCE WORK. TRYING TO STAY BUSY SINCE I'M OFF THE ACTIVE LIST FOR A LITTLE WHILE.
YEAH. LISTEN. I'M REALLY SORRY ABOUT WHAT HAPPENED WITH BREAKER. IT WAS A SHOCK TO ALL OF US. BUT I CAN ONLY IMAGINE.
DON'T WORRY ABOUT IT. I'D REALLY RATHER NOT DISCUSS IT.
NO PROBLEM. I REALLY HAVE TO OPEN THIS ROOM UP, ANYWAY. SINCE THE PIT'S BEEN EVACUATED, WE'RE RUNNING MOST OF THE COMMUNICATIONS UNTIL THEY GET SETTLED IN THE NEW BASE OF OPERATIONS.
NEW BASE? SO SOON?
YOU MEAN YOU HAVEN'T HEARD? OH, MAN, YOU HAVE TO GET DOWN TO THE SITUATION ROOM.

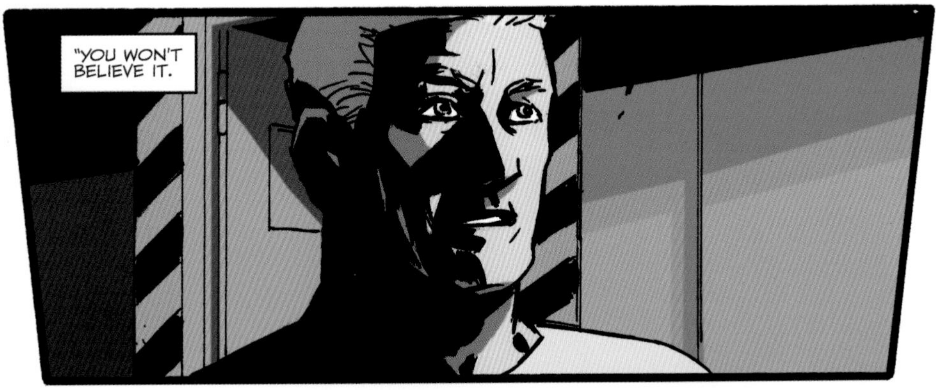
"YOU WON'T BELIEVE IT.

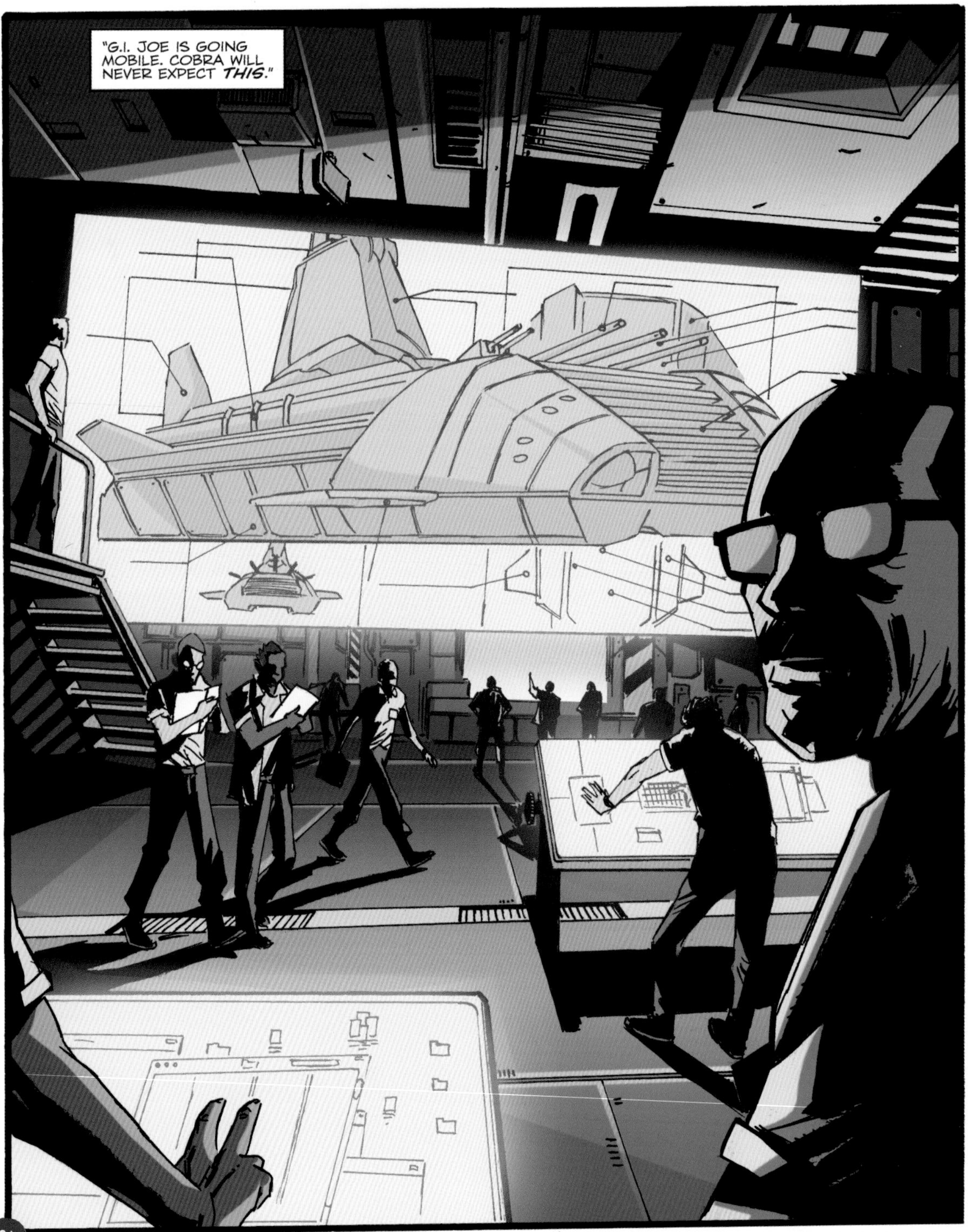
"G.I. JOE IS GOING MOBILE. COBRA WILL NEVER EXPECT THIS."

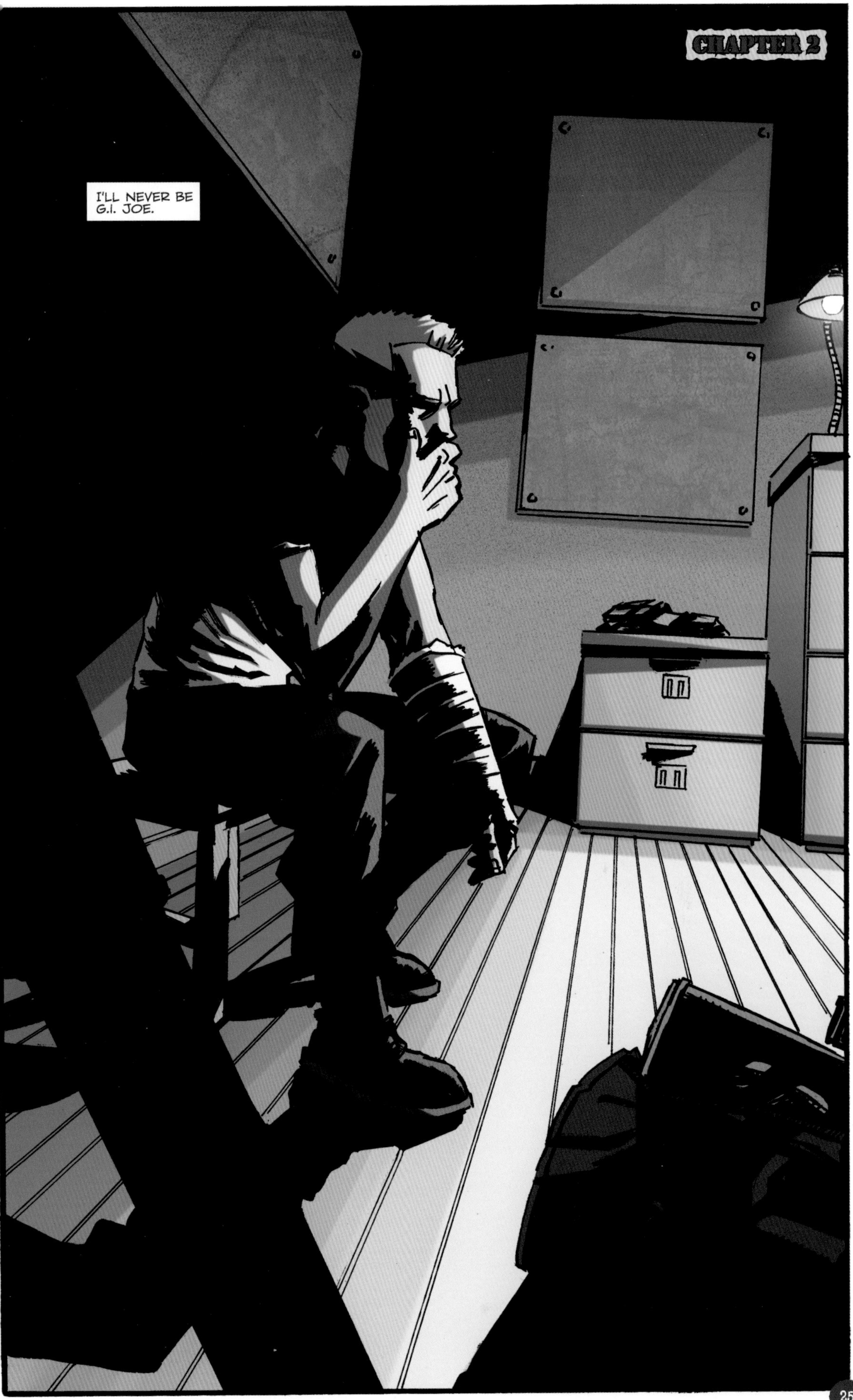
CHAPTER 2
I'LL NEVER BE G.I. JOE.

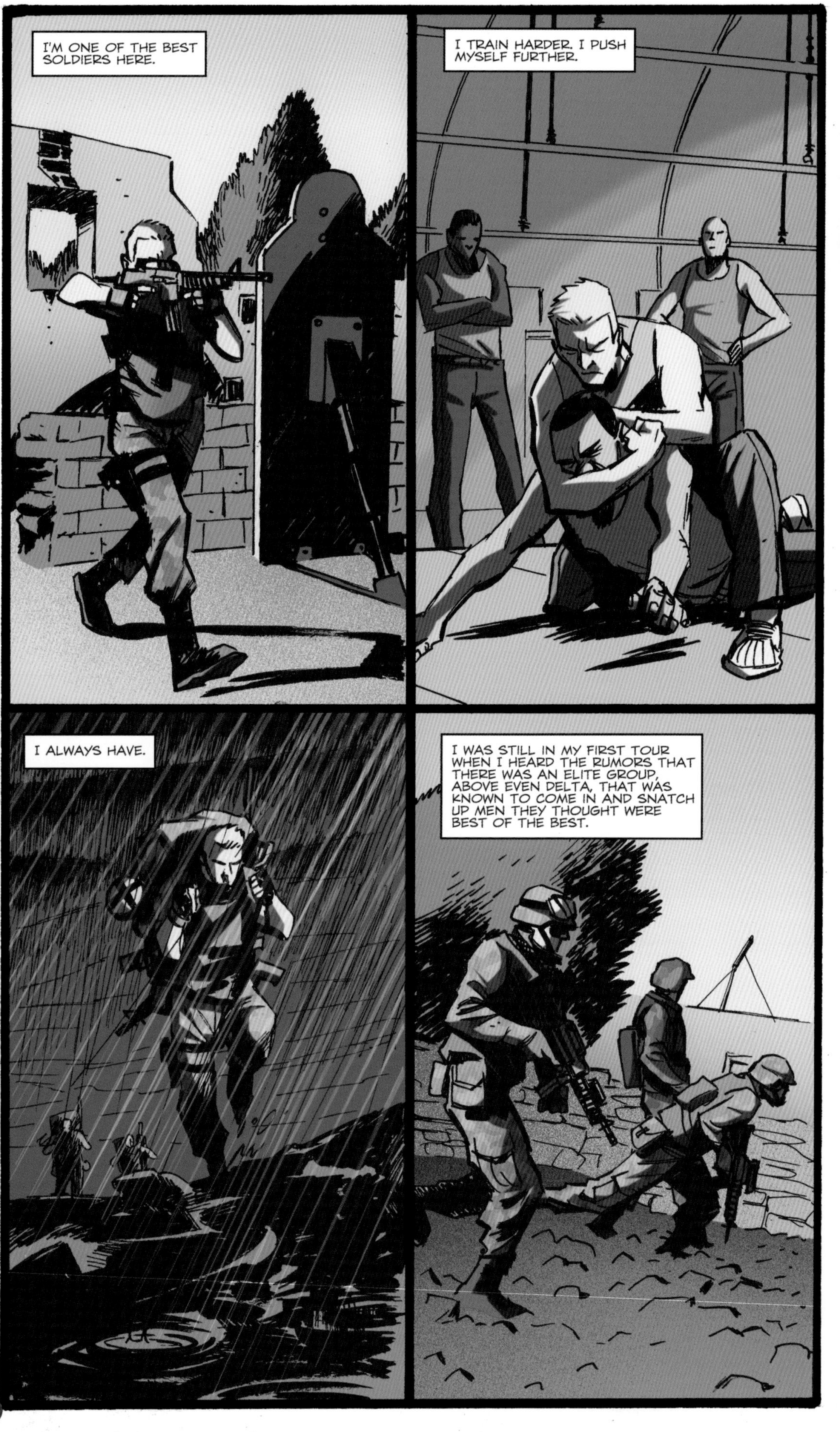
I'M ONE OF THE BEST SOLDIERS HERE.
I TRAIN HARDER. I PUSH MYSELF FURTHER.
I ALWAYS HAVE.
I WAS STILL IN MY FIRST TOUR WHEN I HEARD THE RUMORS THAT THERE WAS AN ELITE GROUP, ABOVE EVEN DELTA, THAT WAS KNOWN TO COME IN AND SNATCH UP MEN THEY THOUGHT WERE BEST OF THE BEST.

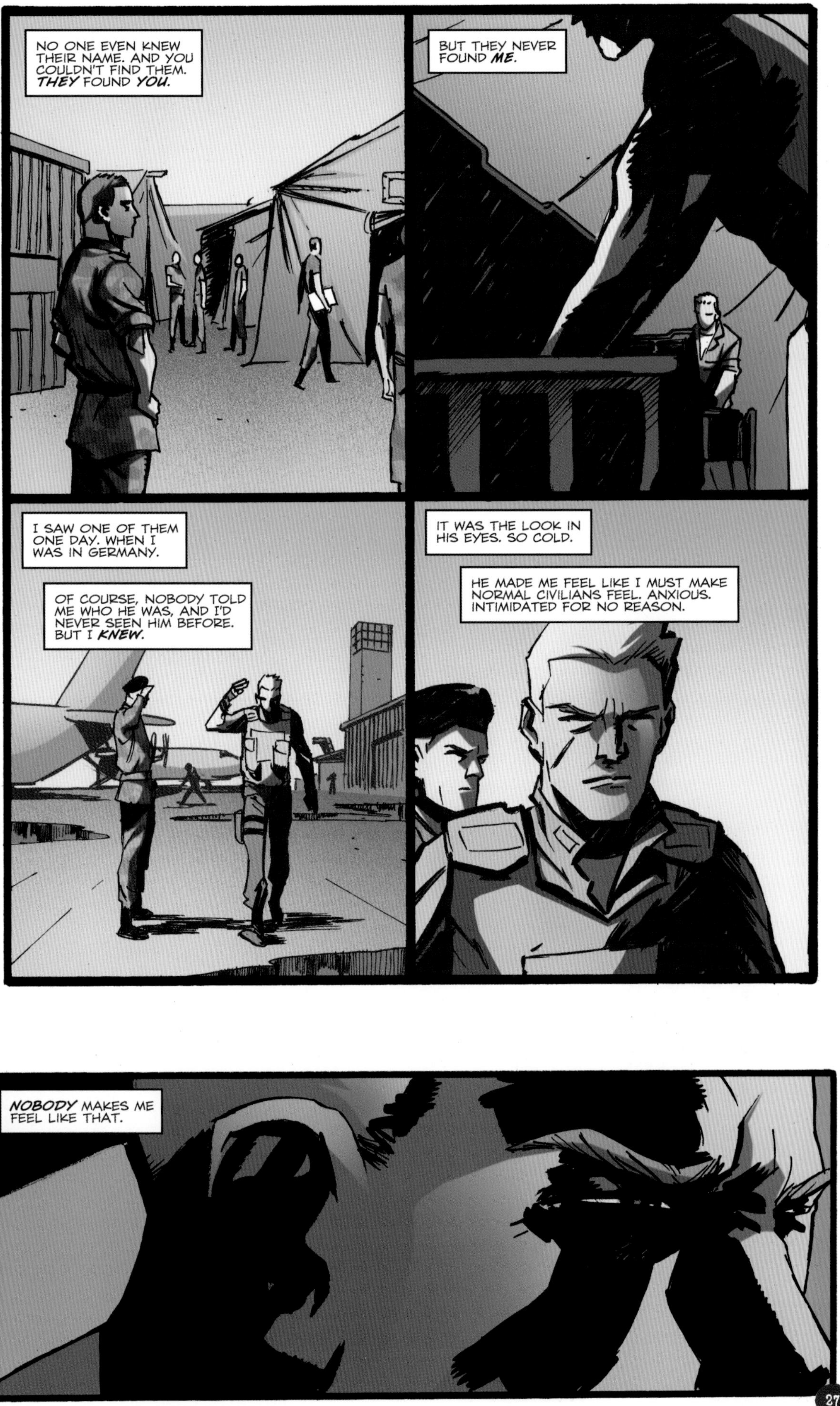
NO ONE EVEN KNEW THEIR NAME. AND YOU COULDN'T FIND THEM. *THEY* FOUND *YOU*.
BUT THEY NEVER FOUND *ME*.
I SAW ONE OF THEM ONE DAY. WHEN I WAS IN GERMANY.
OF COURSE, NOBODY TOLD ME WHO HE WAS, AND I'D NEVER SEEN HIM BEFORE. BUT I *KNEW*.
IT WAS THE LOOK IN HIS EYES. SO COLD.
HE MADE ME FEEL LIKE I MUST MAKE NORMAL CIVILIANS FEEL. ANXIOUS. INTIMIDATED FOR NO REASON.
NOBODY MAKES ME FEEL LIKE THAT.

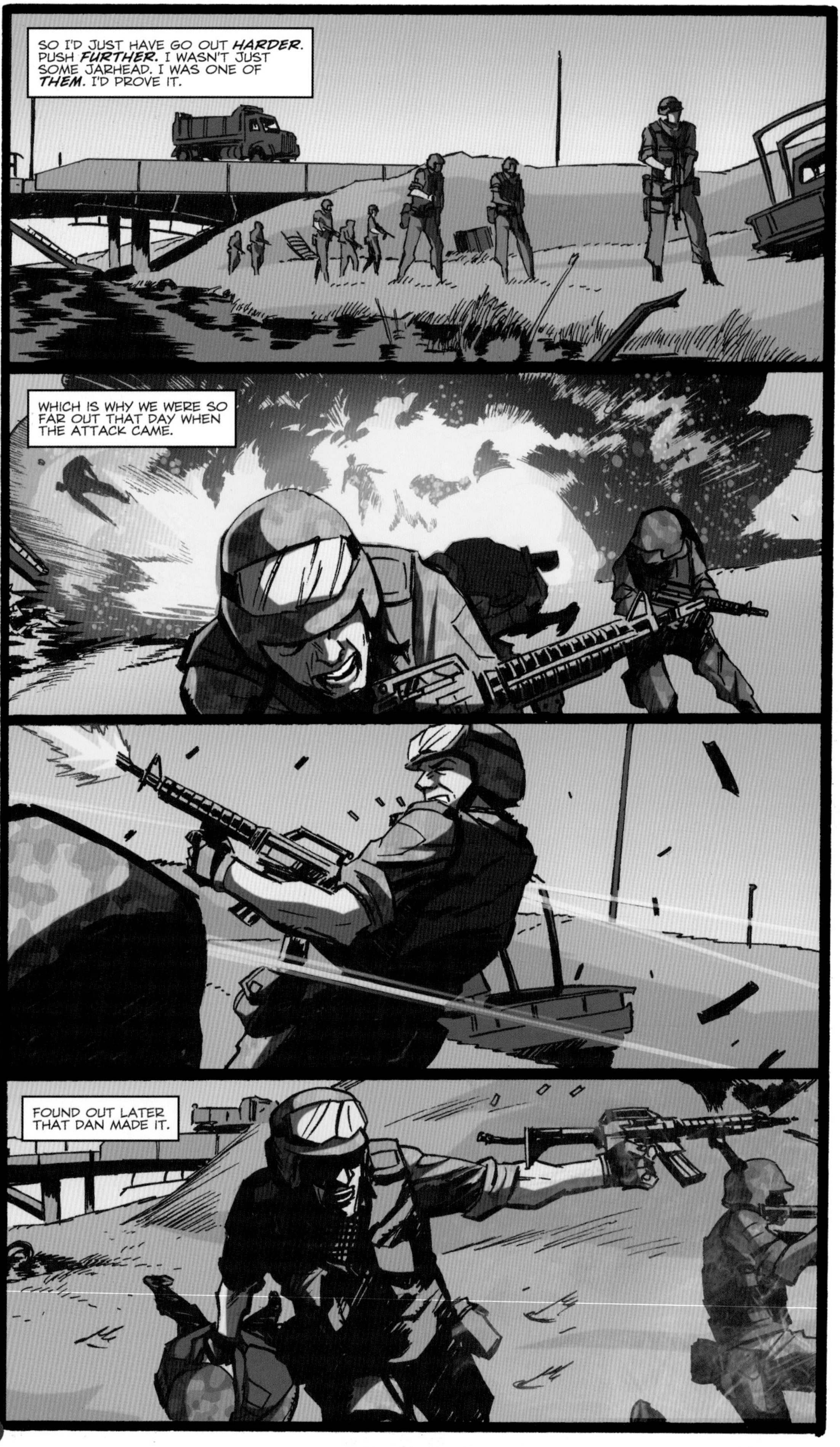
SO I'D JUST HAVE GO OUT ***HARDER***. PUSH ***FURTHER***. I WASN'T JUST SOME JARHEAD. I WAS ONE OF ***THEM***. I'D PROVE IT.
WHICH IS WHY WE WERE SO FAR OUT THAT DAY WHEN THE ATTACK CAME.
FOUND OUT LATER THAT DAN MADE IT.

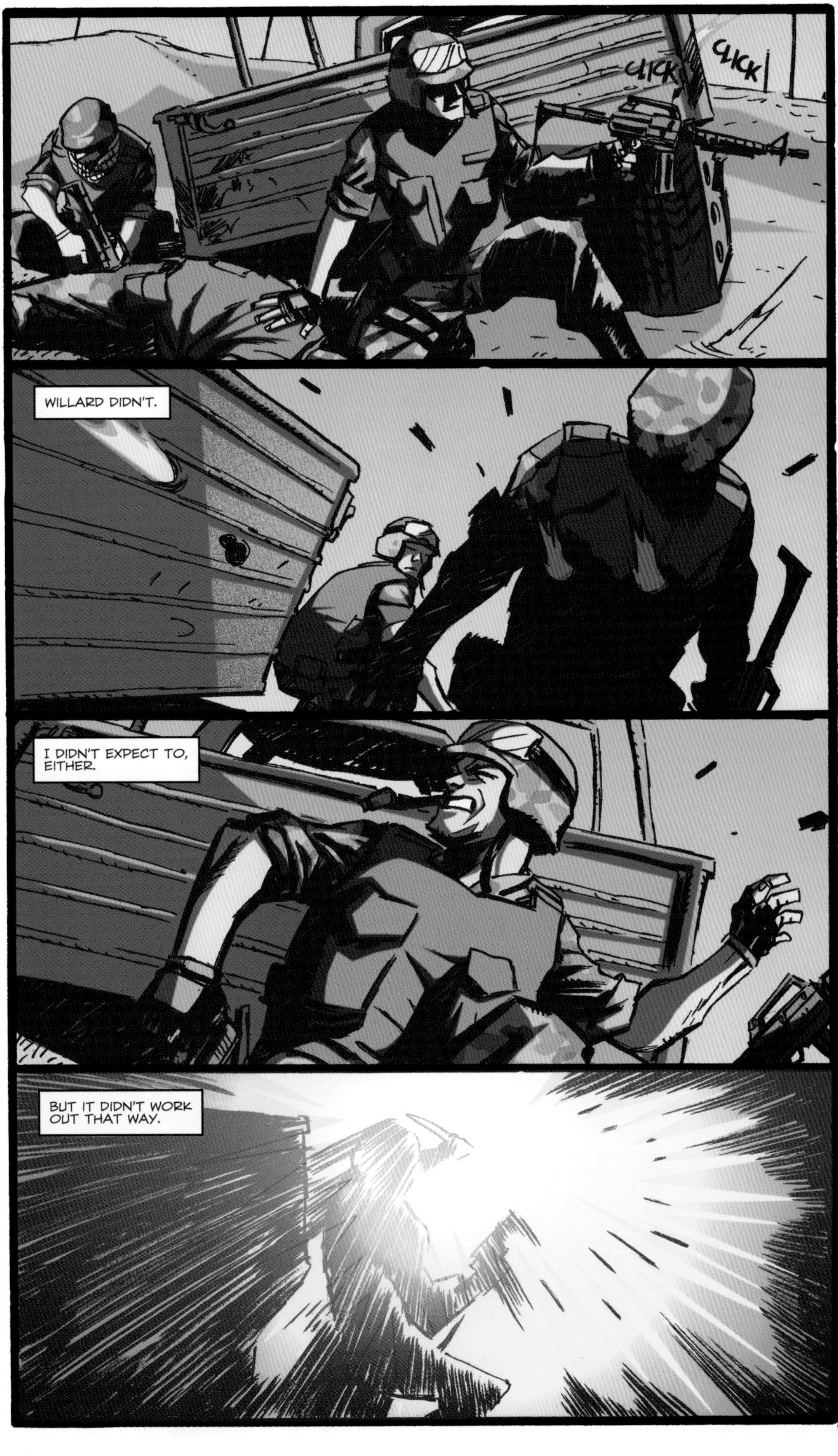
CLICK
CLICK
WILLARD DIDN'T.
I DIDN'T EXPECT TO, EITHER.
BUT IT DIDN'T WORK OUT THAT WAY.

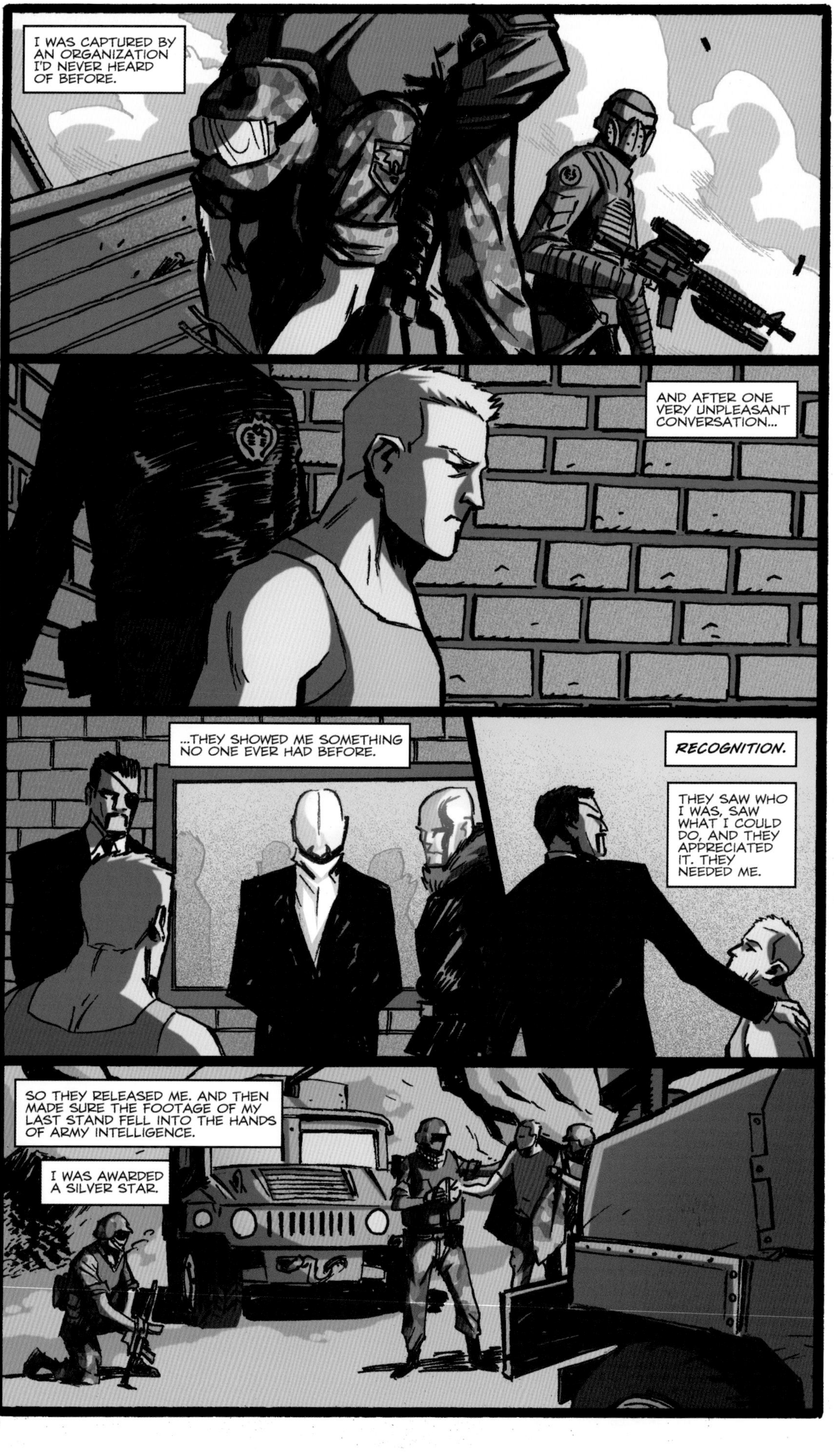
I WAS CAPTURED BY AN ORGANIZATION I'D NEVER HEARD OF BEFORE.
AND AFTER ONE VERY UNPLEASANT CONVERSATION...
...THEY SHOWED ME SOMETHING NO ONE EVER HAD BEFORE.
RECOGNITION.
THEY SAW WHO I WAS, SAW WHAT I COULD DO, AND THEY APPRECIATED IT. THEY NEEDED ME.
SO THEY RELEASED ME. AND THEN MADE SURE THE FOOTAGE OF MY LAST STAND FELL INTO THE HANDS OF ARMY INTELLIGENCE.
I WAS AWARDED A SILVER STAR.

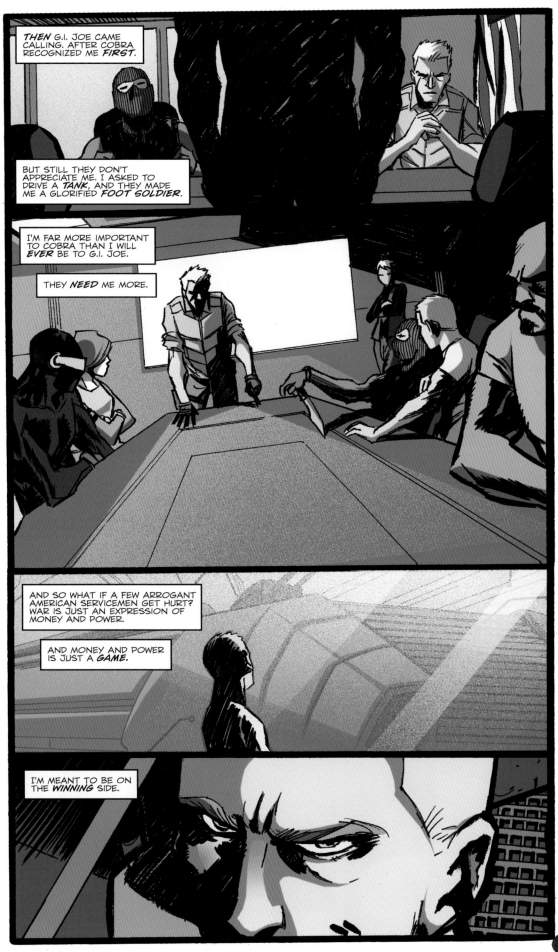

THEN G.I. JOE CAME CALLING. AFTER COBRA RECOGNIZED ME *FIRST*.

BUT STILL THEY DON'T APPRECIATE ME. I ASKED TO DRIVE A *TANK*, AND THEY MADE ME A GLORIFIED *FOOT SOLDIER*.

I'M FAR MORE IMPORTANT TO COBRA THAN I WILL *EVER* BE TO G.I. JOE.

THEY *NEED* ME MORE.

AND SO WHAT IF A FEW ARROGANT AMERICAN SERVICEMEN GET HURT? WAR IS JUST AN EXPRESSION OF MONEY AND POWER.

AND MONEY AND POWER IS JUST A *GAME*.

I'M MEANT TO BE ON THE *WINNING* SIDE.

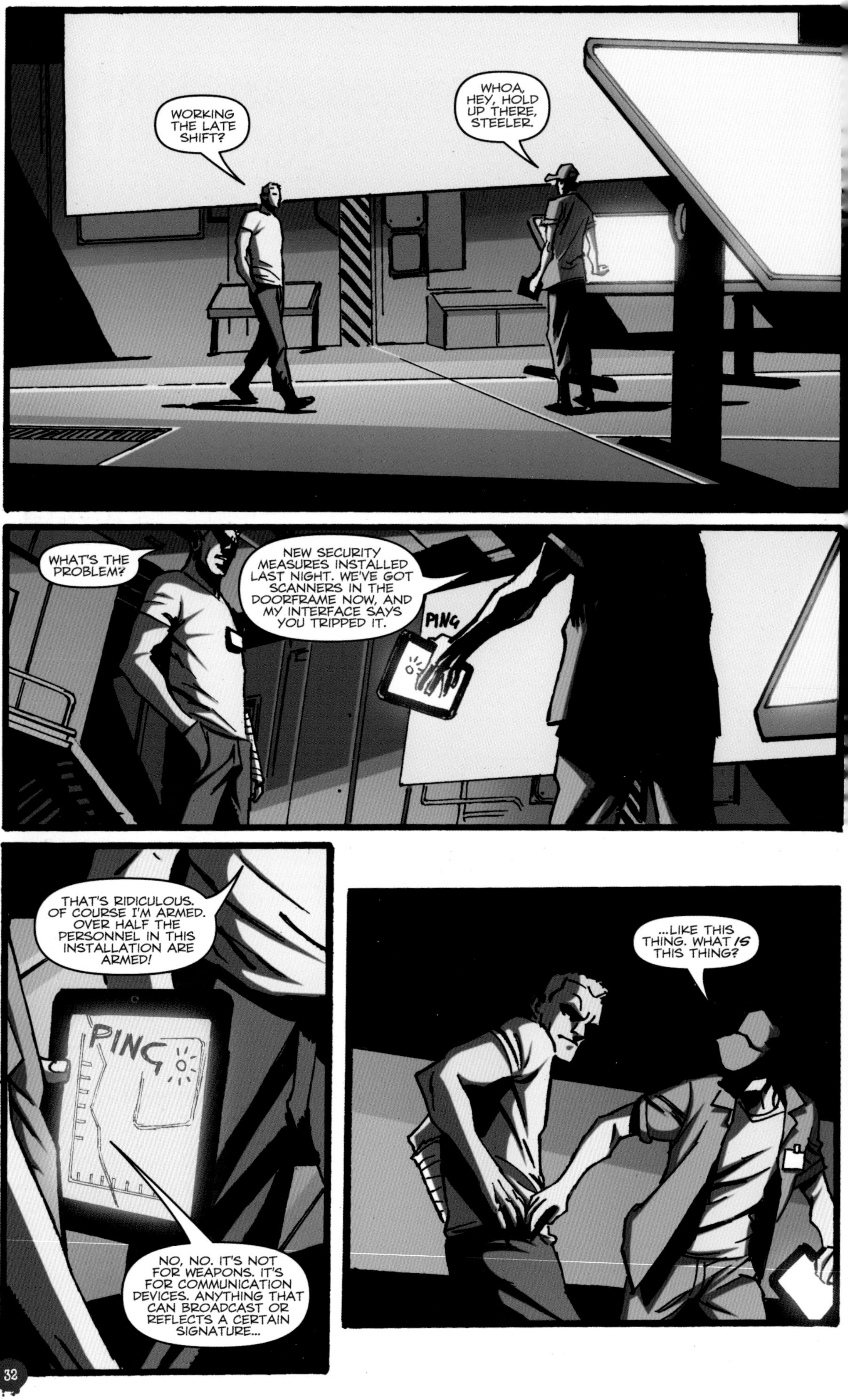
WORKING THE LATE SHIFT?
WHOA, HEY, HOLD UP THERE, STEELER.
WHAT'S THE PROBLEM?
NEW SECURITY MEASURES INSTALLED LAST NIGHT. WE'VE GOT SCANNERS IN THE DOORFRAME NOW, AND MY INTERFACE SAYS YOU TRIPPED IT.
PING
THAT'S RIDICULOUS. OF COURSE I'M ARMED. OVER HALF THE PERSONNEL IN THIS INSTALLATION ARE ARMED!
PING
NO, NO. IT'S NOT FOR WEAPONS. IT'S FOR COMMUNICATION DEVICES. ANYTHING THAT CAN BROADCAST OR REFLECTS A CERTAIN SIGNATURE...
...LIKE THIS THING. WHAT *IS* THIS THING?

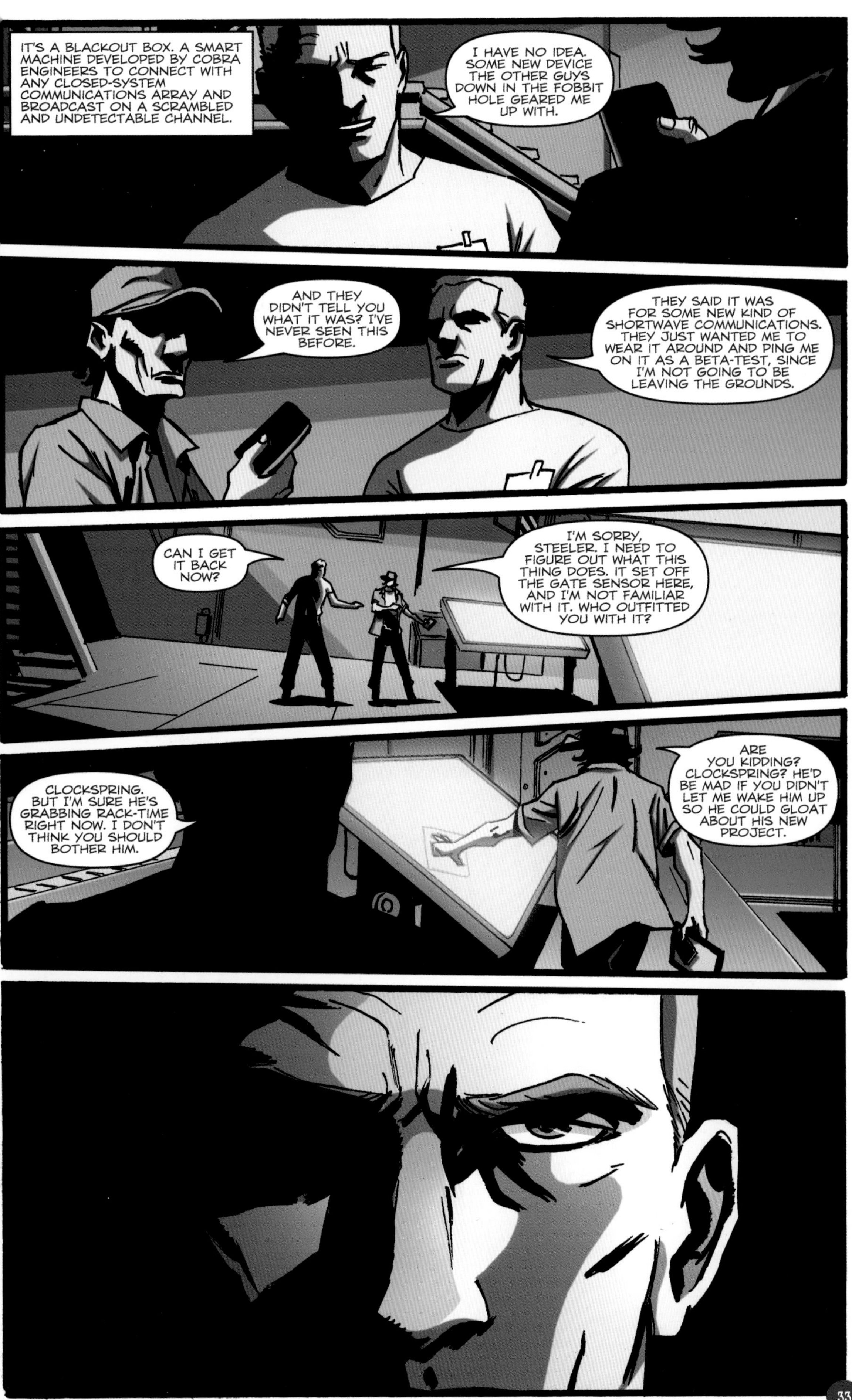
IT'S A BLACKOUT BOX. A SMART MACHINE DEVELOPED BY COBRA ENGINEERS TO CONNECT WITH ANY CLOSED-SYSTEM COMMUNICATIONS ARRAY AND BROADCAST ON A SCRAMBLED AND UNDETECTABLE CHANNEL.
I HAVE NO IDEA. SOME NEW DEVICE THE OTHER GUYS DOWN IN THE FOBBIT HOLE GEARED ME UP WITH.
AND THEY DIDN'T TELL YOU WHAT IT WAS? I'VE NEVER SEEN THIS BEFORE.
THEY SAID IT WAS FOR SOME NEW KIND OF SHORTWAVE COMMUNICATIONS. THEY JUST WANTED ME TO WEAR IT AROUND AND PING ME ON IT AS A BETA-TEST, SINCE I'M NOT GOING TO BE LEAVING THE GROUNDS.
CAN I GET IT BACK NOW?
I'M SORRY, STEELER. I NEED TO FIGURE OUT WHAT THIS THING DOES. IT SET OFF THE GATE SENSOR HERE, AND I'M NOT FAMILIAR WITH IT. WHO OUTFITTED YOU WITH IT?
CLOCKSPRING. BUT I'M SURE HE'S GRABBING RACK-TIME RIGHT NOW. I DON'T THINK YOU SHOULD BOTHER HIM.
ARE YOU KIDDING? CLOCKSPRING? HE'D BE MAD IF YOU DIDN'T LET ME WAKE HIM UP SO HE COULD GLOAT ABOUT HIS NEW PROJECT.

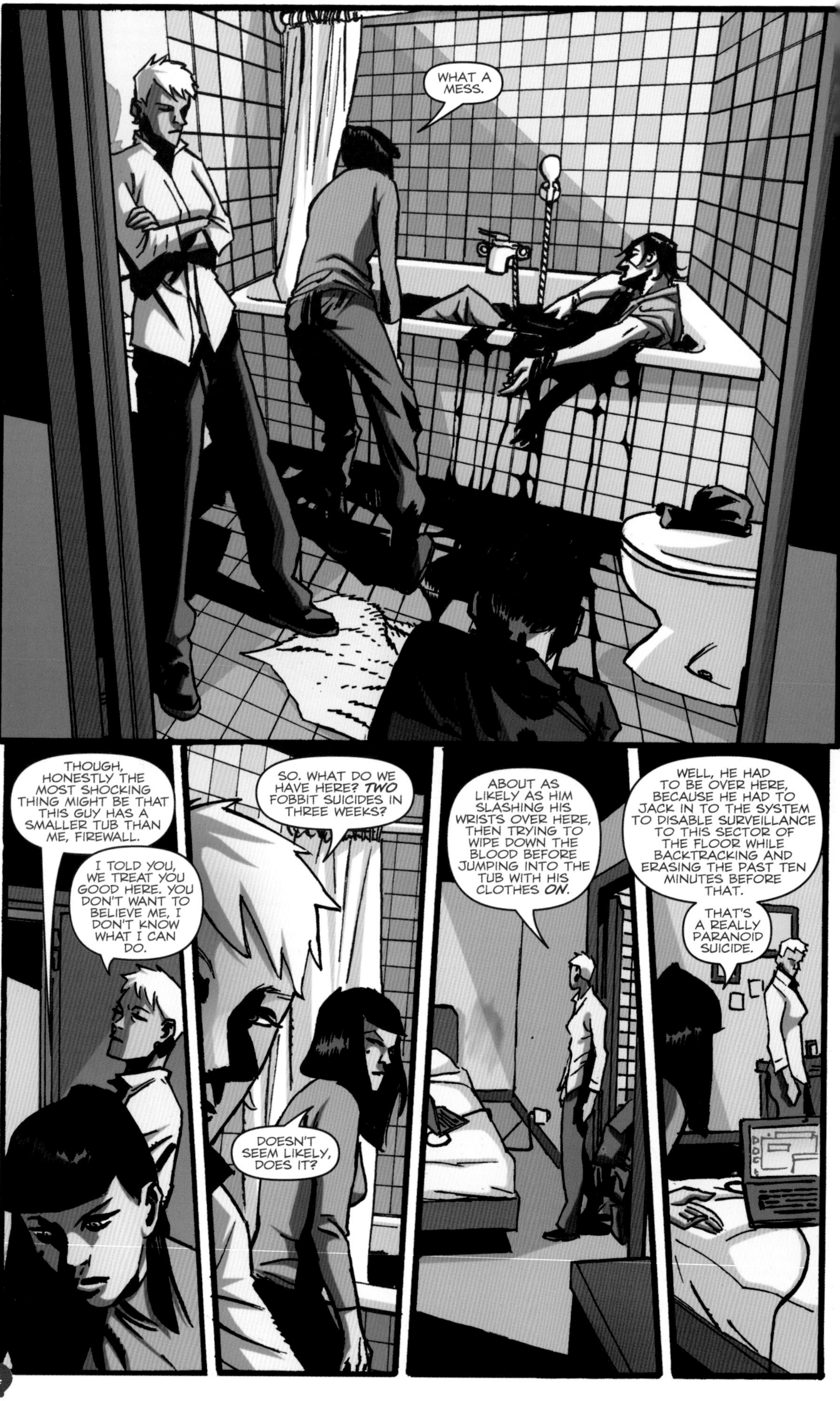
WHAT A MESS.
THOUGH, HONESTLY THE MOST SHOCKING THING MIGHT BE THAT THIS GUY HAS A SMALLER TUB THAN ME, FIREWALL.
I TOLD YOU, WE TREAT YOU GOOD HERE. YOU DON'T WANT TO BELIEVE ME, I DON'T KNOW WHAT I CAN DO.
SO. WHAT DO WE HAVE HERE? *TWO* FOBBIT SUICIDES IN THREE WEEKS?
DOESN'T SEEM LIKELY, DOES IT?
ABOUT AS LIKELY AS HIM SLASHING HIS WRISTS OVER HERE, THEN TRYING TO WIPE DOWN THE BLOOD BEFORE JUMPING INTO THE TUB WITH HIS CLOTHES *ON*.
WELL, HE HAD TO BE OVER HERE, BECAUSE HE HAD TO JACK IN TO THE SYSTEM TO DISABLE SURVEILLANCE TO THIS SECTOR OF THE FLOOR WHILE BACKTRACKING AND ERASING THE PAST TEN MINUTES BEFORE THAT.
THAT'S A REALLY PARANOID SUICIDE.

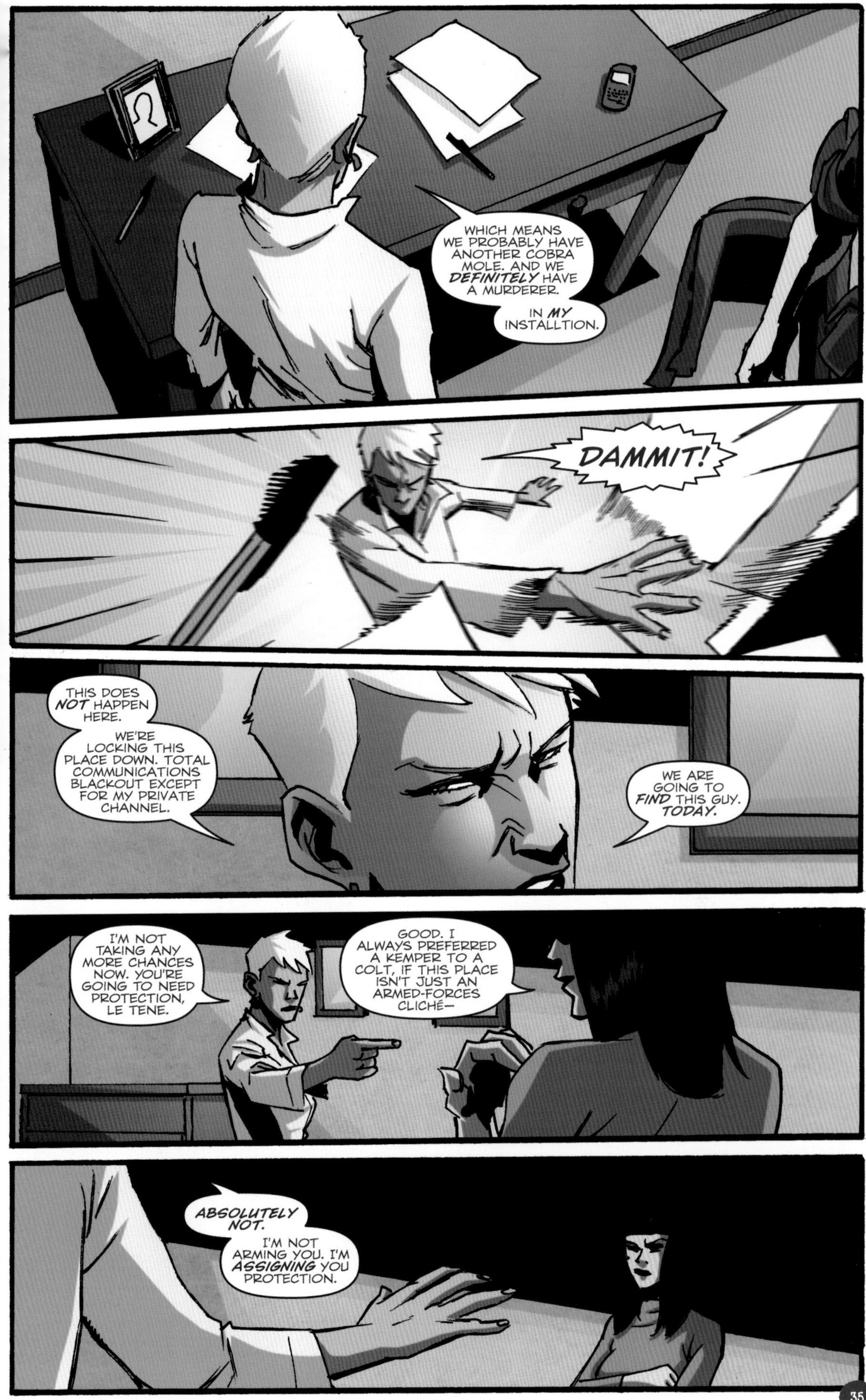

WHICH MEANS WE PROBABLY HAVE ANOTHER COBRA MOLE. AND WE DEFINITELY HAVE A MURDERER.
IN MY INSTALLTION.
DAMMIT!
THIS DOES NOT HAPPEN HERE.
WE'RE LOCKING THIS PLACE DOWN. TOTAL COMMUNICATIONS BLACKOUT EXCEPT FOR MY PRIVATE CHANNEL.
WE ARE GOING TO FIND THIS GUY. TODAY.
I'M NOT TAKING ANY MORE CHANCES NOW. YOU'RE GOING TO NEED PROTECTION, LE TENE.
GOOD. I ALWAYS PREFERRED A KEMPER TO A COLT, IF THIS PLACE ISN'T JUST AN ARMED-FORCES CLICHÉ—
ABSOLUTELY NOT.
I'M NOT ARMING YOU. I'M ASSIGNING YOU PROTECTION.

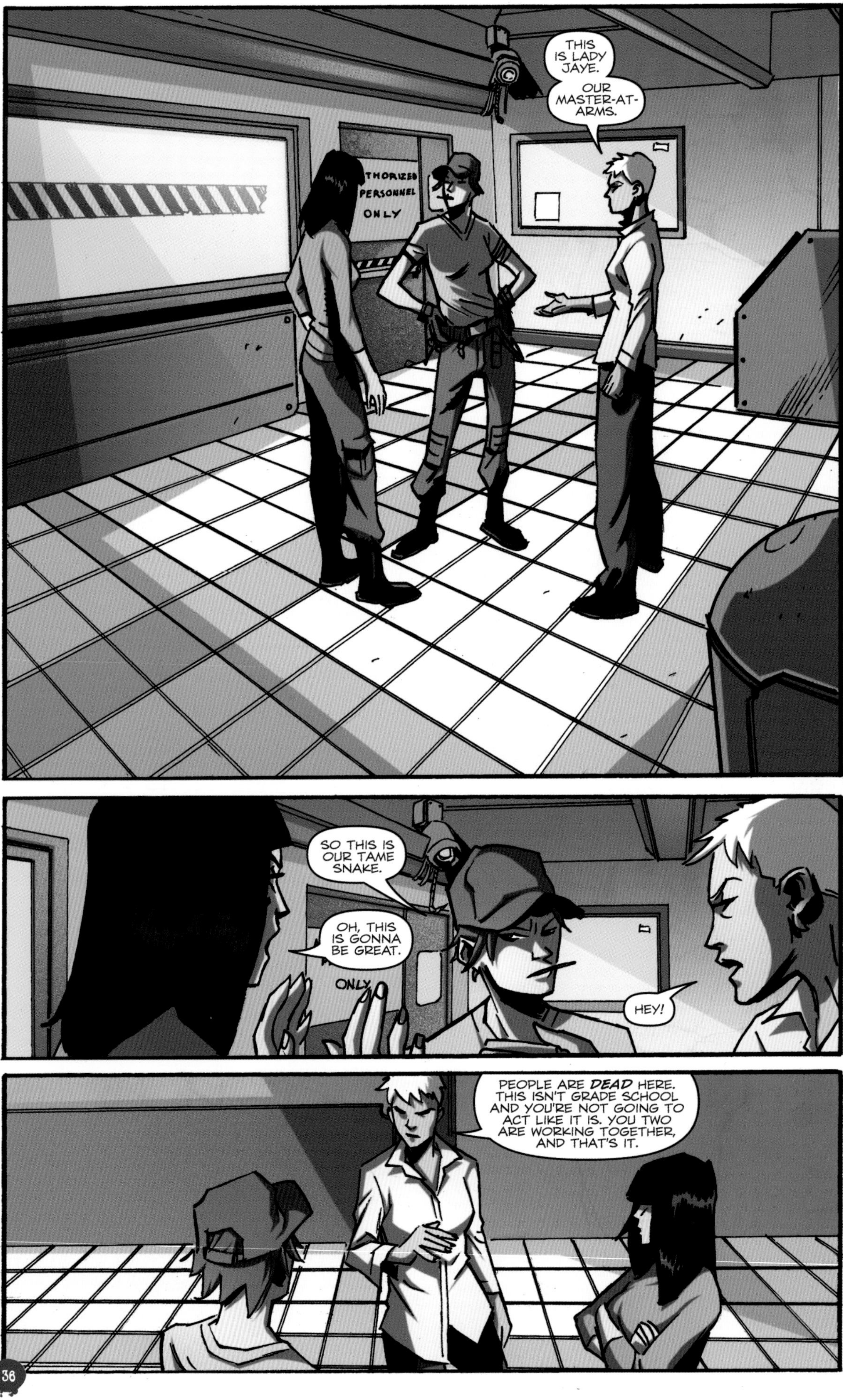

THIS IS LADY JAYE.
OUR MASTER-AT-ARMS.
THORIZED PERSONNEL ONLY
SO THIS IS OUR TAME SNAKE.
OH, THIS IS GONNA BE GREAT.
ONLY
HEY!
PEOPLE ARE DEAD HERE. THIS ISN'T GRADE SCHOOL AND YOU'RE NOT GOING TO ACT LIKE IT IS. YOU TWO ARE WORKING TOGETHER, AND THAT'S IT.

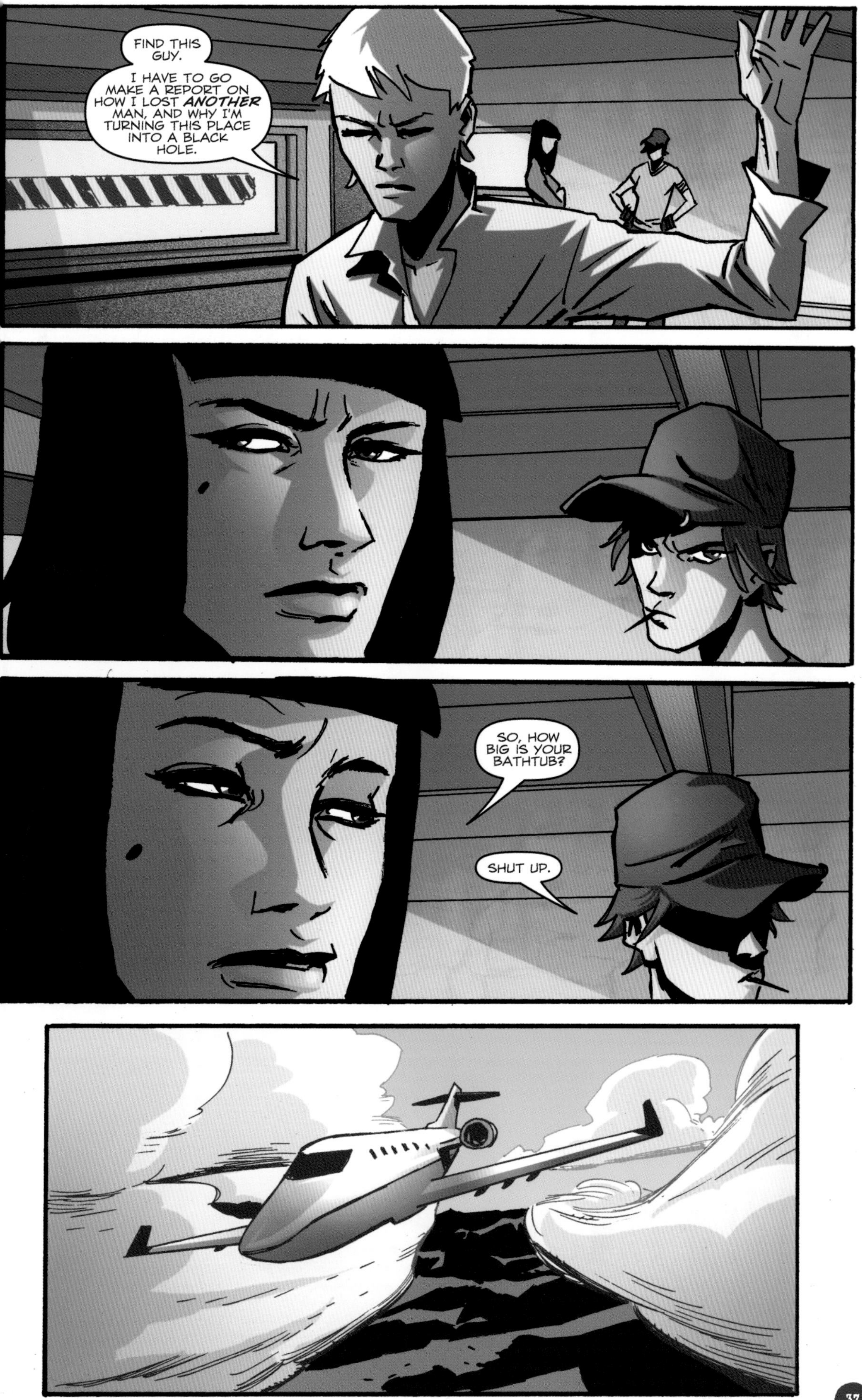
FIND THIS GUY.
I HAVE TO GO MAKE A REPORT ON HOW I LOST ANOTHER MAN, AND WHY I'M TURNING THIS PLACE INTO A BLACK HOLE.
SO, HOW BIG IS YOUR BATHTUB?
SHUT UP.

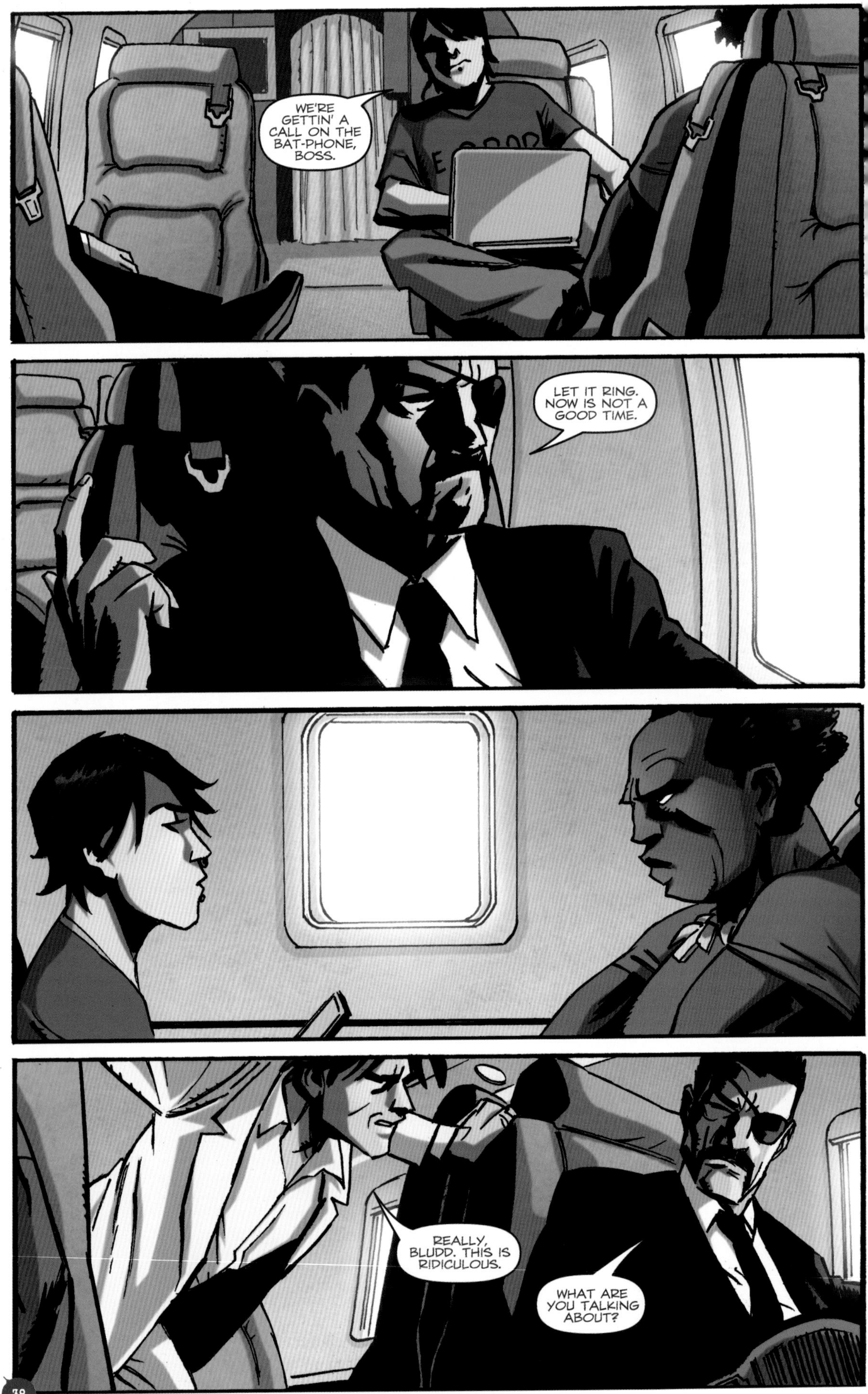
WE'RE GETTIN' A CALL ON THE BAT-PHONE, BOSS.
LET IT RING. NOW IS NOT A GOOD TIME.
REALLY, BLUDD. THIS IS RIDICULOUS.
WHAT ARE YOU TALKING ABOUT?

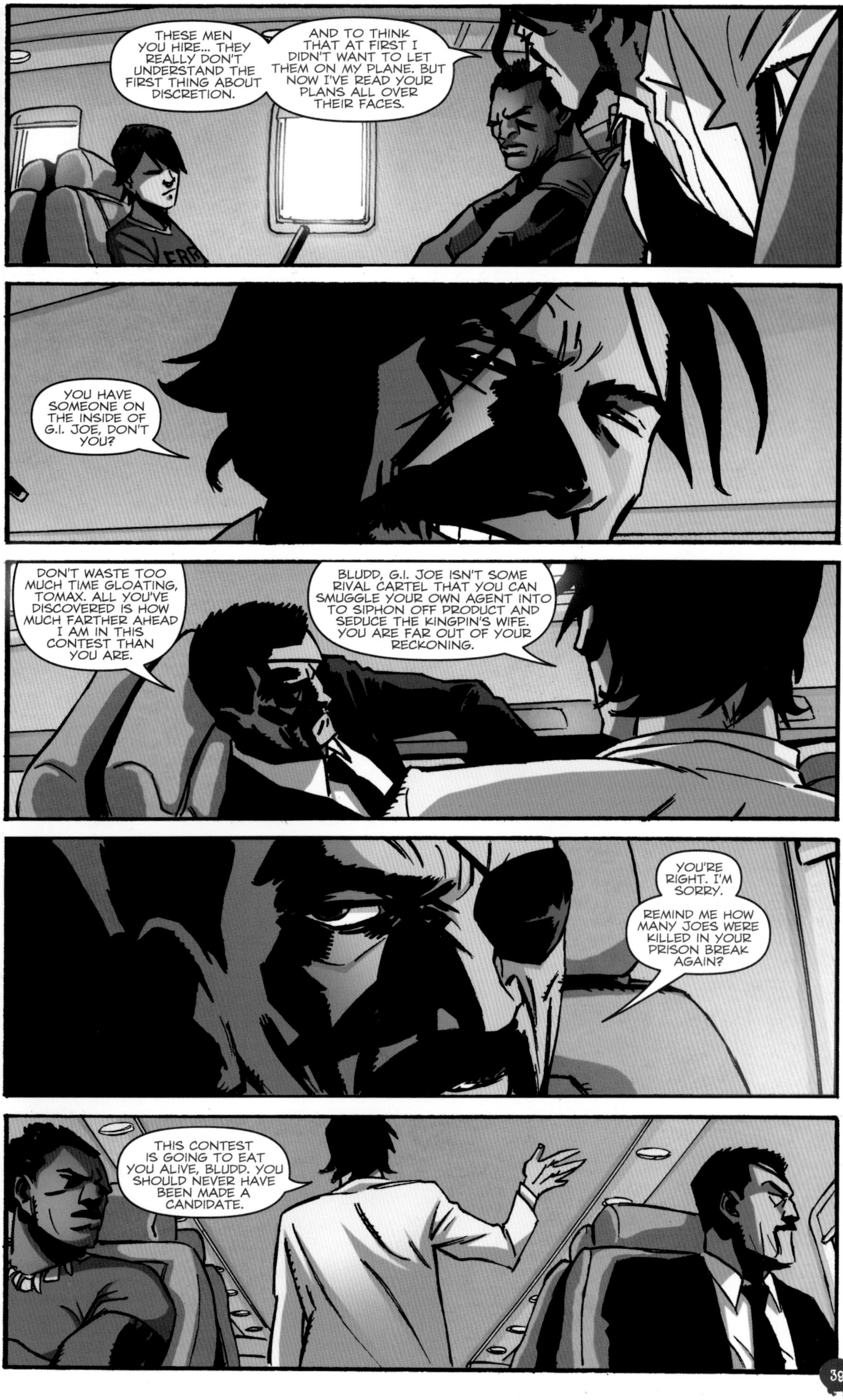
THESE MEN YOU HIRE... THEY REALLY DON'T UNDERSTAND THE FIRST THING ABOUT DISCRETION.
AND TO THINK THAT AT FIRST I DIDN'T WANT TO LET THEM ON MY PLANE. BUT NOW I'VE READ YOUR PLANS ALL OVER THEIR FACES.
YOU HAVE SOMEONE ON THE INSIDE OF G.I. JOE, DON'T YOU?
DON'T WASTE TOO MUCH TIME GLOATING, TOMAX. ALL YOU'VE DISCOVERED IS HOW MUCH FARTHER AHEAD I AM IN THIS CONTEST THAN YOU ARE.
BLUDD, G.I. JOE ISN'T SOME RIVAL CARTEL THAT YOU CAN SMUGGLE YOUR OWN AGENT INTO TO SIPHON OFF PRODUCT AND SEDUCE THE KINGPIN'S WIFE. YOU ARE FAR OUT OF YOUR RECKONING.
YOU'RE RIGHT. I'M SORRY.
REMIND ME HOW MANY JOES WERE KILLED IN YOUR PRISON BREAK AGAIN?
THIS CONTEST IS GOING TO EAT YOU ALIVE, BLUDD. YOU SHOULD NEVER HAVE BEEN MADE A CANDIDATE.

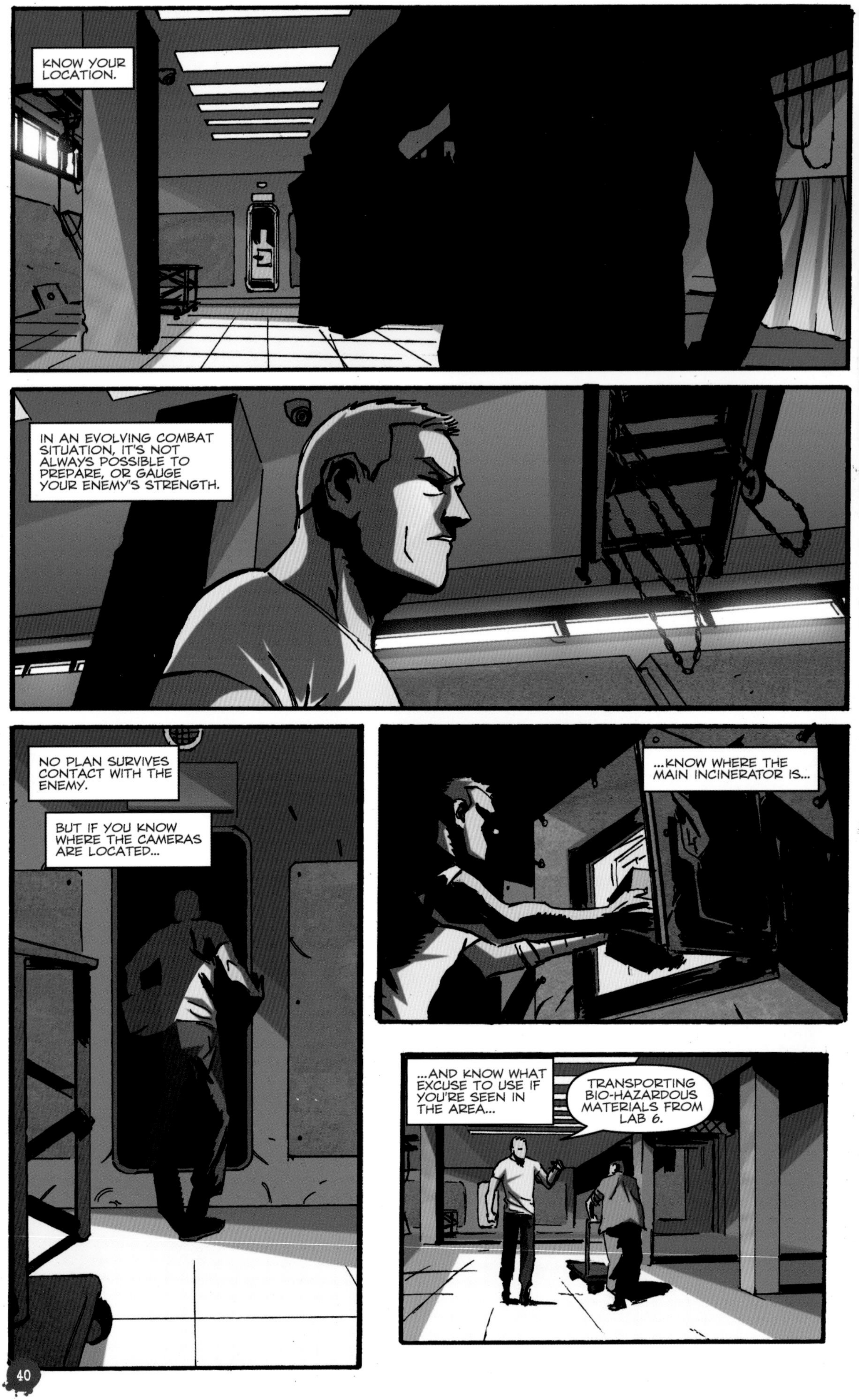
KNOW YOUR LOCATION.
IN AN EVOLVING COMBAT SITUATION, IT'S NOT ALWAYS POSSIBLE TO PREPARE, OR GAUGE YOUR ENEMY'S STRENGTH.
NO PLAN SURVIVES CONTACT WITH THE ENEMY.
BUT IF YOU KNOW WHERE THE CAMERAS ARE LOCATED...
...KNOW WHERE THE MAIN INCINERATOR IS...
...AND KNOW WHAT EXCUSE TO USE IF YOU'RE SEEN IN THE AREA...
TRANSPORTING BIO-HAZARDOUS MATERIALS FROM LAB 6.

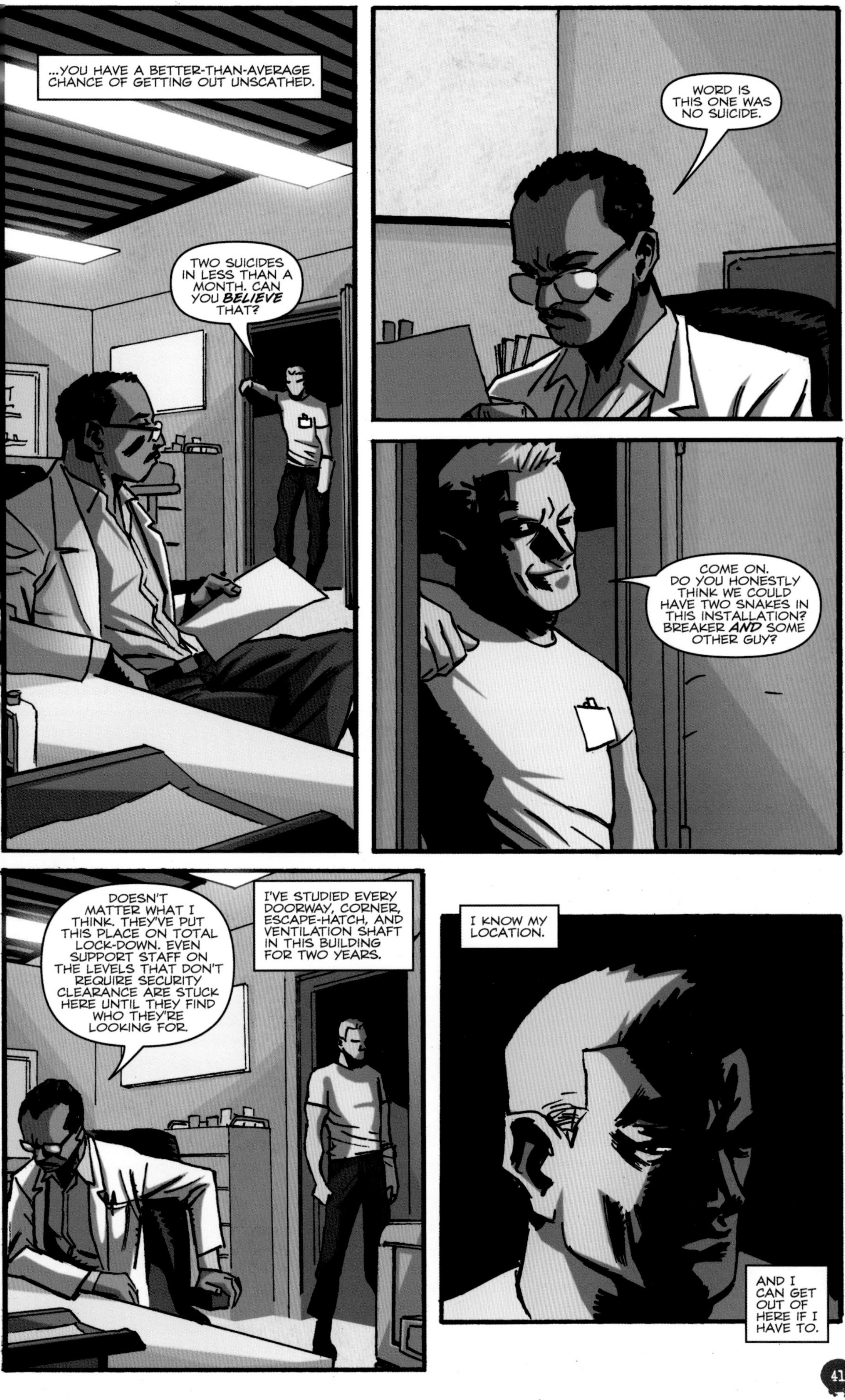
...YOU HAVE A BETTER-THAN-AVERAGE CHANCE OF GETTING OUT UNSCATHED.
TWO SUICIDES IN LESS THAN A MONTH. CAN YOU BELIEVE THAT?
WORD IS THIS ONE WAS NO SUICIDE.
COME ON. DO YOU HONESTLY THINK WE COULD HAVE TWO SNAKES IN THIS INSTALLATION? BREAKER AND SOME OTHER GUY?
DOESN'T MATTER WHAT I THINK. THEY'VE PUT THIS PLACE ON TOTAL LOCK-DOWN. EVEN SUPPORT STAFF ON THE LEVELS THAT DON'T REQUIRE SECURITY CLEARANCE ARE STUCK HERE UNTIL THEY FIND WHO THEY'RE LOOKING FOR.
I'VE STUDIED EVERY DOORWAY, CORNER, ESCAPE-HATCH, AND VENTILATION SHAFT IN THIS BUILDING FOR TWO YEARS.
I KNOW MY LOCATION.
AND I CAN GET OUT OF HERE IF I HAVE TO.

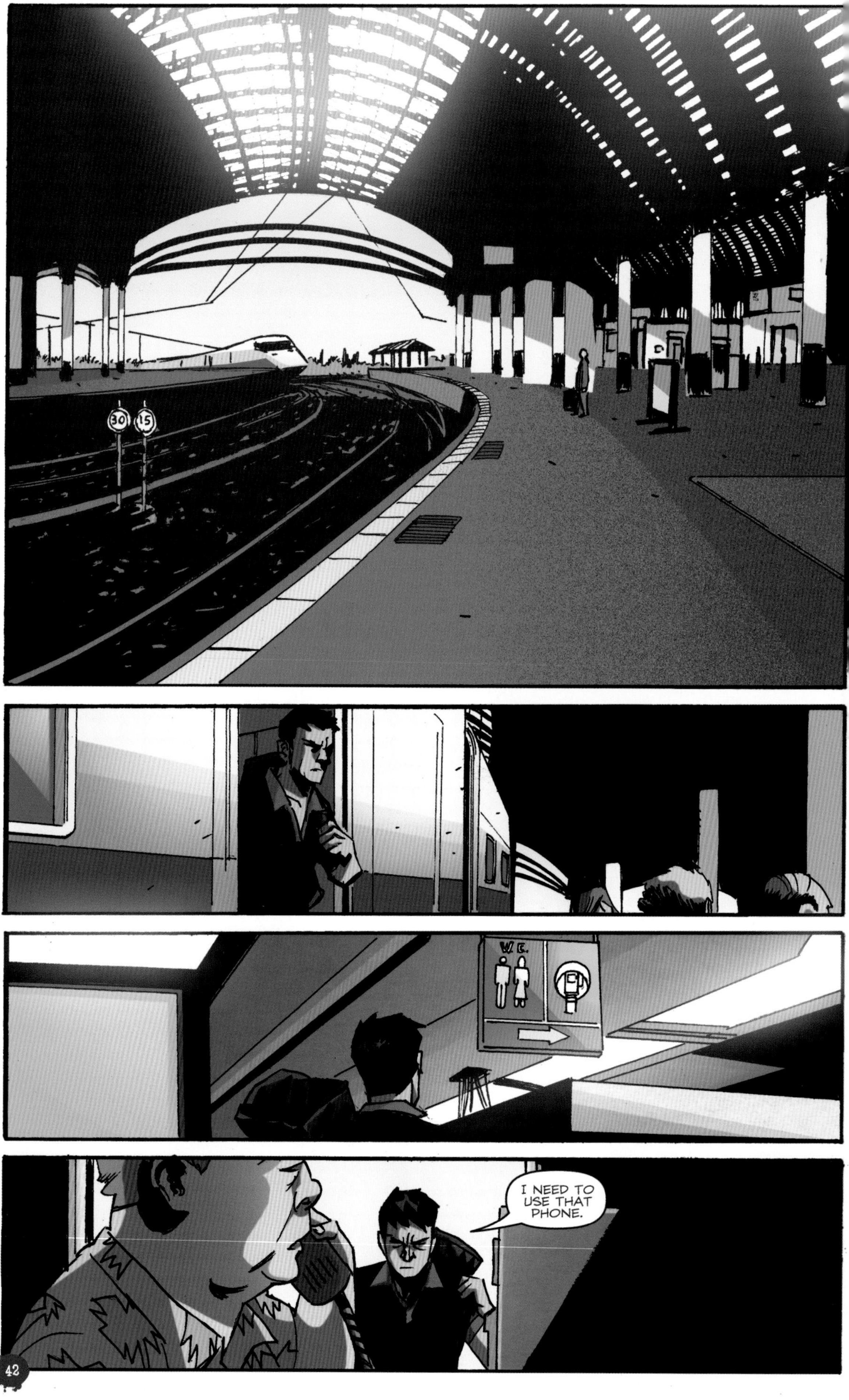
30
15
W.C.
I NEED TO USE THAT PHONE.

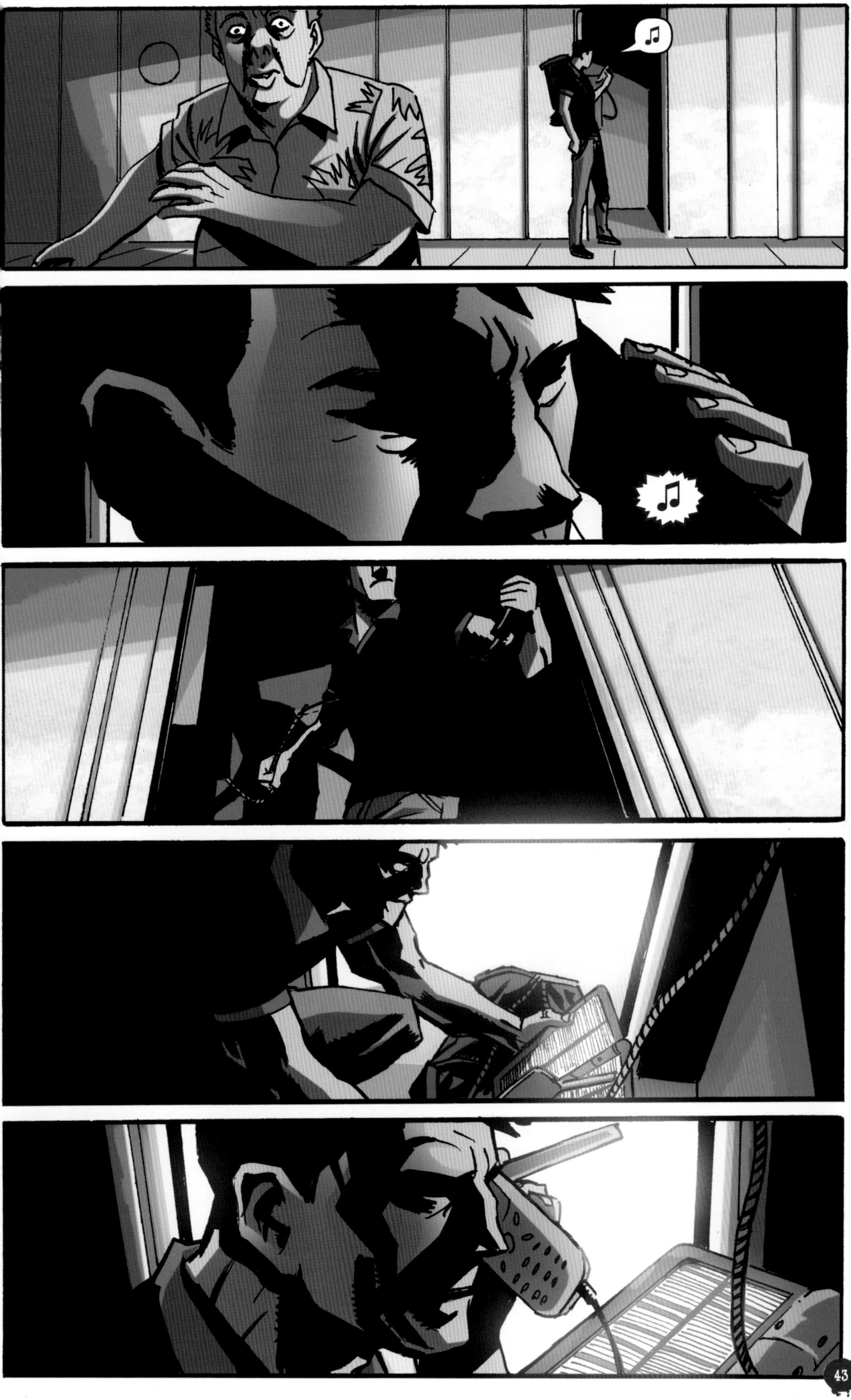

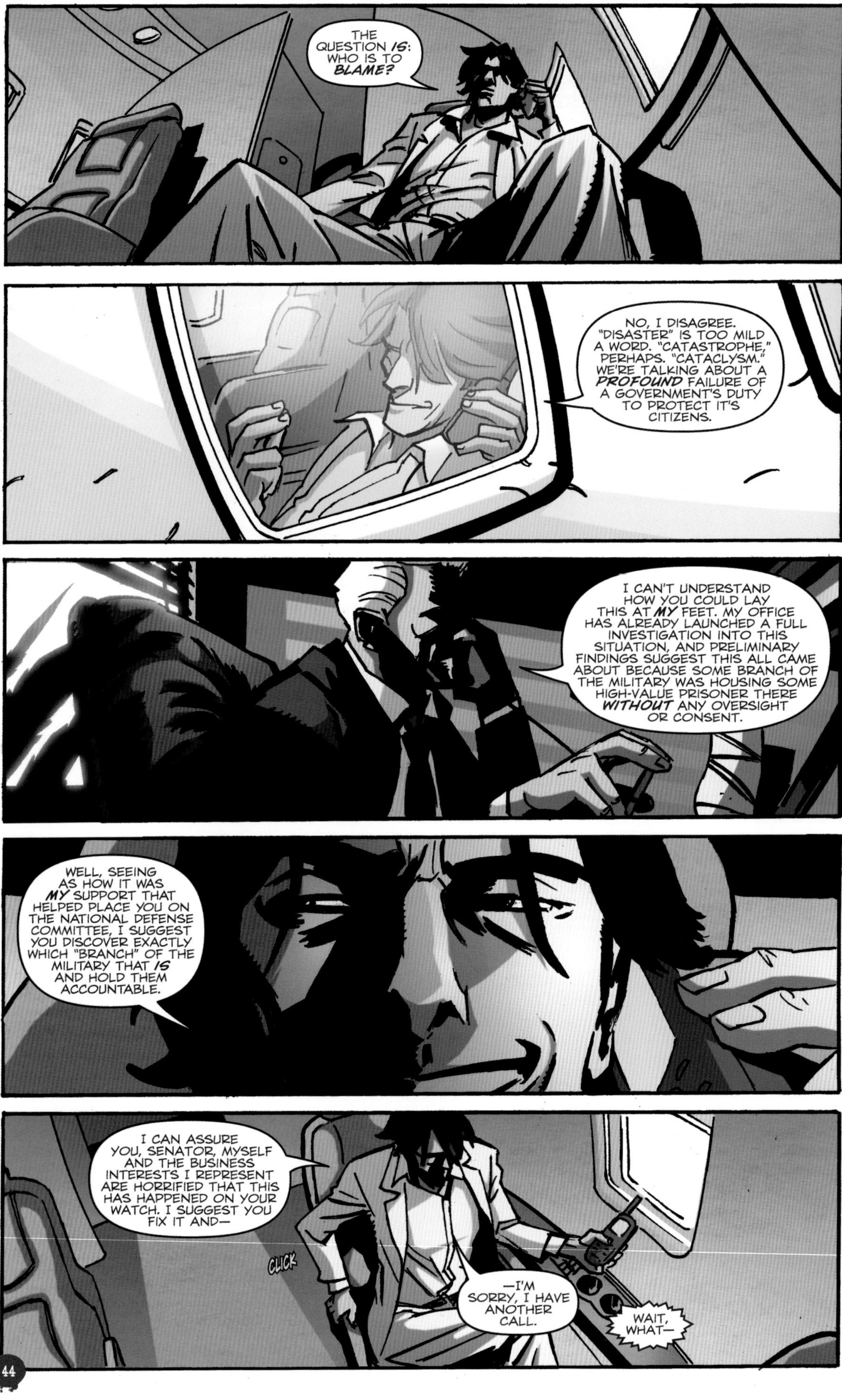
THE QUESTION IS: WHO IS TO BLAME?
NO, I DISAGREE. "DISASTER" IS TOO MILD A WORD. "CATASTROPHE," PERHAPS. "CATACLYSM." WE'RE TALKING ABOUT A PROFOUND FAILURE OF A GOVERNMENT'S DUTY TO PROTECT IT'S CITIZENS.
I CAN'T UNDERSTAND HOW YOU COULD LAY THIS AT MY FEET. MY OFFICE HAS ALREADY LAUNCHED A FULL INVESTIGATION INTO THIS SITUATION, AND PRELIMINARY FINDINGS SUGGEST THIS ALL CAME ABOUT BECAUSE SOME BRANCH OF THE MILITARY WAS HOUSING SOME HIGH-VALUE PRISONER THERE WITHOUT ANY OVERSIGHT OR CONSENT.
WELL, SEEING AS HOW IT WAS MY SUPPORT THAT HELPED PLACE YOU ON THE NATIONAL DEFENSE COMMITTEE, I SUGGEST YOU DISCOVER EXACTLY WHICH "BRANCH" OF THE MILITARY THAT IS AND HOLD THEM ACCOUNTABLE.
I CAN ASSURE YOU, SENATOR, MYSELF AND THE BUSINESS INTERESTS I REPRESENT ARE HORRIFIED THAT THIS HAS HAPPENED ON YOUR WATCH. I SUGGEST YOU FIX IT AND—
CLICK
—I'M SORRY, I HAVE ANOTHER CALL.
WAIT, WHAT—

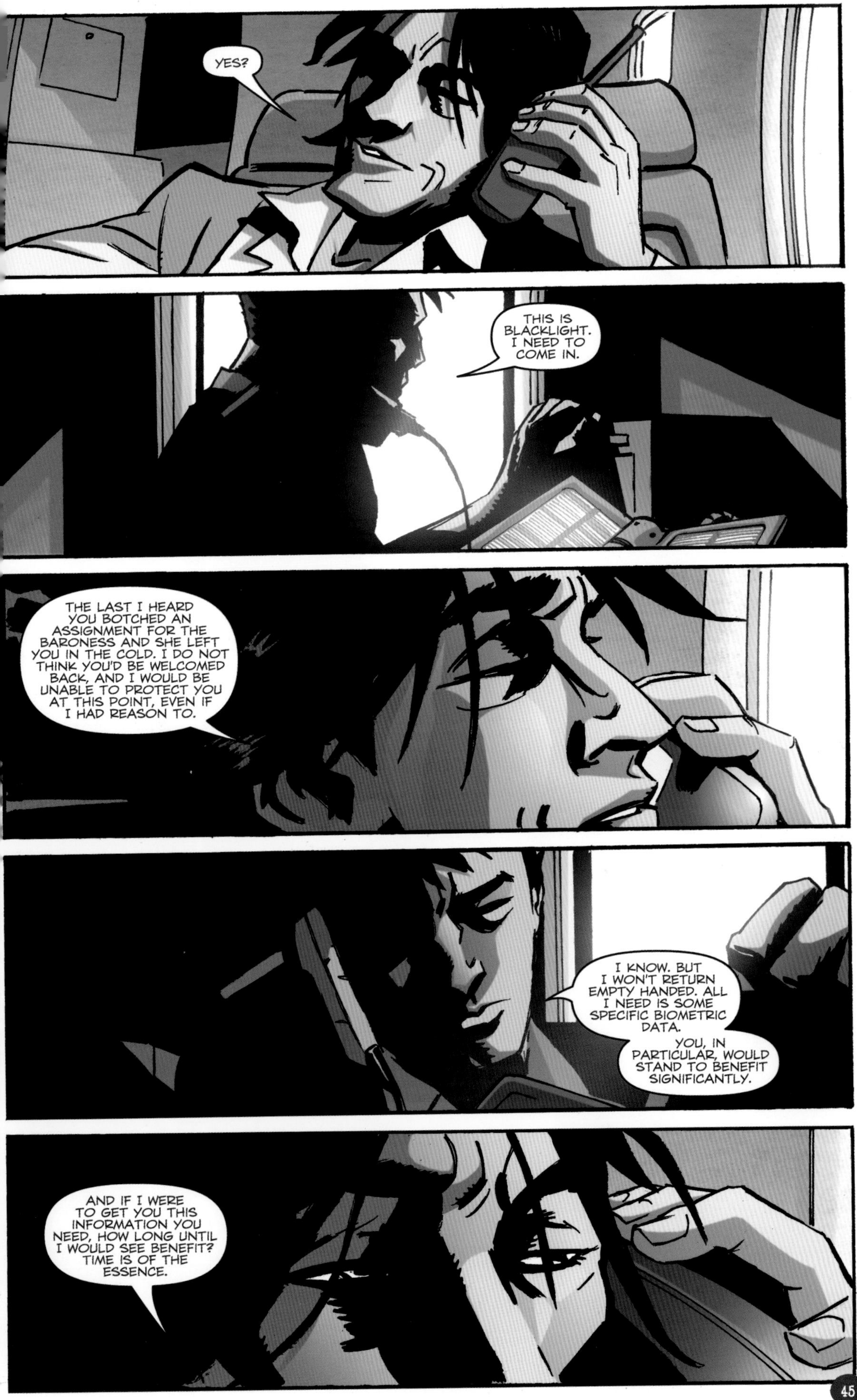
YES?
THIS IS BLACKLIGHT. I NEED TO COME IN.
THE LAST I HEARD YOU BOTCHED AN ASSIGNMENT FOR THE BARONESS AND SHE LEFT YOU IN THE COLD. I DO NOT THINK YOU'D BE WELCOMED BACK, AND I WOULD BE UNABLE TO PROTECT YOU AT THIS POINT, EVEN IF I HAD REASON TO.
I KNOW. BUT I WON'T RETURN EMPTY HANDED. ALL I NEED IS SOME SPECIFIC BIOMETRIC DATA.
YOU, IN PARTICULAR, WOULD STAND TO BENEFIT SIGNIFICANTLY.
AND IF I WERE TO GET YOU THIS INFORMATION YOU NEED, HOW LONG UNTIL I WOULD SEE BENEFIT? TIME IS OF THE ESSENCE.

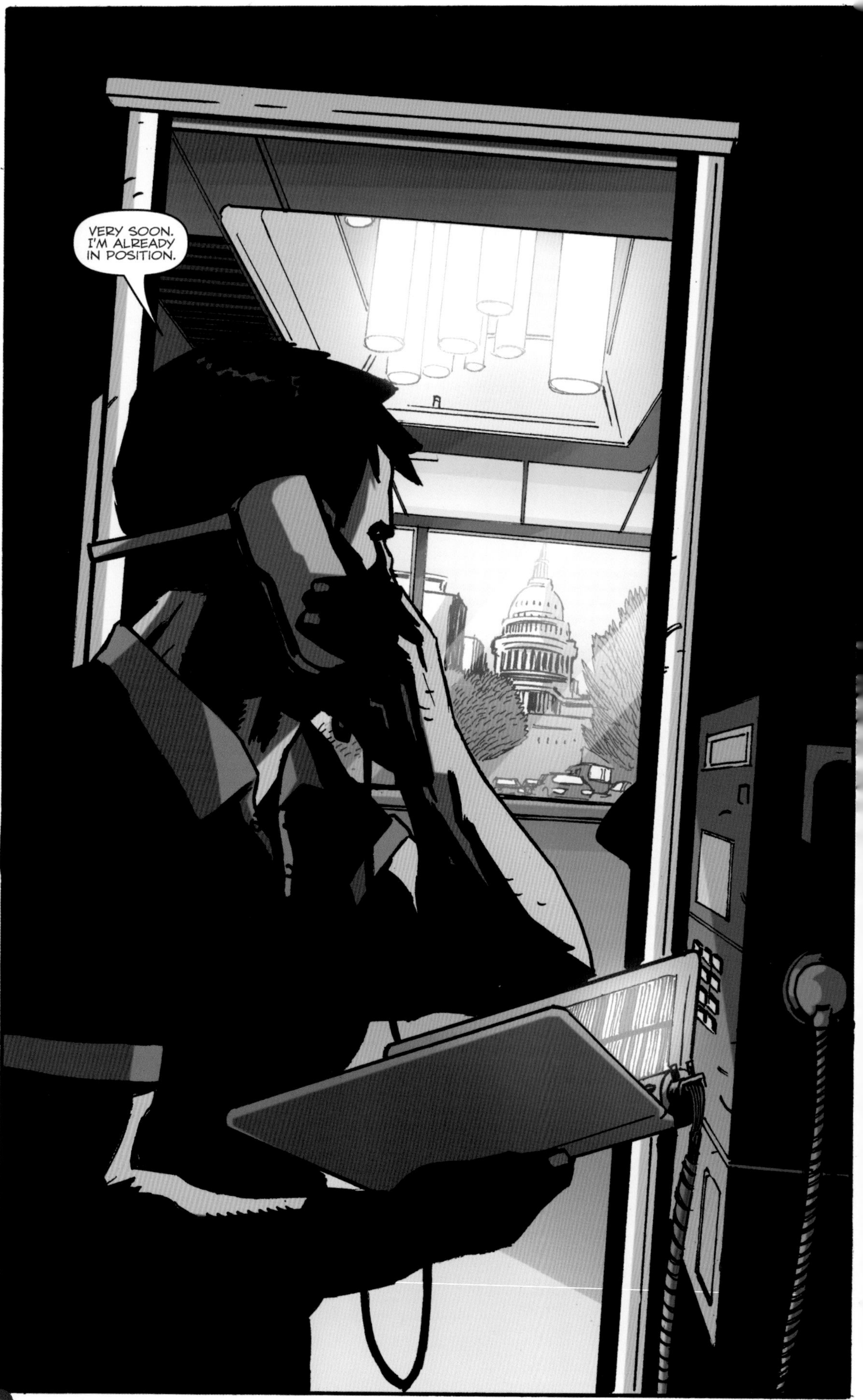
VERY SOON. I'M ALREADY IN POSITION.

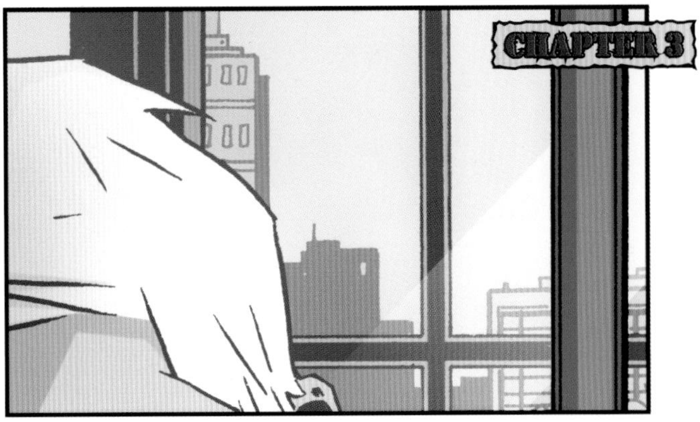
CHAPTER 3

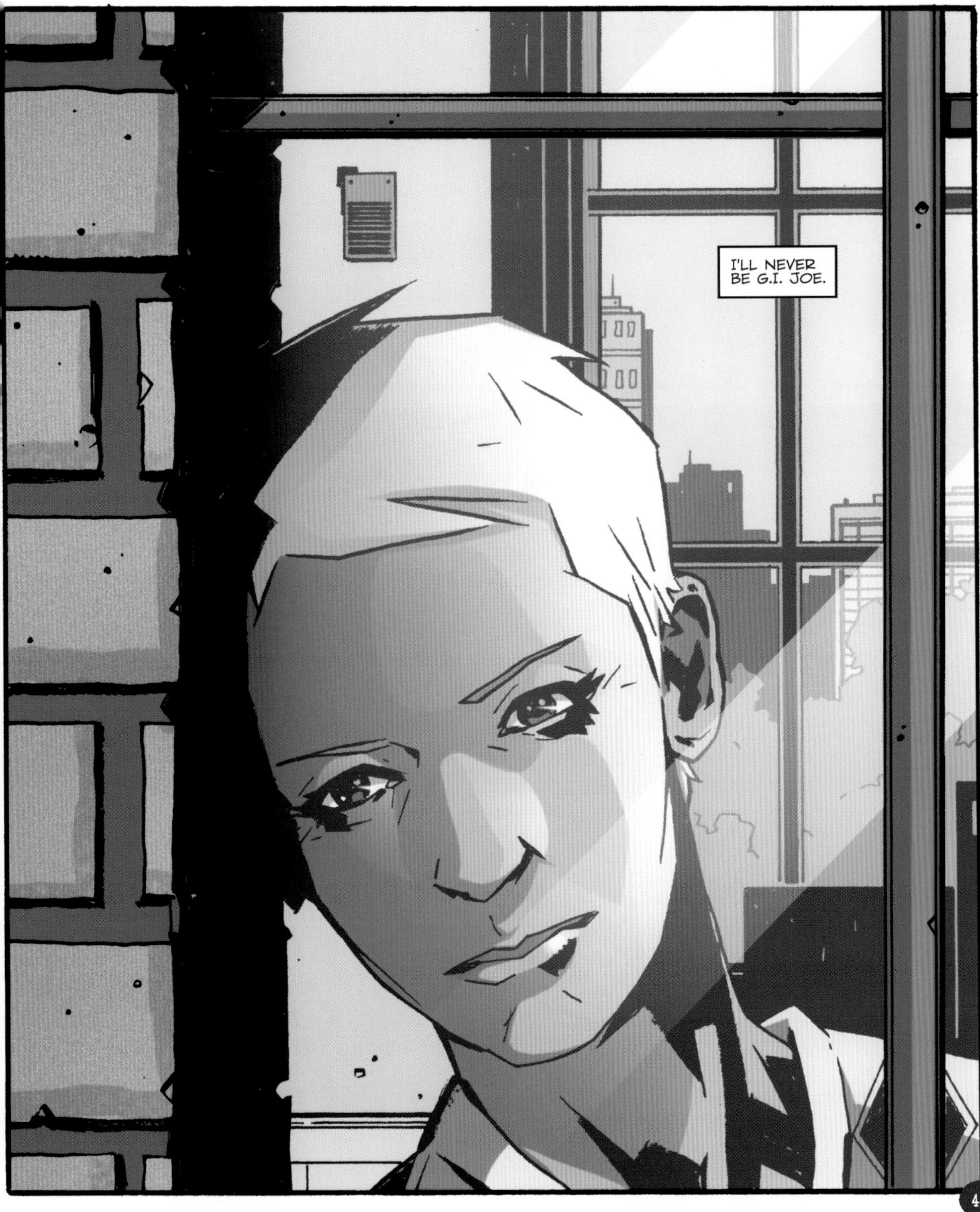
I'LL NEVER
BE G.I. JOE.

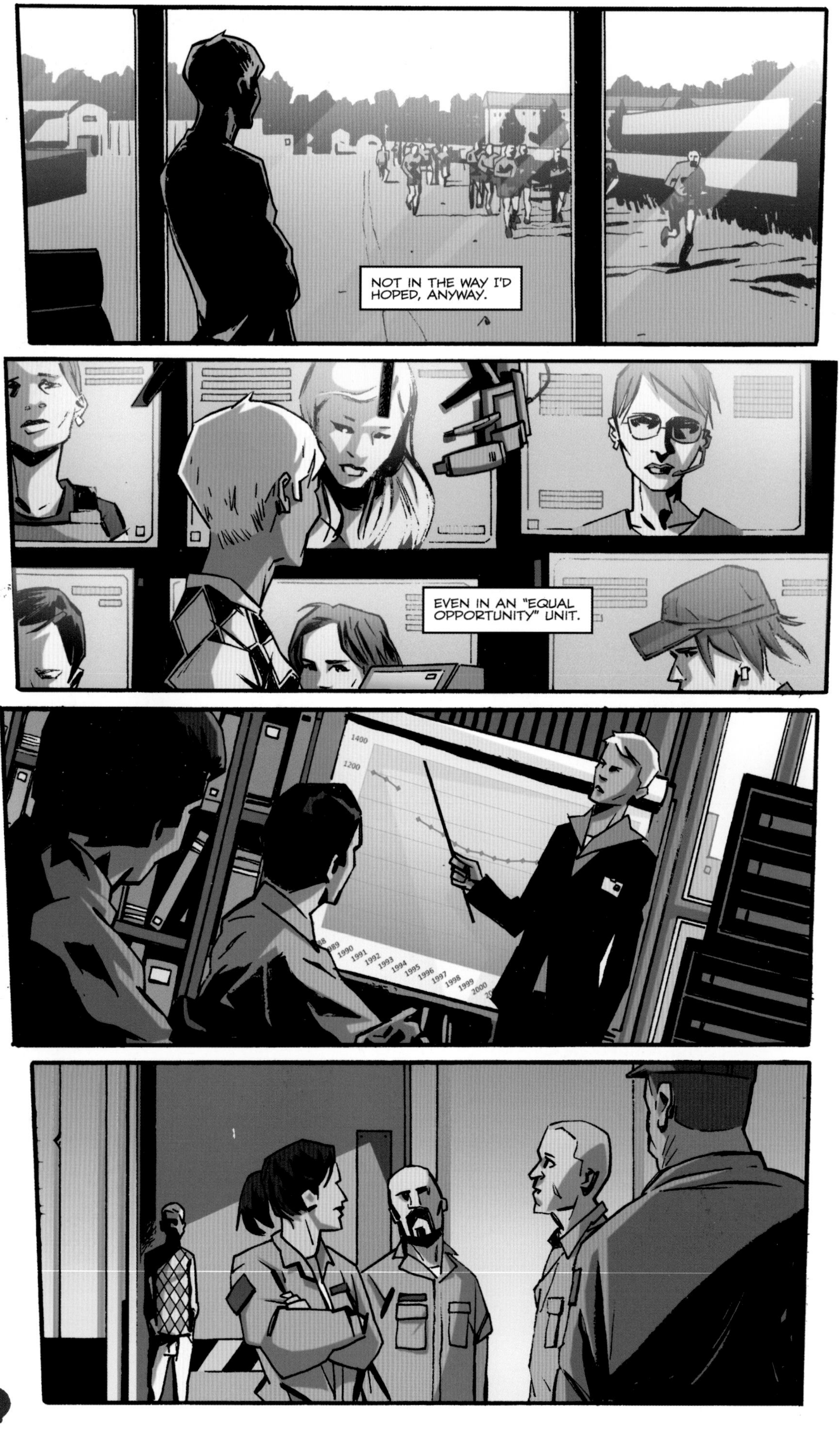
NOT IN THE WAY I'D HOPED, ANYWAY.
EVEN IN AN "EQUAL OPPORTUNITY" UNIT.
1400
1200
1990
1991
1992
1993
1994
1995
1996
1997
1998
1999
2000

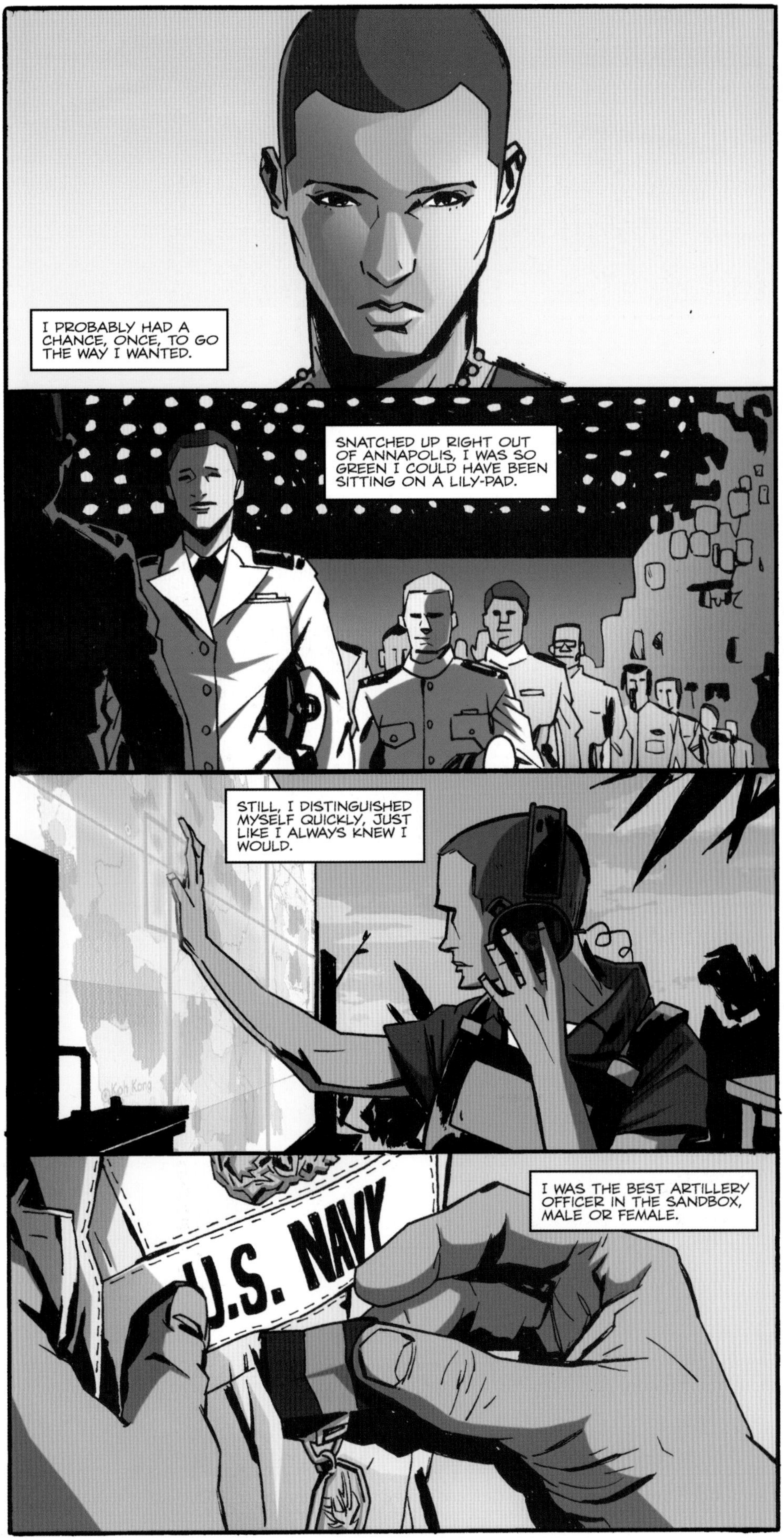
I PROBABLY HAD A CHANCE, ONCE, TO GO THE WAY I WANTED.
SNATCHED UP RIGHT OUT OF ANNAPOLIS, I WAS SO GREEN I COULD HAVE BEEN SITTING ON A LILY-PAD.
STILL, I DISTINGUISHED MYSELF QUICKLY, JUST LIKE I ALWAYS KNEW I WOULD.
I WAS THE BEST ARTILLERY OFFICER IN THE SANDBOX, MALE OR FEMALE.
U.S. NAVY

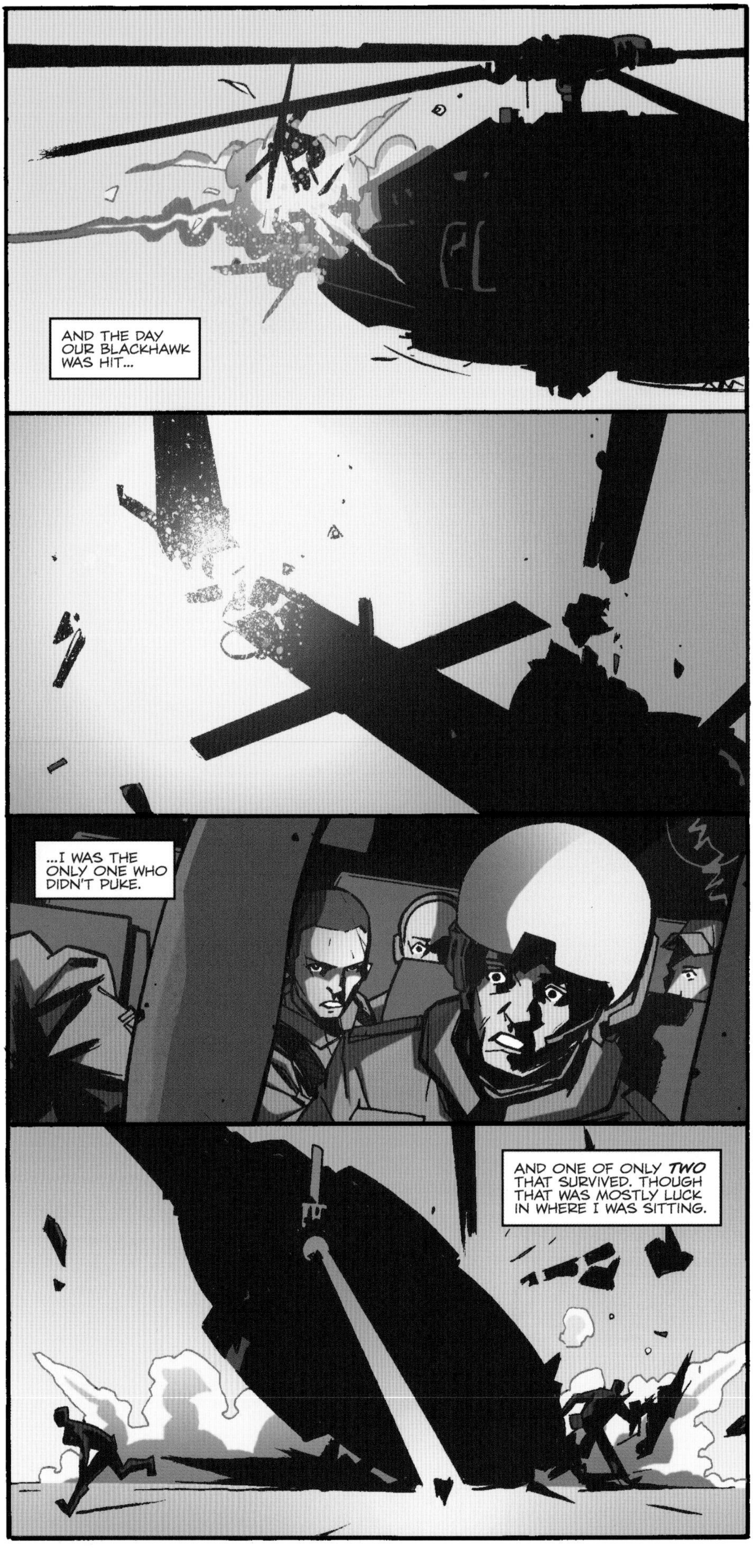
AND THE DAY OUR BLACKHAWK WAS HIT...
...I WAS THE ONLY ONE WHO DIDN'T PUKE.
AND ONE OF ONLY *TWO* THAT SURVIVED. THOUGH THAT WAS MOSTLY LUCK IN WHERE I WAS SITTING.

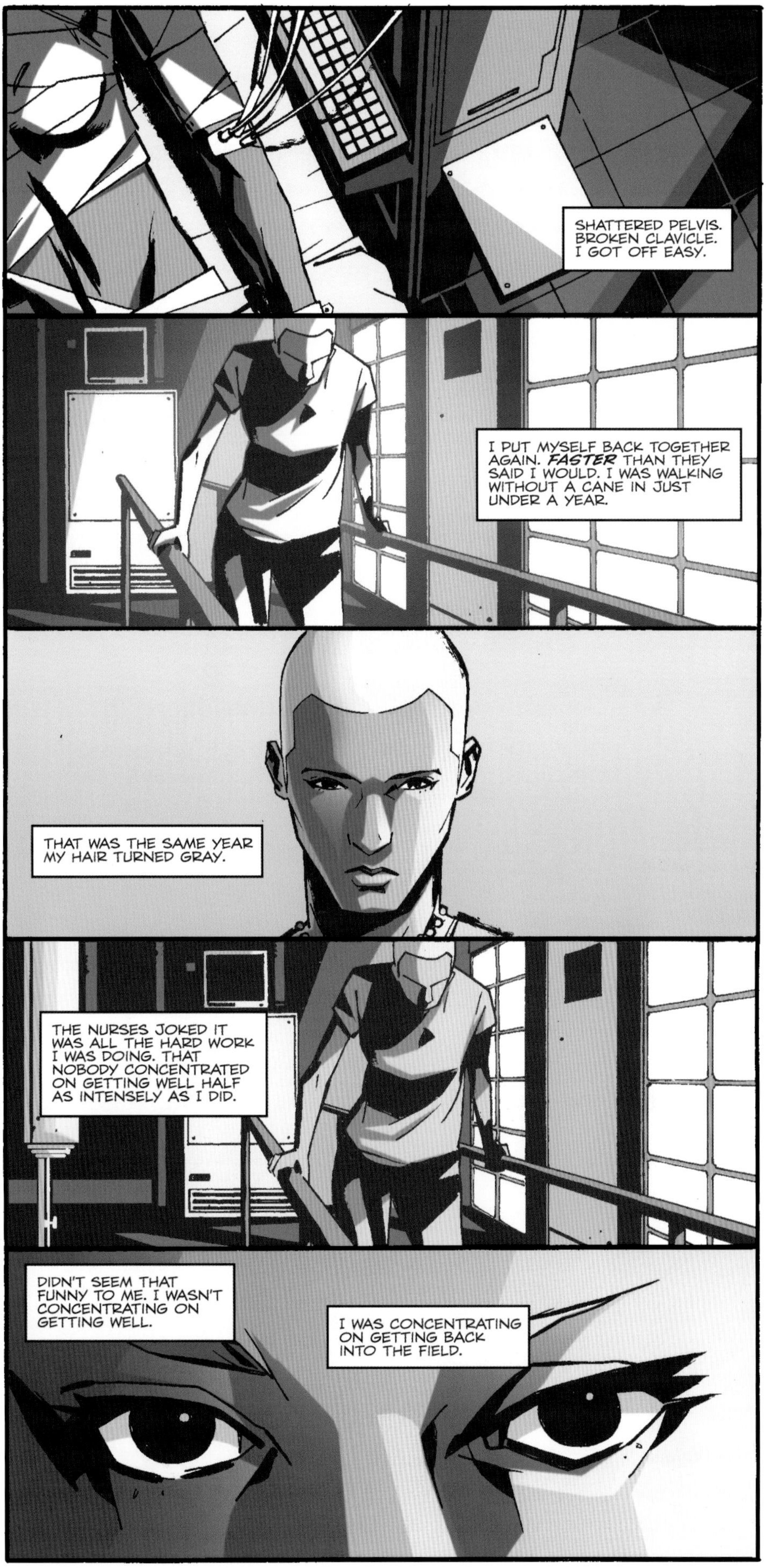
SHATTERED PELVIS. BROKEN CLAVICLE. I GOT OFF EASY.
I PUT MYSELF BACK TOGETHER AGAIN. FASTER THAN THEY SAID I WOULD. I WAS WALKING WITHOUT A CANE IN JUST UNDER A YEAR.
THAT WAS THE SAME YEAR MY HAIR TURNED GRAY.
THE NURSES JOKED IT WAS ALL THE HARD WORK I WAS DOING. THAT NOBODY CONCENTRATED ON GETTING WELL HALF AS INTENSELY AS I DID.
DIDN'T SEEM THAT FUNNY TO ME. I WASN'T CONCENTRATING ON GETTING WELL.
I WAS CONCENTRATING ON GETTING BACK INTO THE FIELD.

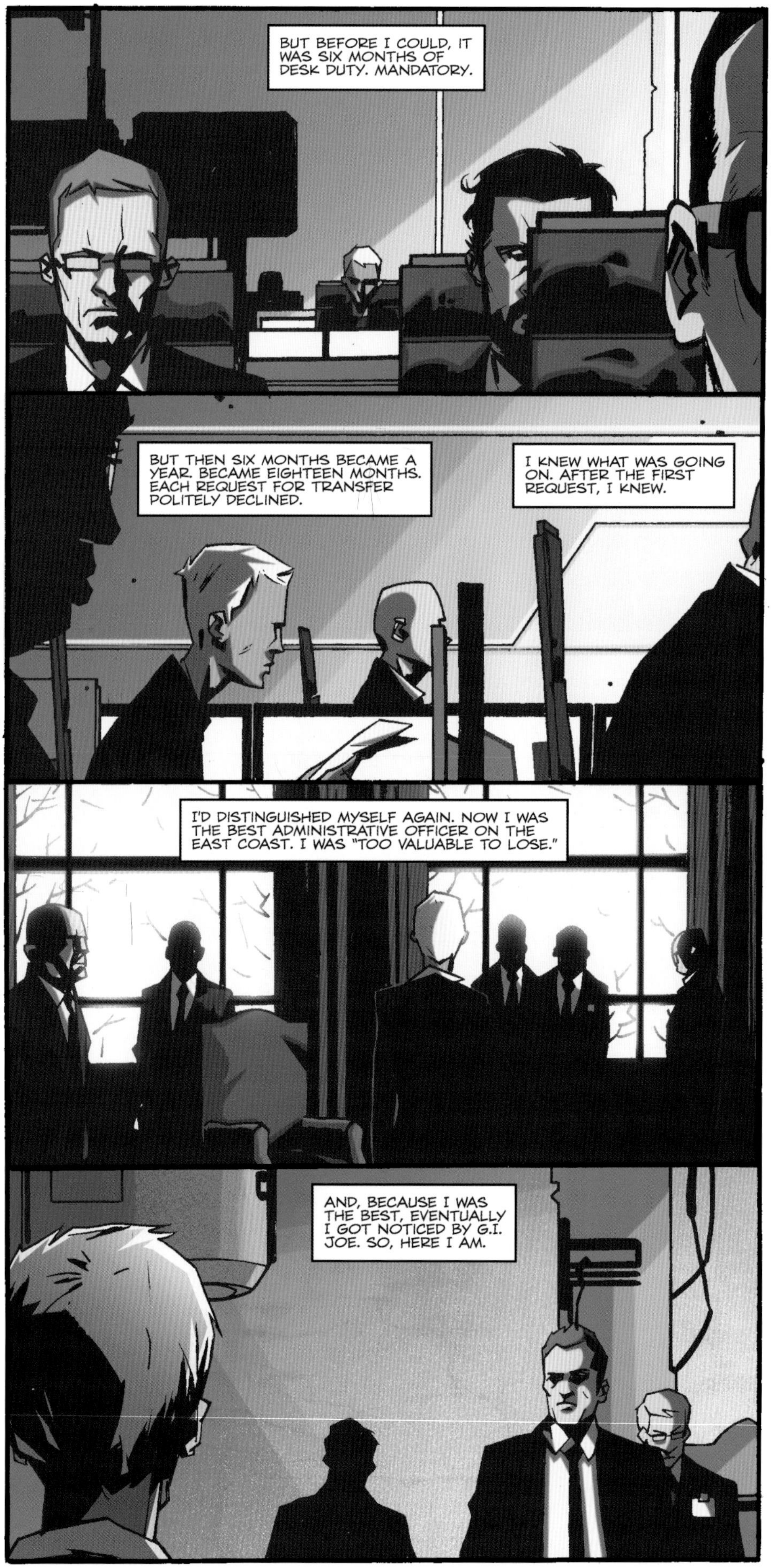
BUT BEFORE I COULD, IT WAS SIX MONTHS OF DESK DUTY. MANDATORY.
BUT THEN SIX MONTHS BECAME A YEAR. BECAME EIGHTEEN MONTHS. EACH REQUEST FOR TRANSFER POLITELY DECLINED.
I KNEW WHAT WAS GOING ON. AFTER THE FIRST REQUEST, I KNEW.
I'D DISTINGUISHED MYSELF AGAIN. NOW I WAS THE BEST ADMINISTRATIVE OFFICER ON THE EAST COAST. I WAS "TOO VALUABLE TO LOSE."
AND, BECAUSE I WAS THE BEST, EVENTUALLY I GOT NOTICED BY G.I. JOE. SO, HERE I AM.

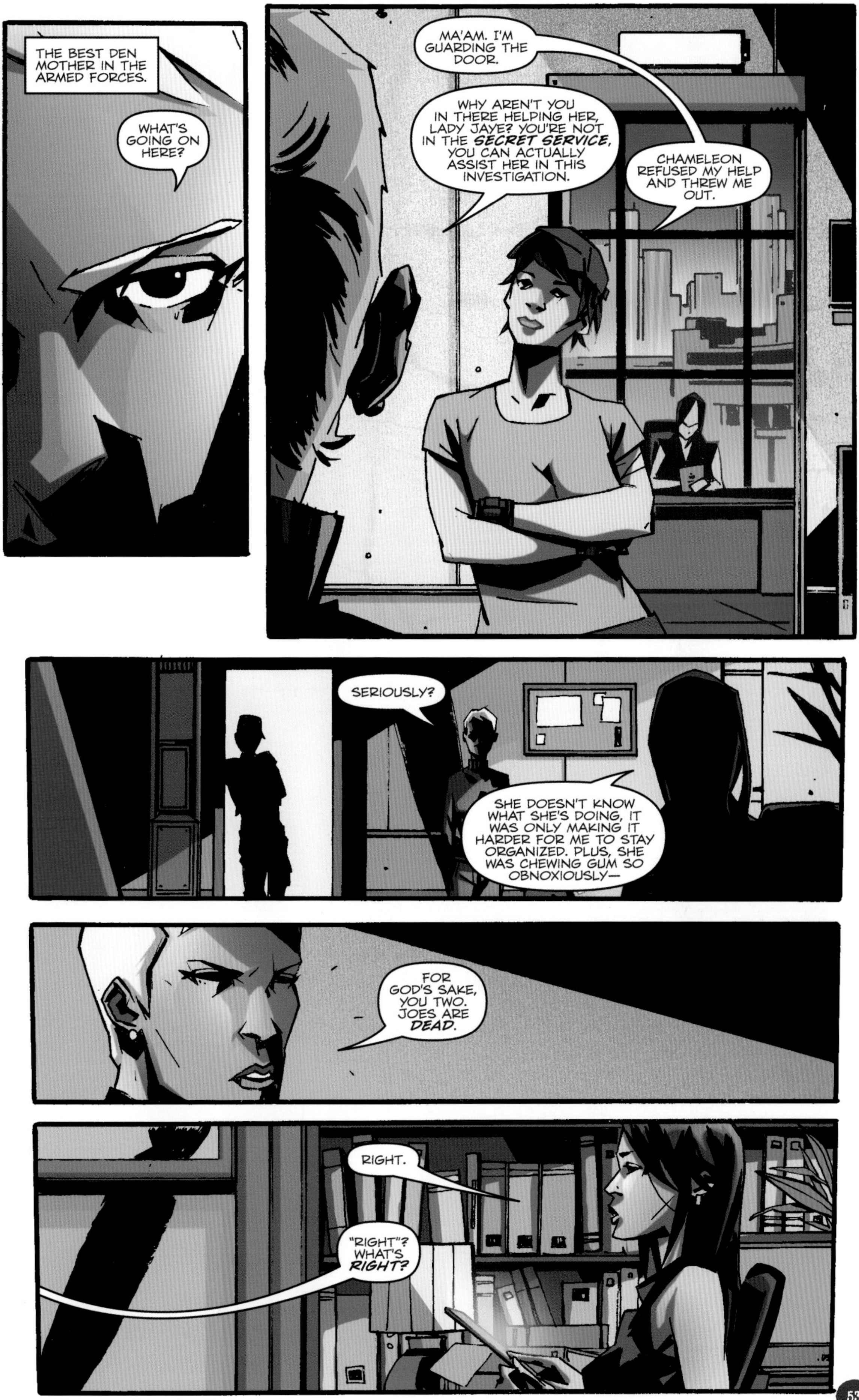

THE BEST DEN MOTHER IN THE ARMED FORCES.
WHAT'S GOING ON HERE?
MA'AM. I'M GUARDING THE DOOR.
WHY AREN'T YOU IN THERE HELPING HER, LADY JAYE? YOU'RE NOT IN THE ***SECRET SERVICE***, YOU CAN ACTUALLY ASSIST HER IN THIS INVESTIGATION.
CHAMELEON REFUSED MY HELP AND THREW ME OUT.
SERIOUSLY?
SHE DOESN'T KNOW WHAT SHE'S DOING, IT WAS ONLY MAKING IT HARDER FOR ME TO STAY ORGANIZED. PLUS, SHE WAS CHEWING GUM SO OBNOXIOUSLY—
FOR GOD'S SAKE, YOU TWO. JOES ARE ***DEAD***.
RIGHT.
"RIGHT"? WHAT'S ***RIGHT***?

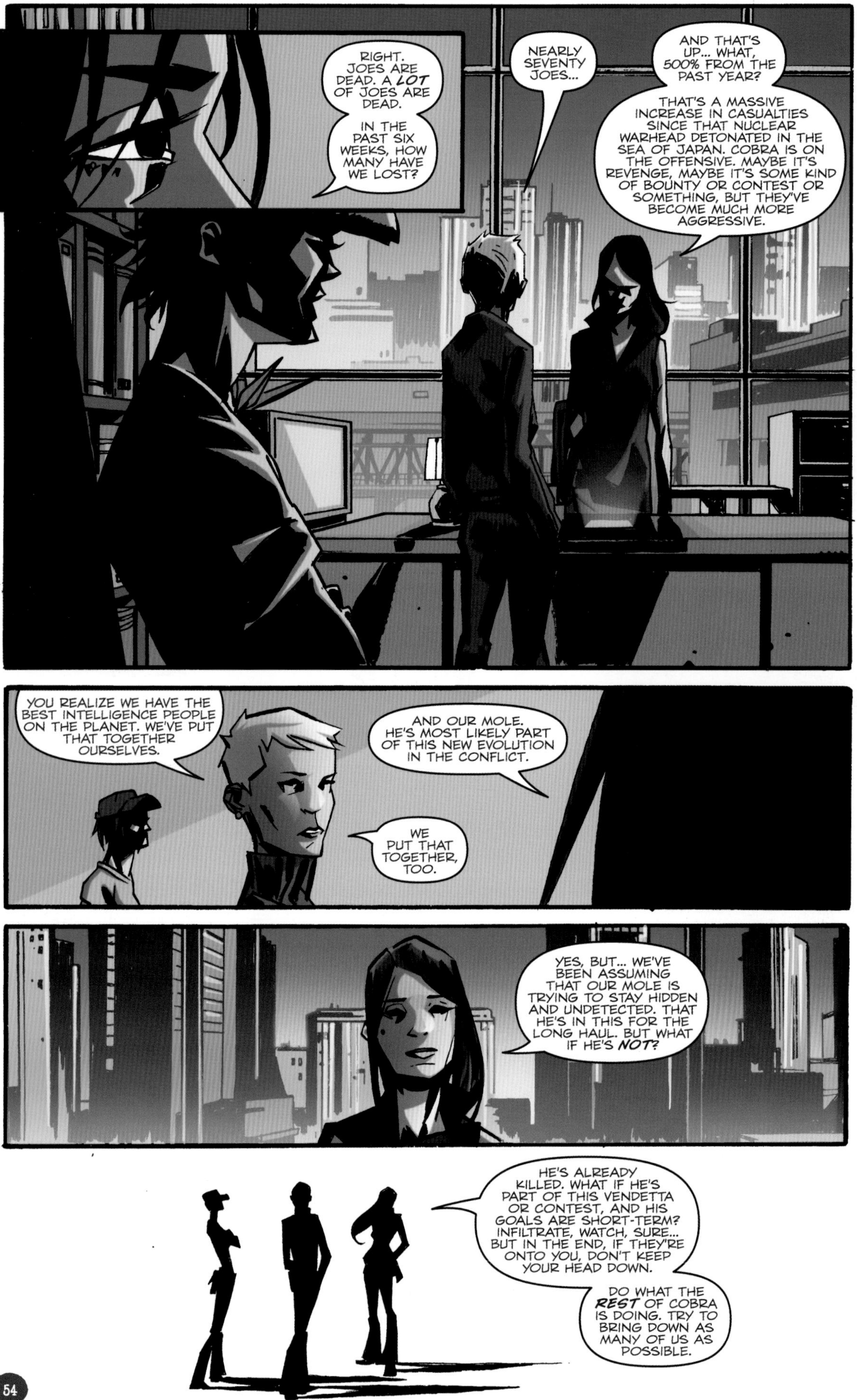
RIGHT. JOES ARE DEAD. A LOT OF JOES ARE DEAD.
IN THE PAST SIX WEEKS, HOW MANY HAVE WE LOST?
NEARLY SEVENTY JOES...
AND THAT'S UP... WHAT, 500% FROM THE PAST YEAR?
THAT'S A MASSIVE INCREASE IN CASUALTIES SINCE THAT NUCLEAR WARHEAD DETONATED IN THE SEA OF JAPAN. COBRA IS ON THE OFFENSIVE. MAYBE IT'S REVENGE, MAYBE IT'S SOME KIND OF BOUNTY OR CONTEST OR SOMETHING, BUT THEY'VE BECOME MUCH MORE AGGRESSIVE.
YOU REALIZE WE HAVE THE BEST INTELLIGENCE PEOPLE ON THE PLANET. WE'VE PUT THAT TOGETHER OURSELVES.
AND OUR MOLE. HE'S MOST LIKELY PART OF THIS NEW EVOLUTION IN THE CONFLICT.
WE PUT THAT TOGETHER, TOO.
YES, BUT... WE'VE BEEN ASSUMING THAT OUR MOLE IS TRYING TO STAY HIDDEN AND UNDETECTED. THAT HE'S IN THIS FOR THE LONG HAUL. BUT WHAT IF HE'S NOT?
HE'S ALREADY KILLED. WHAT IF HE'S PART OF THIS VENDETTA OR CONTEST, AND HIS GOALS ARE SHORT-TERM? INFILTRATE, WATCH, SURE... BUT IN THE END, IF THEY'RE ONTO YOU, DON'T KEEP YOUR HEAD DOWN.
DO WHAT THE REST OF COBRA IS DOING. TRY TO BRING DOWN AS MANY OF US AS POSSIBLE.

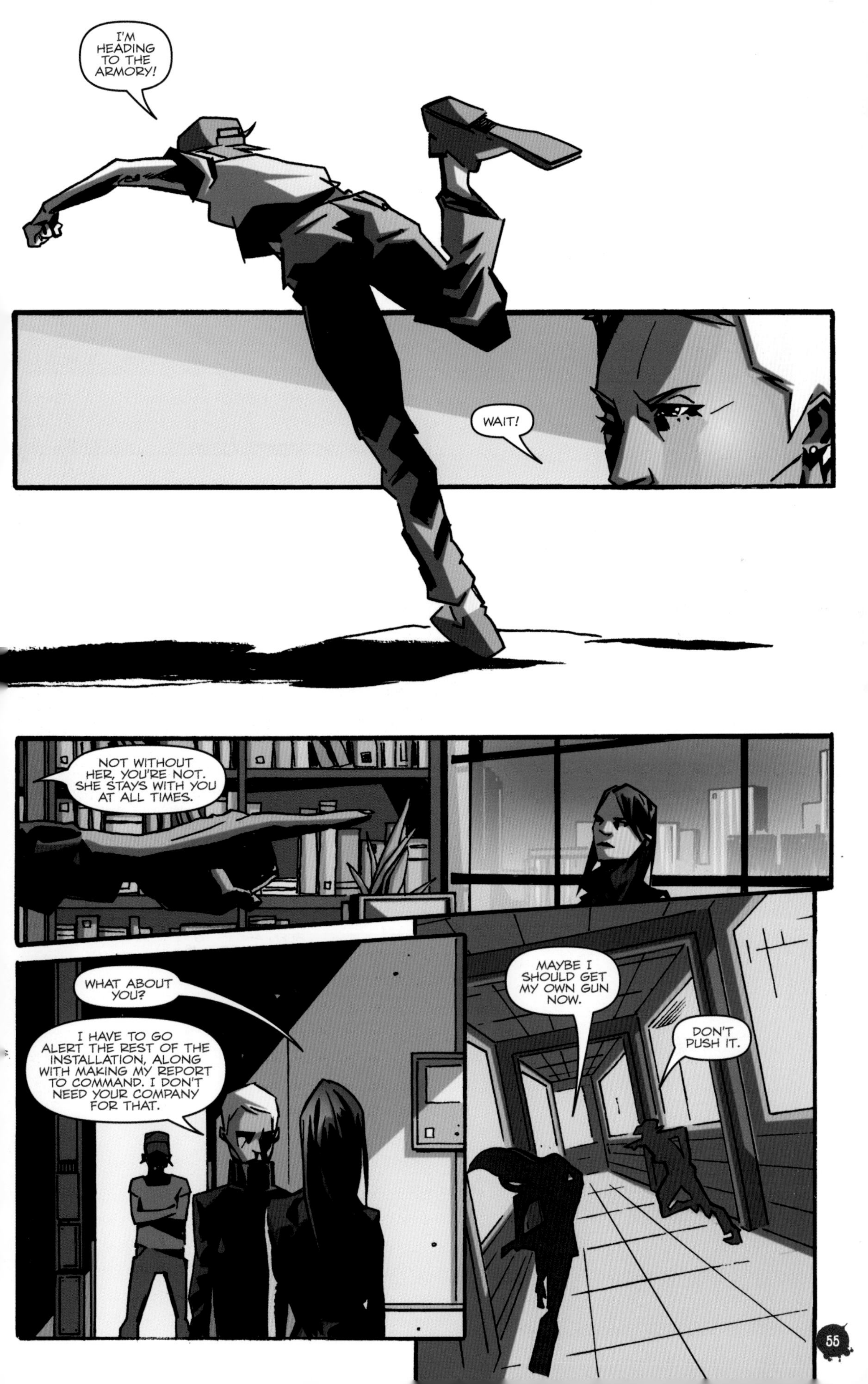
I'M HEADING TO THE ARMORY!
WAIT!
NOT WITHOUT HER, YOU'RE NOT. SHE STAYS WITH YOU AT ALL TIMES.
WHAT ABOUT YOU?
I HAVE TO GO ALERT THE REST OF THE INSTALLATION, ALONG WITH MAKING MY REPORT TO COMMAND. I DON'T NEED YOUR COMPANY FOR THAT.
MAYBE I SHOULD GET MY OWN GUN NOW.
DON'T PUSH IT.

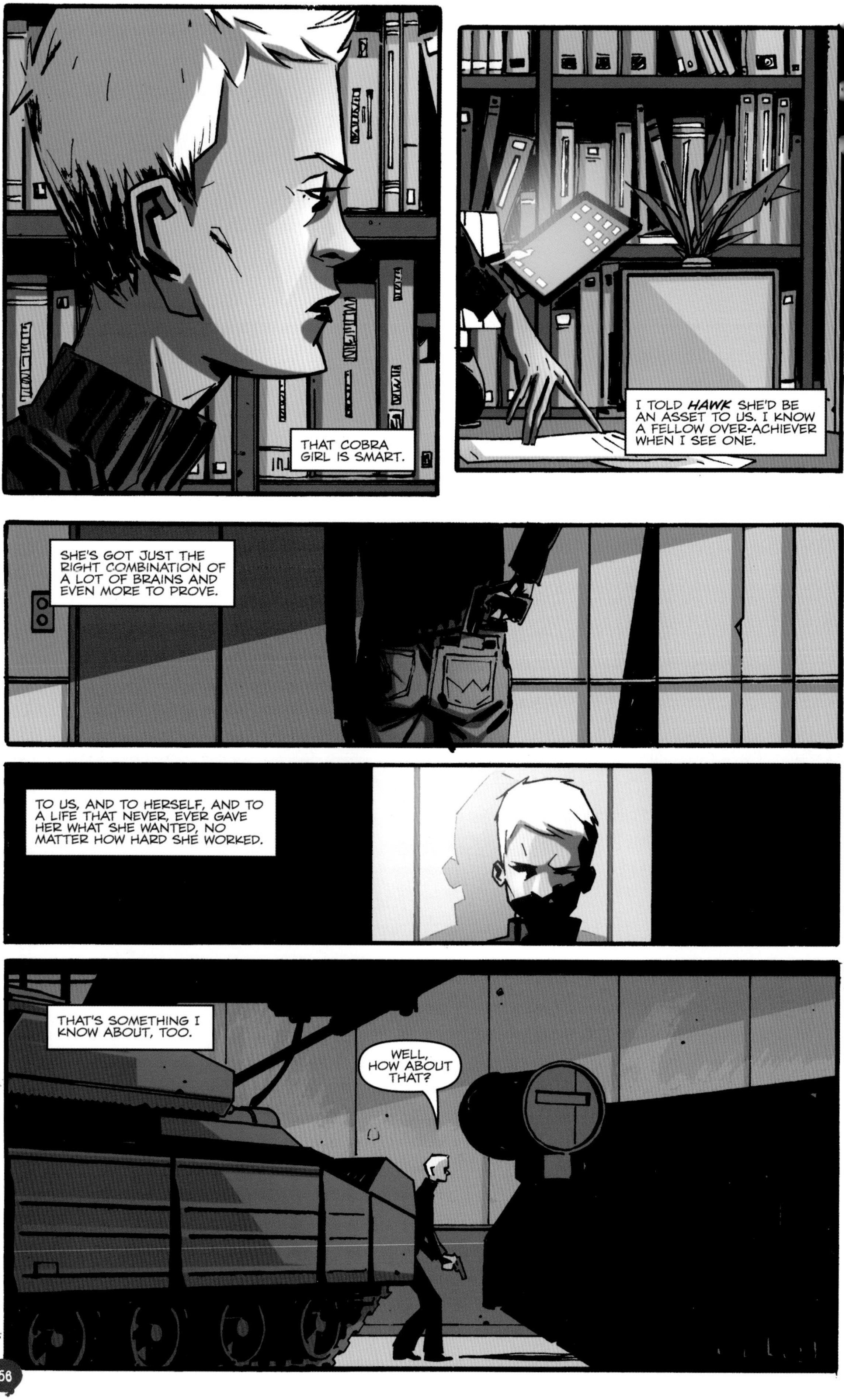
THAT COBRA GIRL IS SMART.
I TOLD HAWK SHE'D BE AN ASSET TO US. I KNOW A FELLOW OVER-ACHIEVER WHEN I SEE ONE.
SHE'S GOT JUST THE RIGHT COMBINATION OF A LOT OF BRAINS AND EVEN MORE TO PROVE.
TO US, AND TO HERSELF, AND TO A LIFE THAT NEVER, EVER GAVE HER WHAT SHE WANTED, NO MATTER HOW HARD SHE WORKED.
THAT'S SOMETHING I KNOW ABOUT, TOO.
WELL, HOW ABOUT THAT?

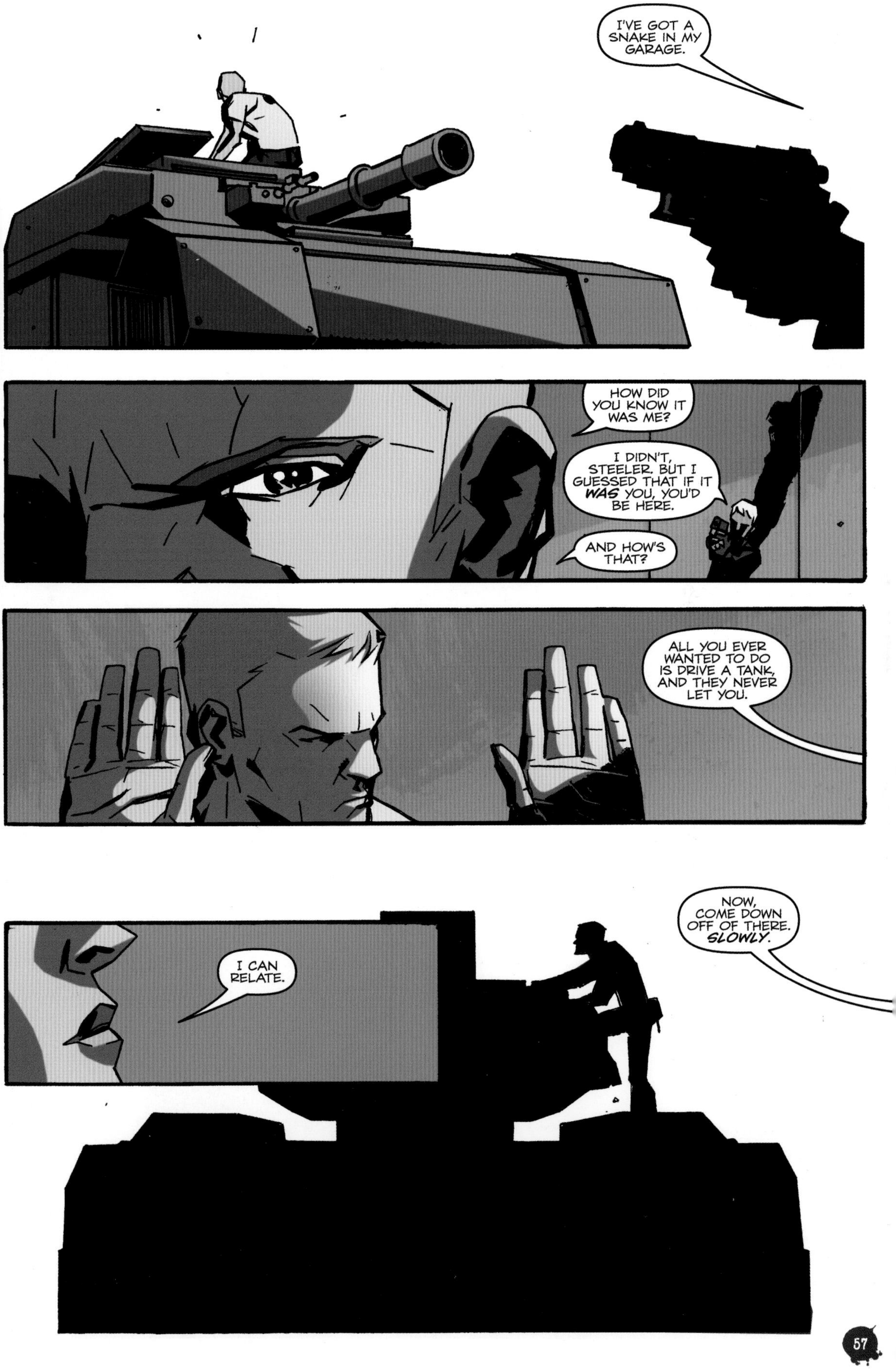
I'VE GOT A SNAKE IN MY GARAGE.
HOW DID YOU KNOW IT WAS ME?
I DIDN'T, STEELER. BUT I GUESSED THAT IF IT WAS YOU, YOU'D BE HERE.
AND HOW'S THAT?
ALL YOU EVER WANTED TO DO IS DRIVE A TANK, AND THEY NEVER LET YOU.
I CAN RELATE.
NOW, COME DOWN OFF OF THERE. SLOWLY.

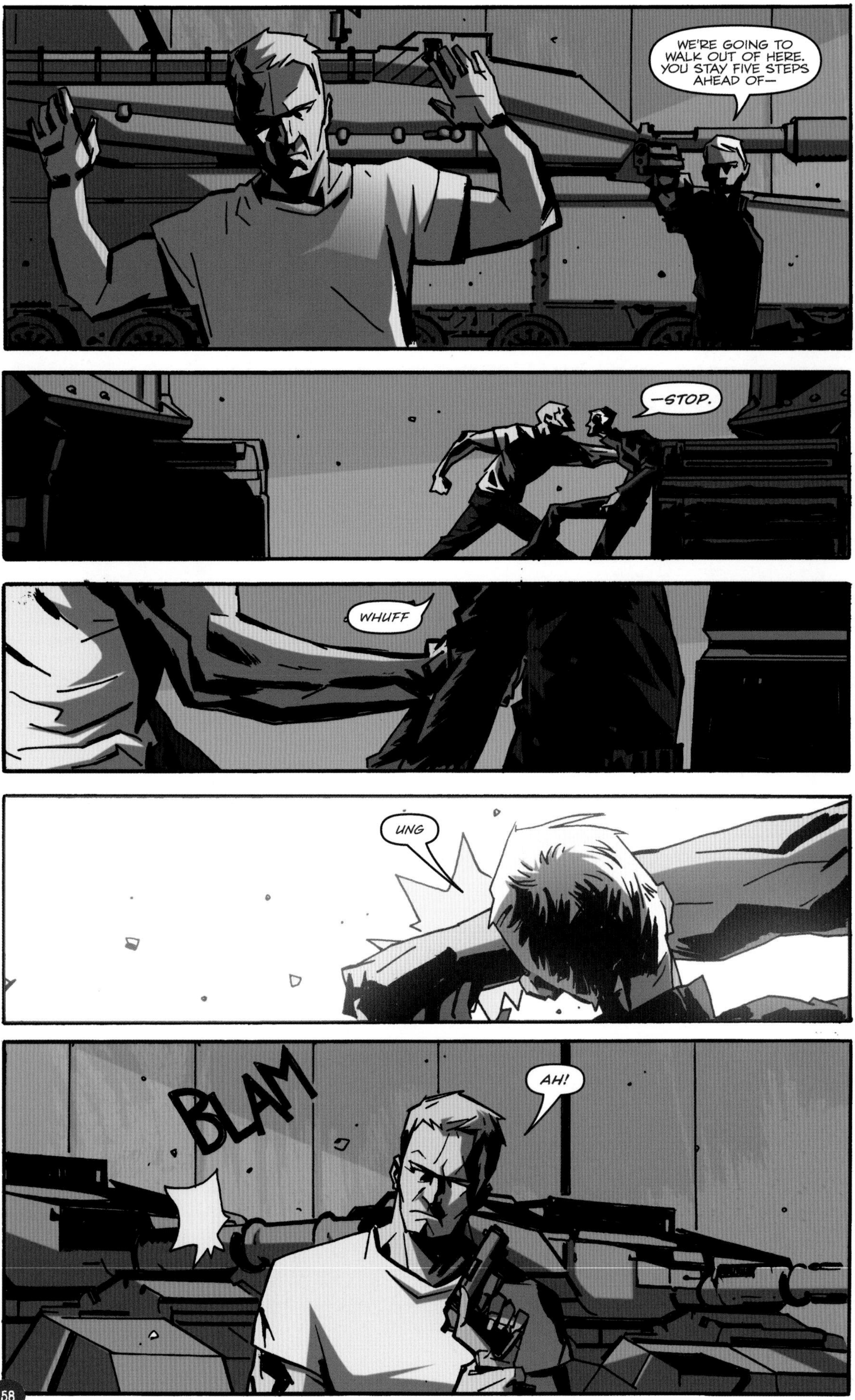
WE'RE GOING TO WALK OUT OF HERE. YOU STAY FIVE STEPS AHEAD OF—
—STOP.
WHUFF
UNG
BLAM
AH!

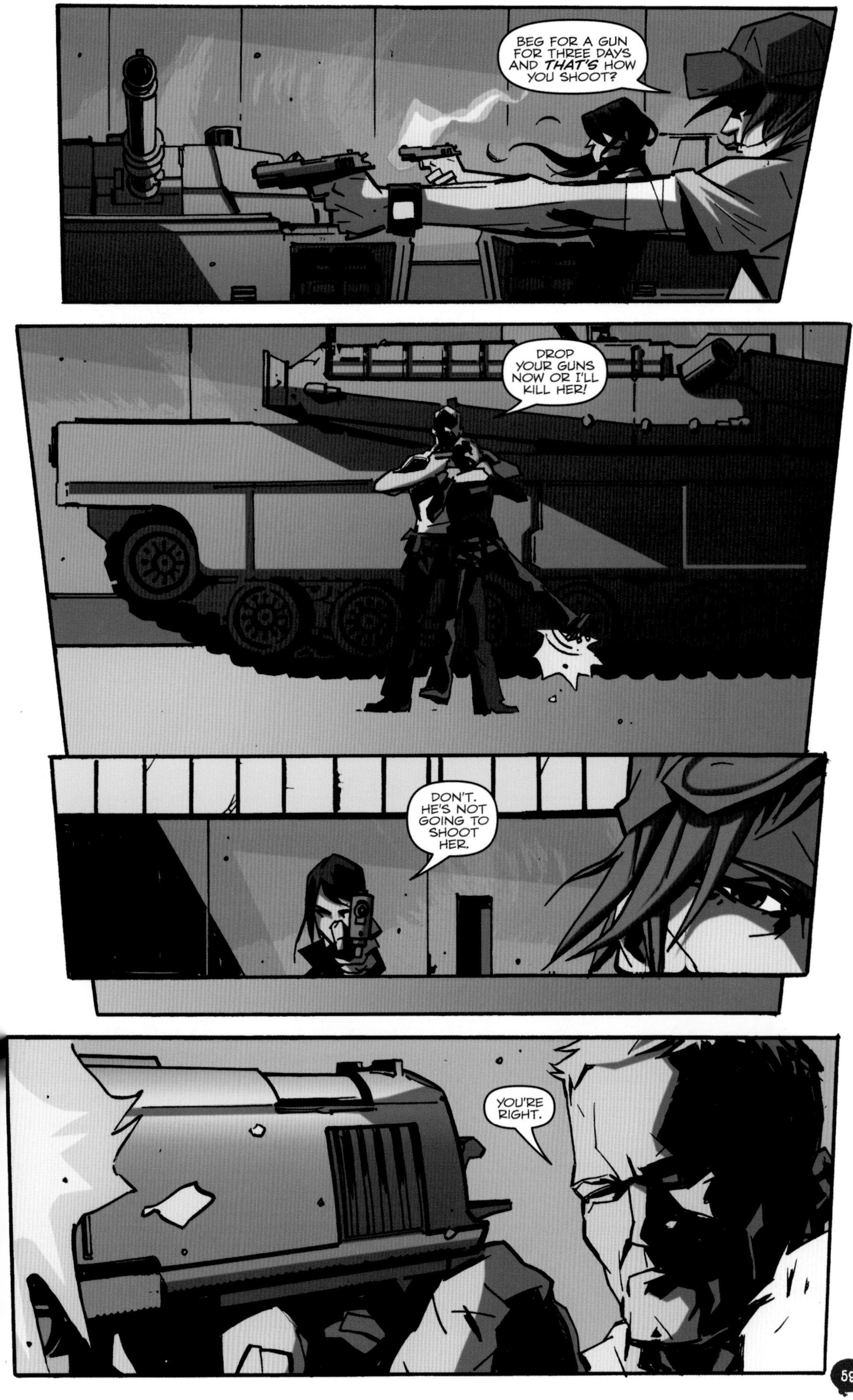
BEG FOR A GUN FOR THREE DAYS AND *THAT'S* HOW YOU SHOOT?
DROP YOUR GUNS NOW OR I'LL KILL HER!
DON'T. HE'S NOT GOING TO SHOOT HER.
YOU'RE RIGHT.

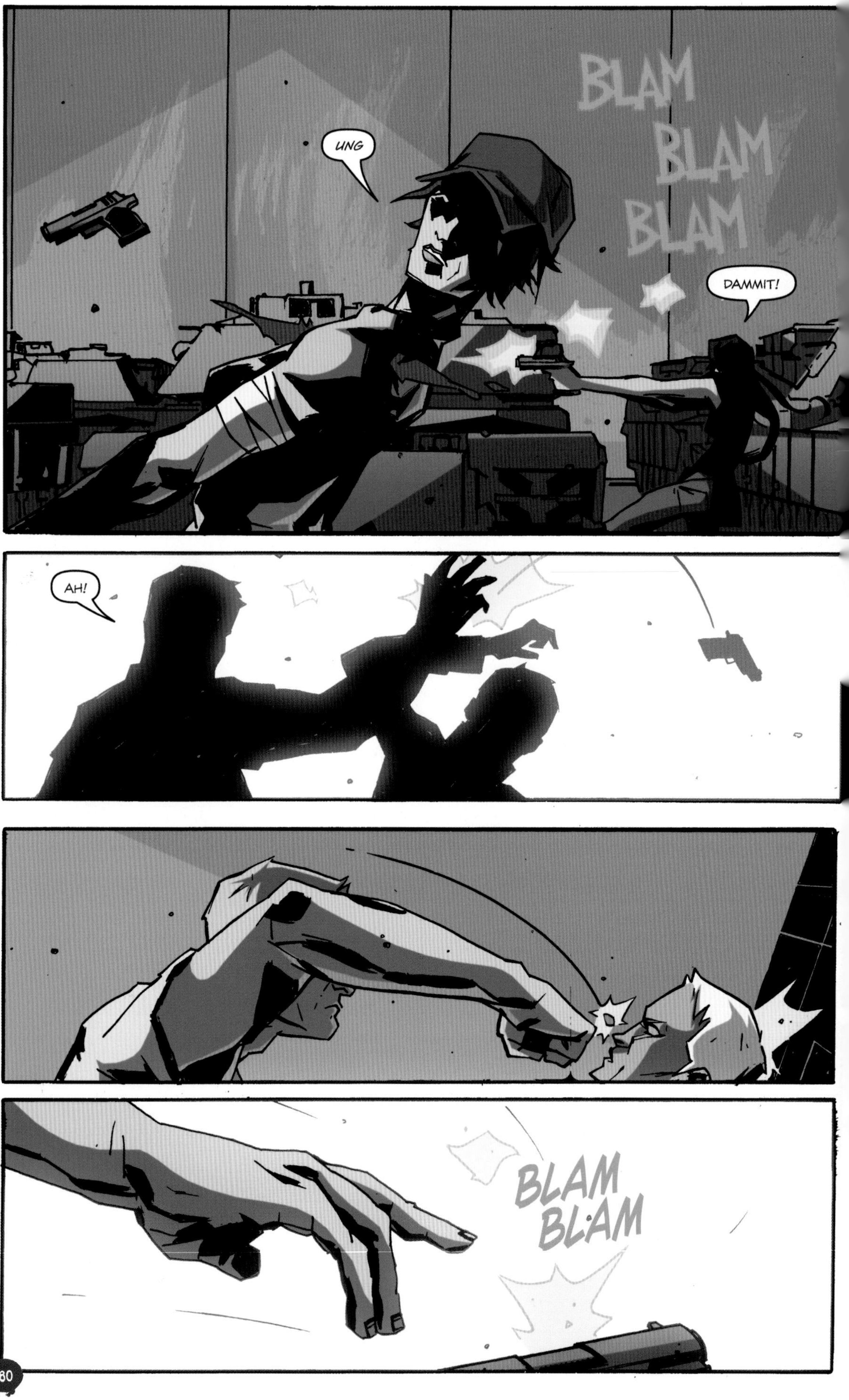

BLAM
BLAM
BLAM
UNG
DAMMIT!
AH!
BLAM
BLAM

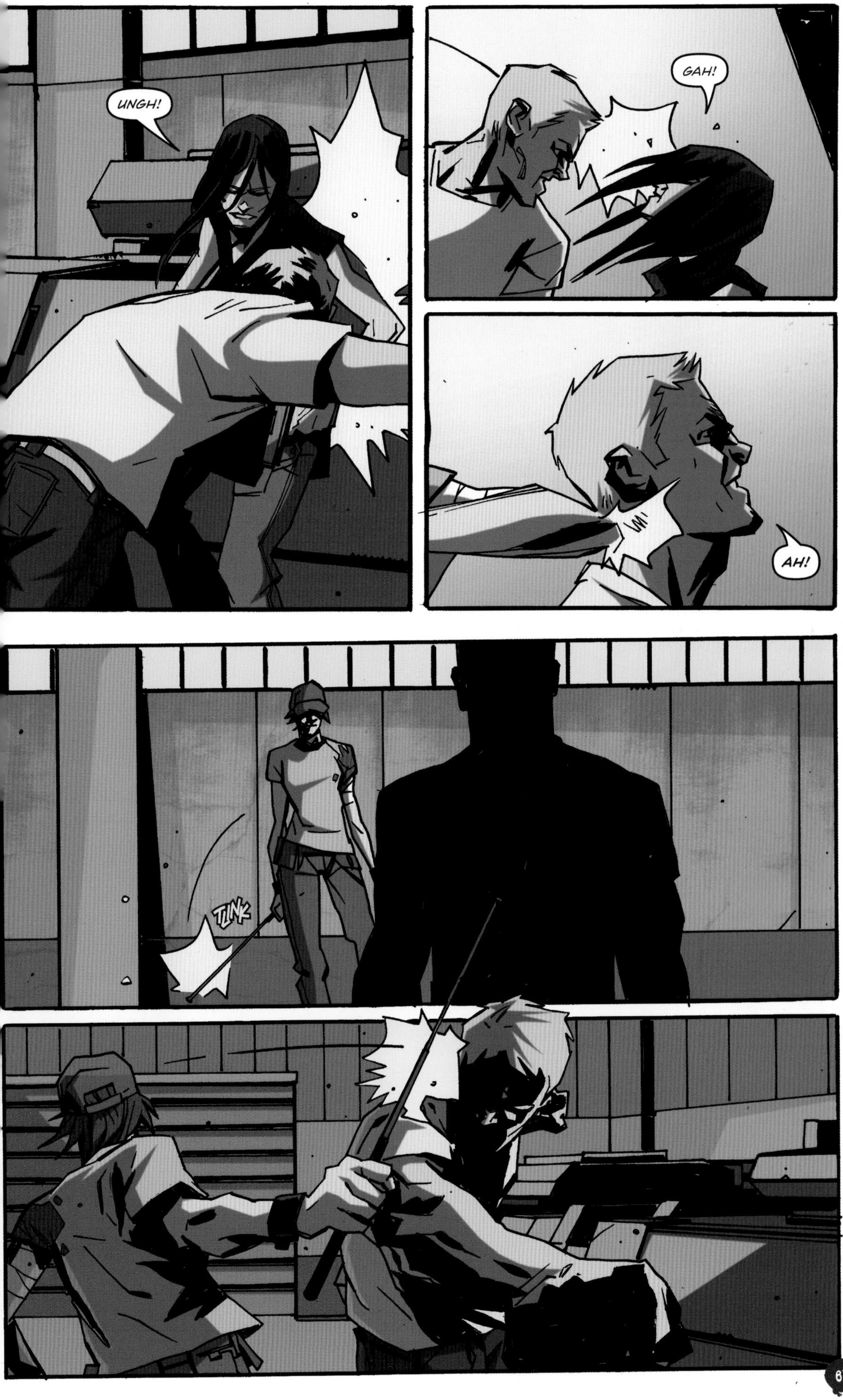
UNGH!
GAH!
AH!
TLINK

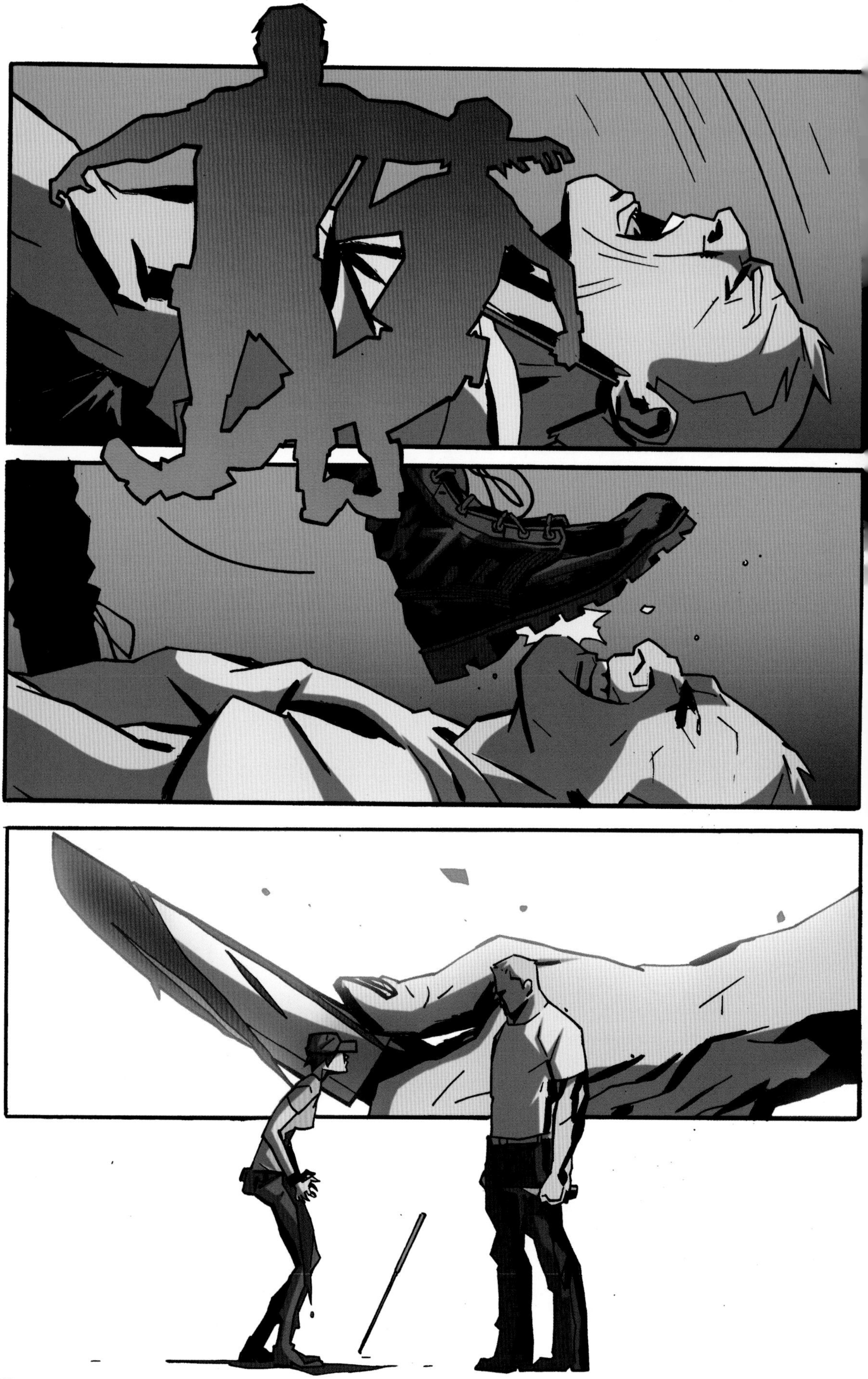

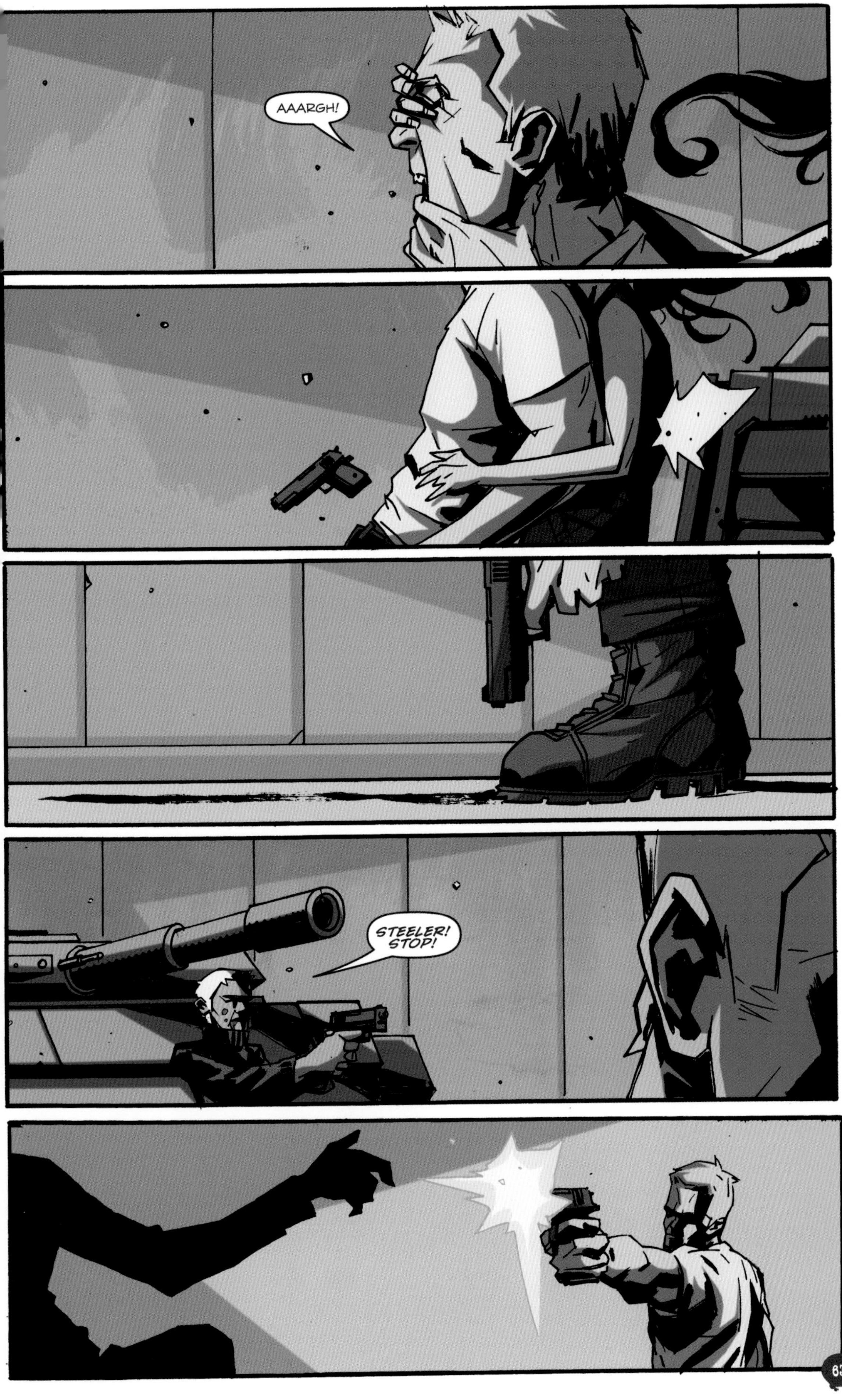
AAARGH!
STEELER! STOP!

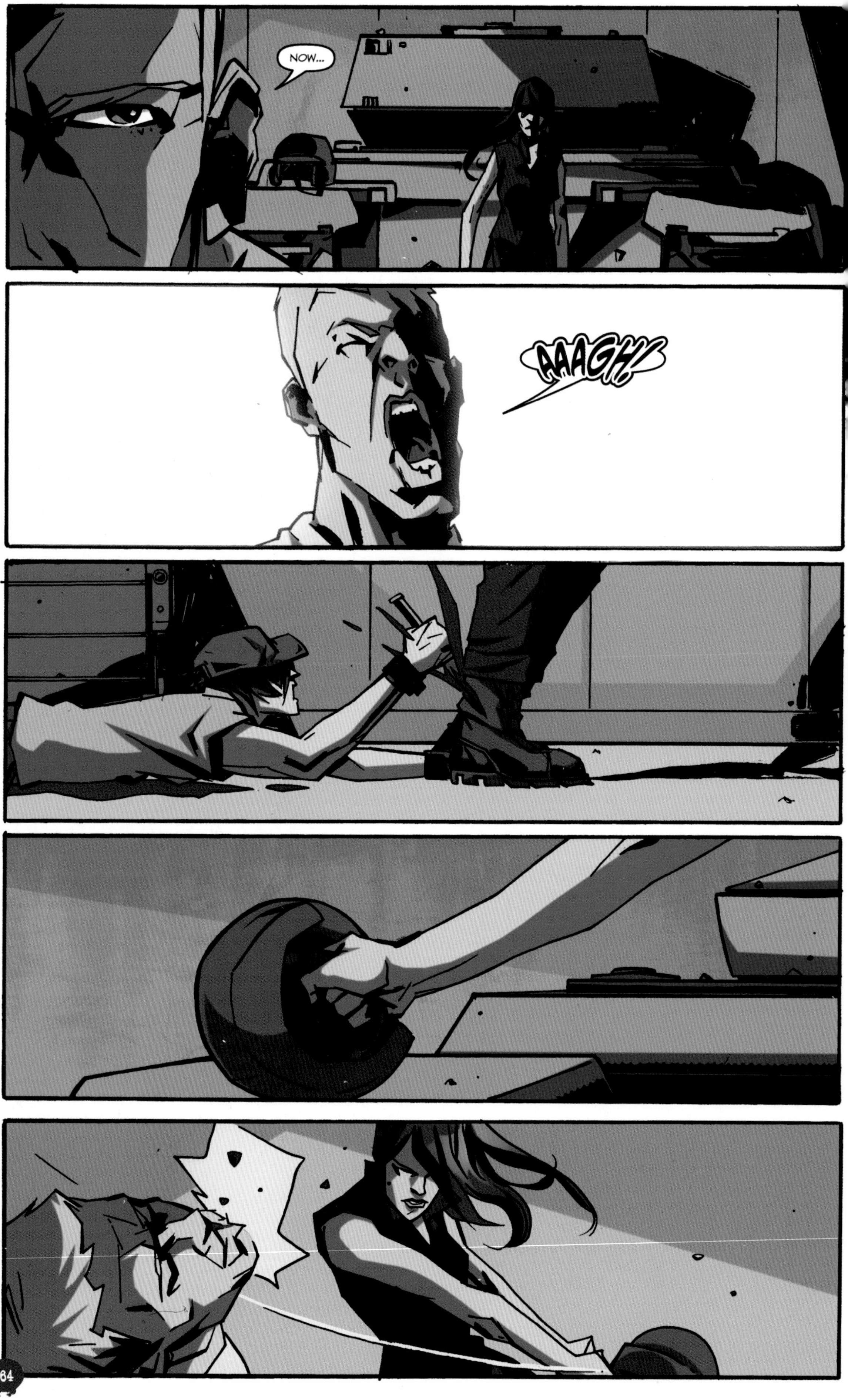
NOW...
AAAGH!

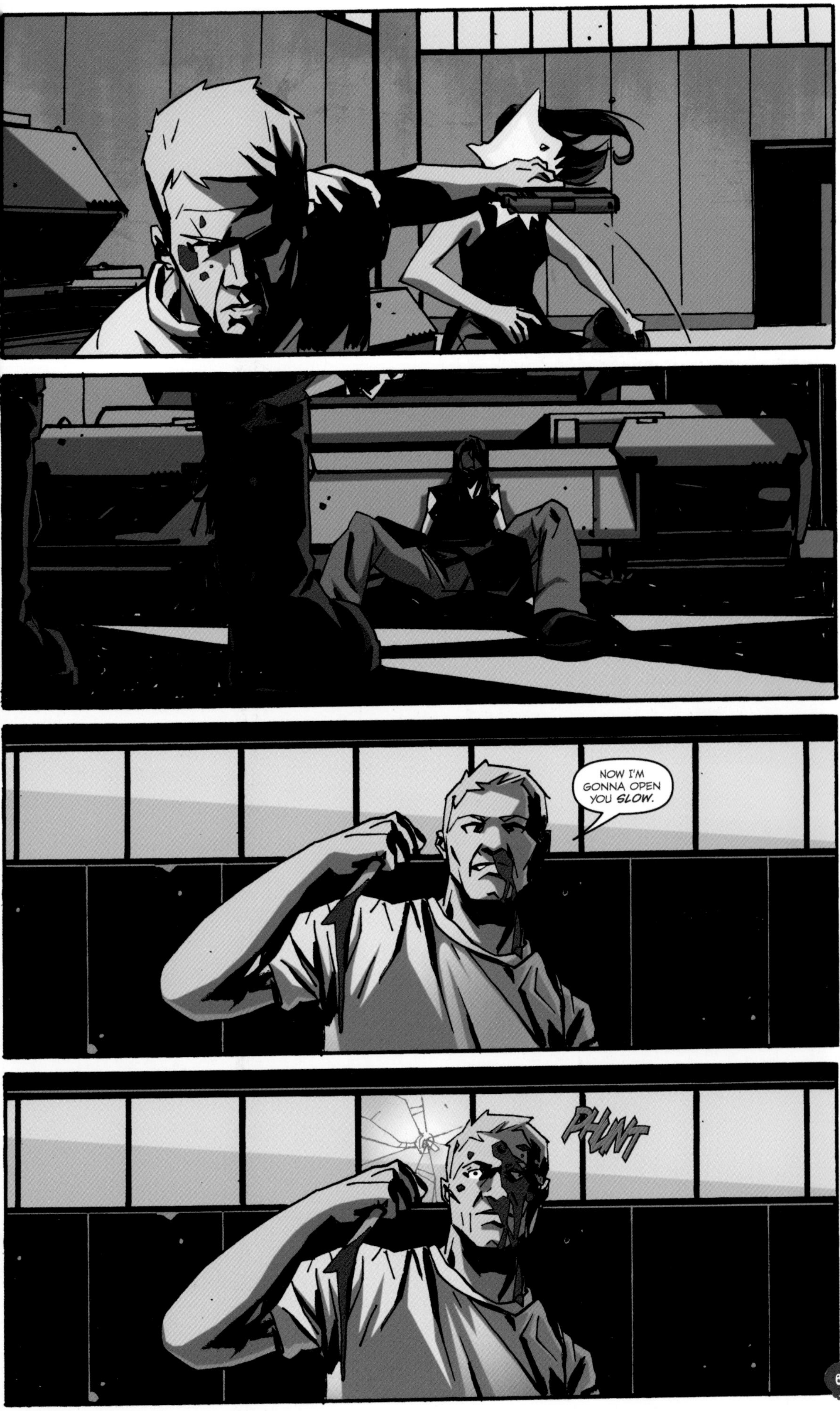
NOW I'M GONNA OPEN YOU *SLOW*.
PHUNT

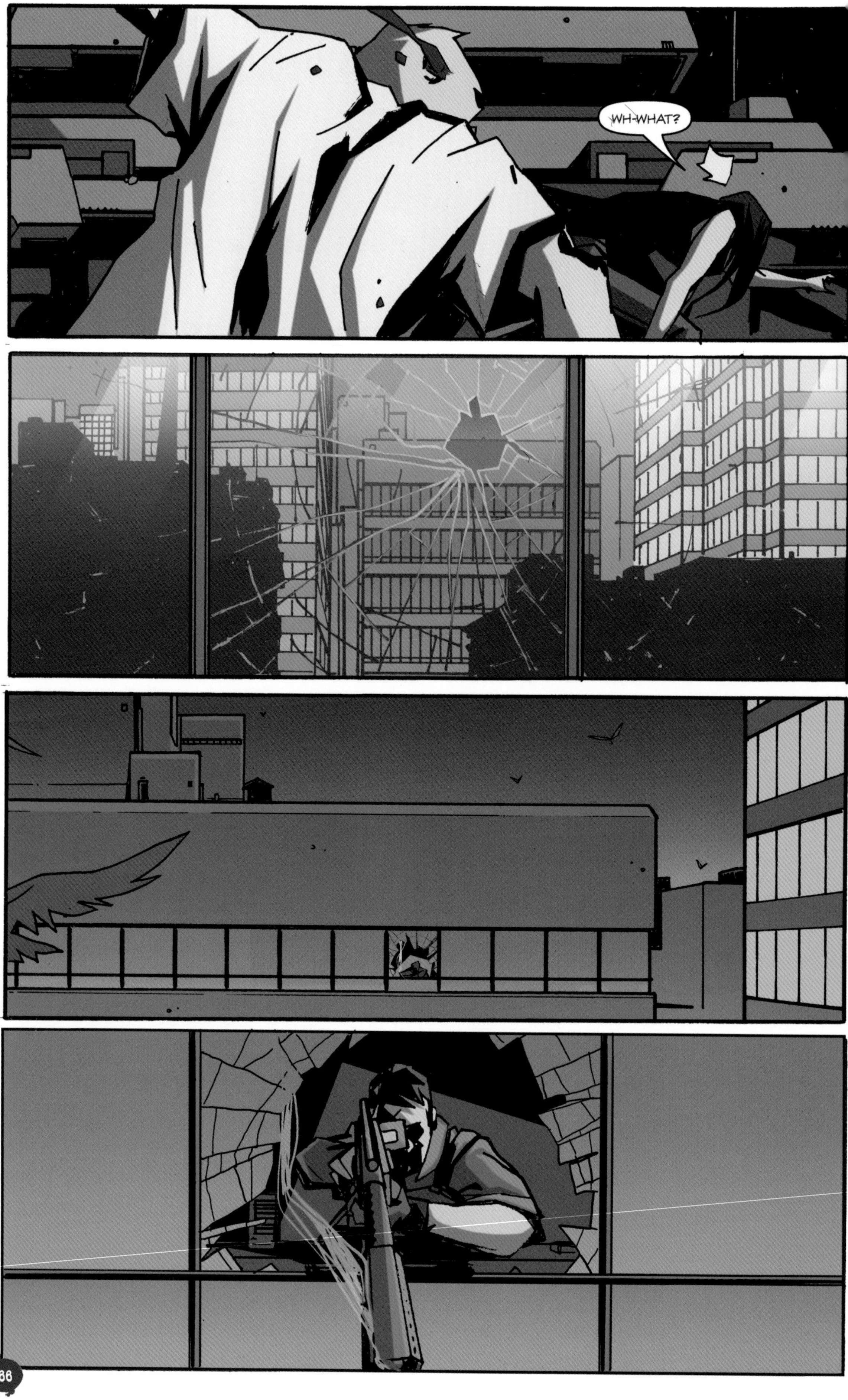
WH-WHAT?

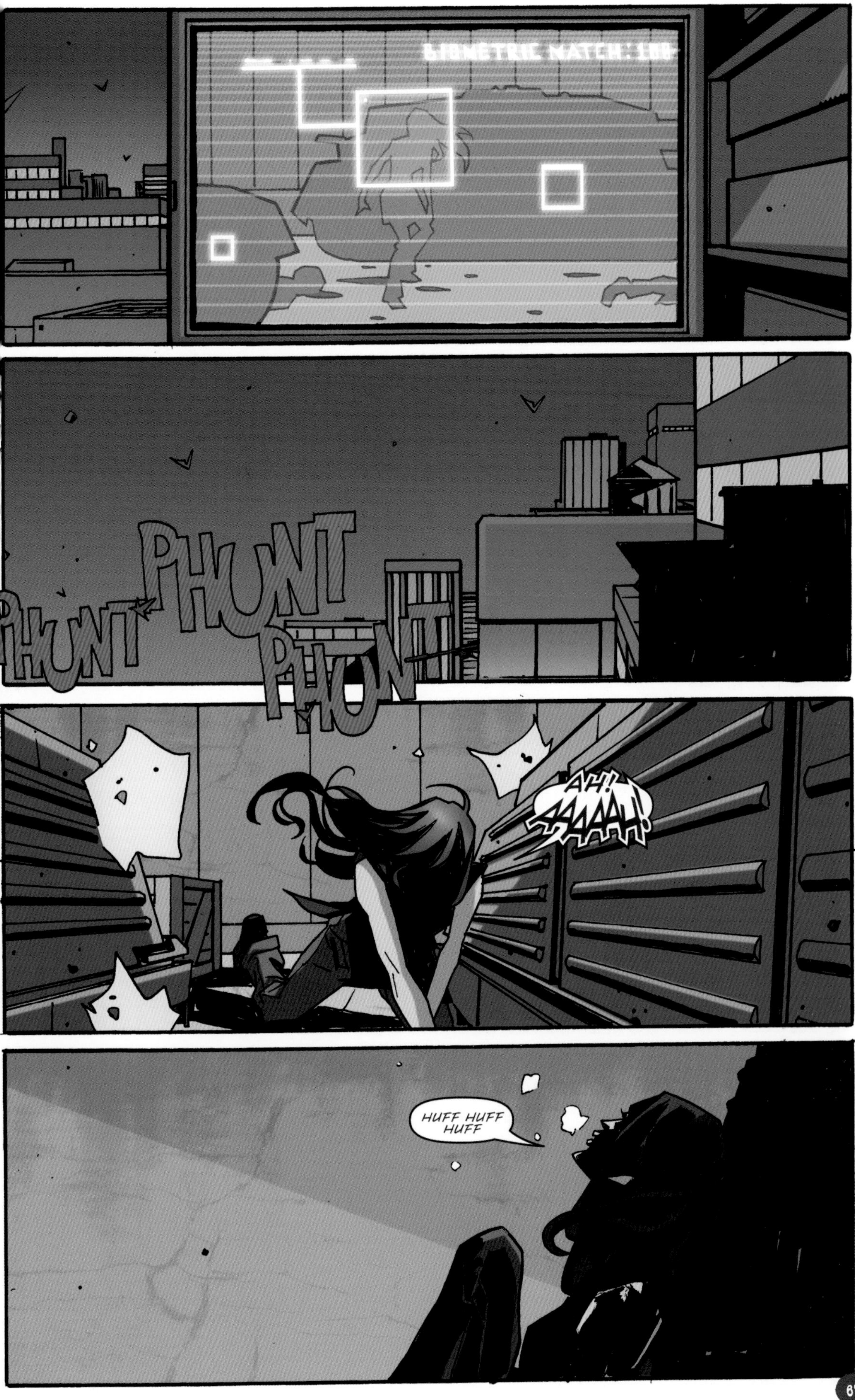

BIOMETRIC MATCH: 100
PHUNT
PHUNT
PHUNT
PHUNT
AH! AAAAAH!
HUFF HUFF HUFF

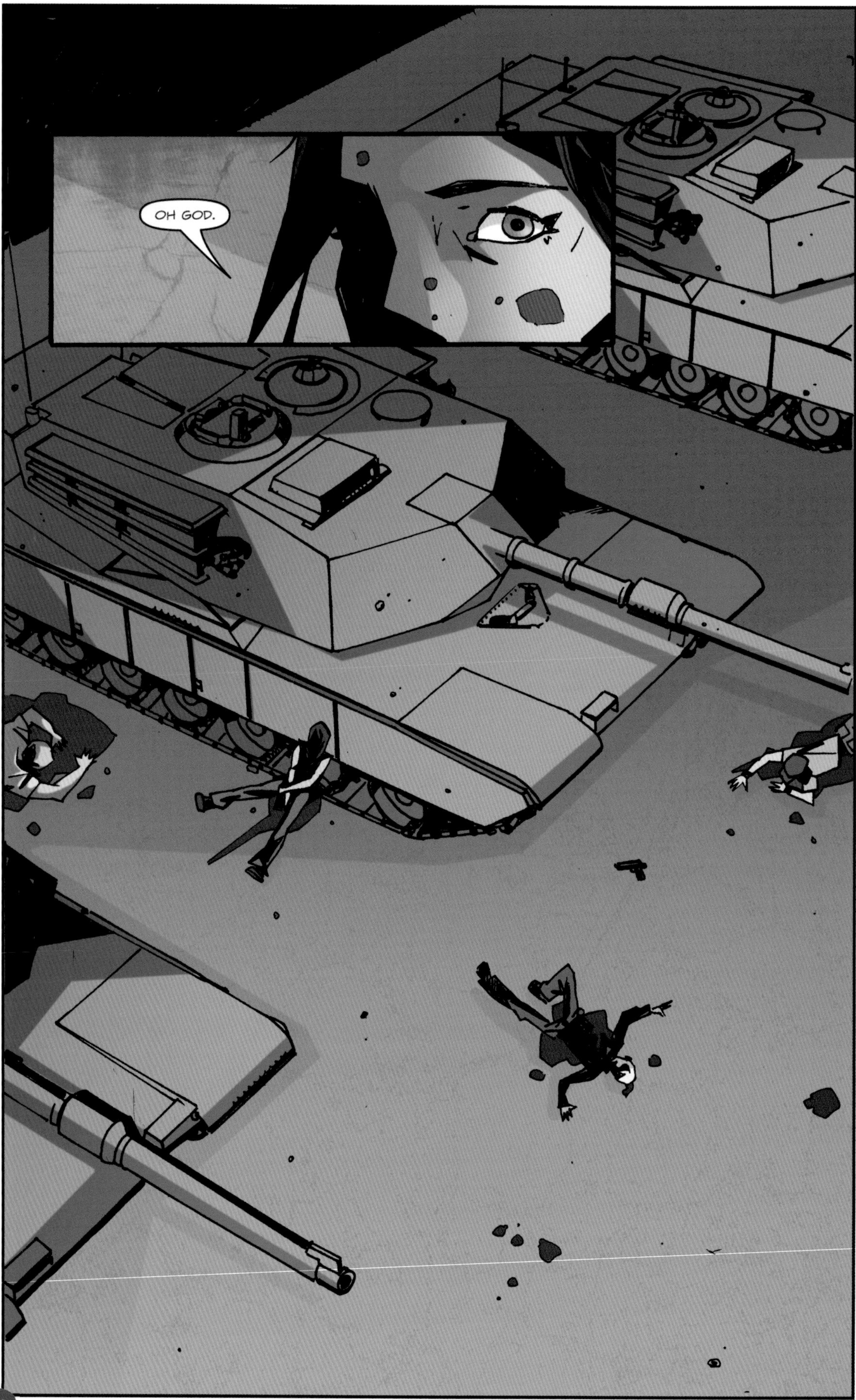
OH GOD.

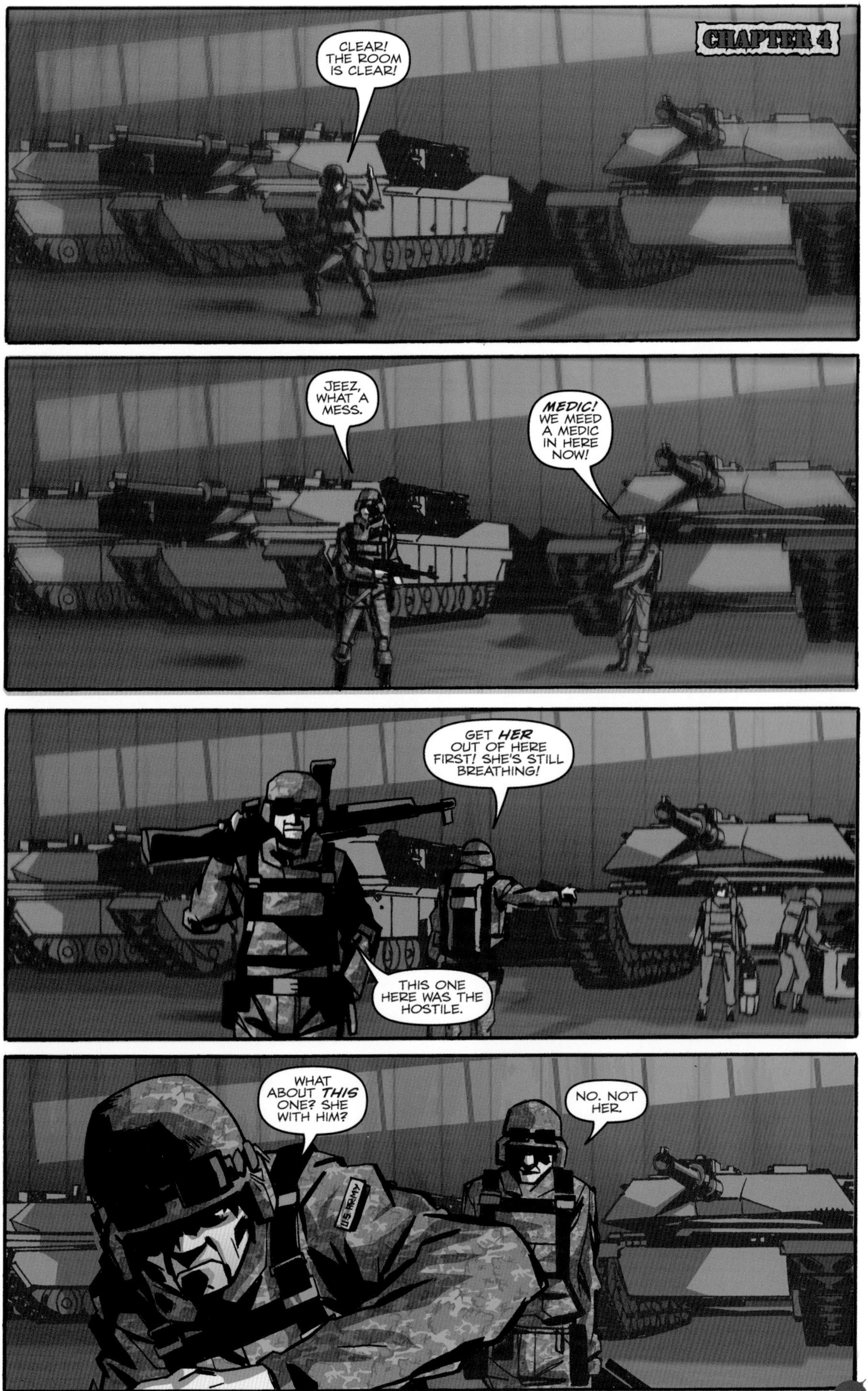
CHAPTER 4
CLEAR! THE ROOM IS CLEAR!
JEEZ, WHAT A MESS.
MEDIC! WE MEED A MEDIC IN HERE NOW!
GET HER OUT OF HERE FIRST! SHE'S STILL BREATHING!
THIS ONE HERE WAS THE HOSTILE.
WHAT ABOUT THIS ONE? SHE WITH HIM?
NO. NOT HER.
U.S. ARMY

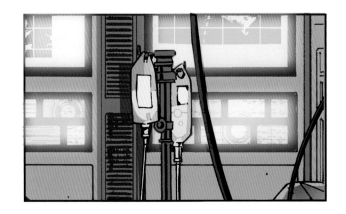

"SHE'S *G.I. JOE.*"

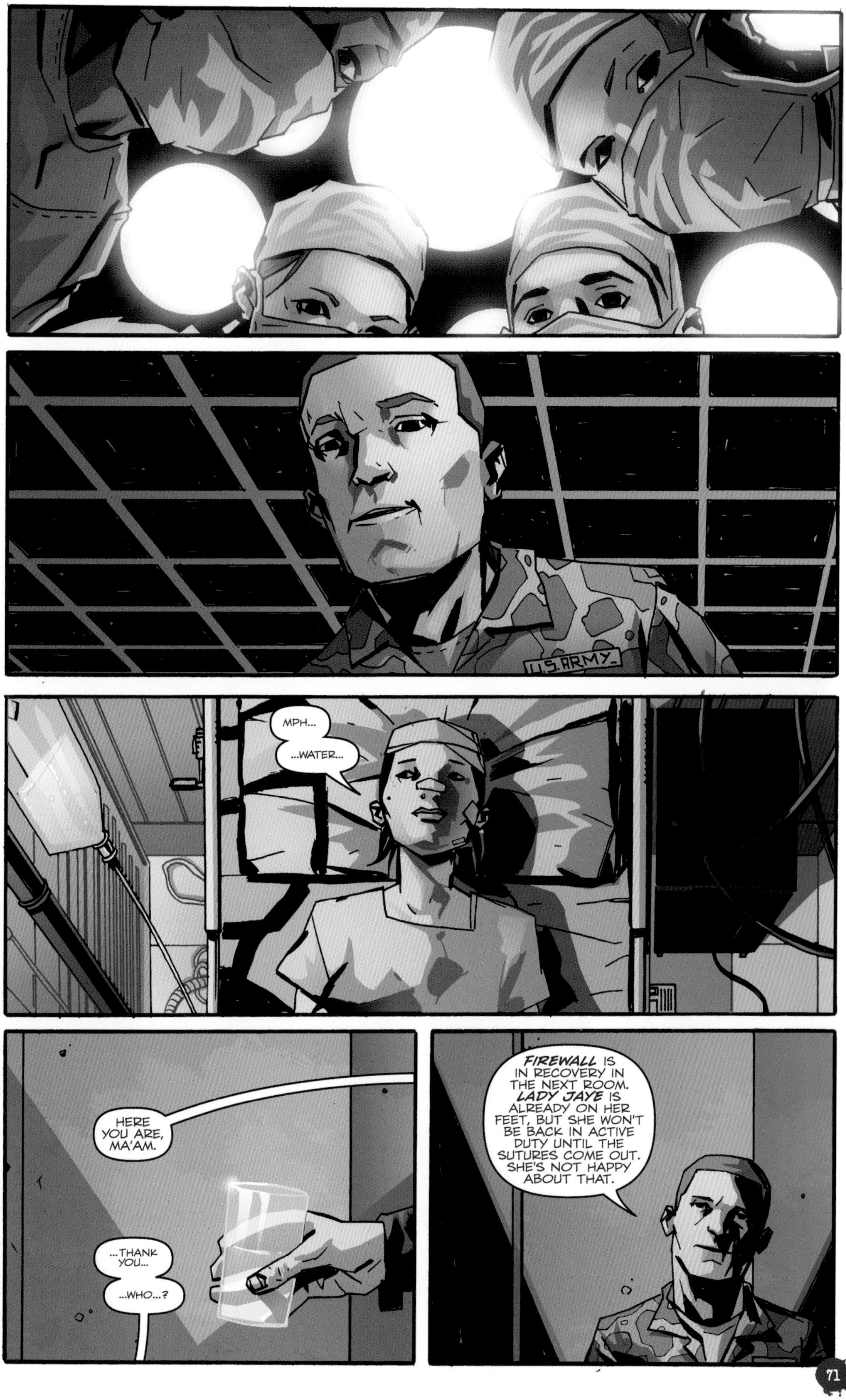
U.S. ARMY
MPH...
...WATER...
HERE YOU ARE, MA'AM.
...THANK YOU...
...WHO...?
FIREWALL IS IN RECOVERY IN THE NEXT ROOM. LADY JAYE IS ALREADY ON HER FEET, BUT SHE WON'T BE BACK IN ACTIVE DUTY UNTIL THE SUTURES COME OUT. SHE'S NOT HAPPY ABOUT THAT.

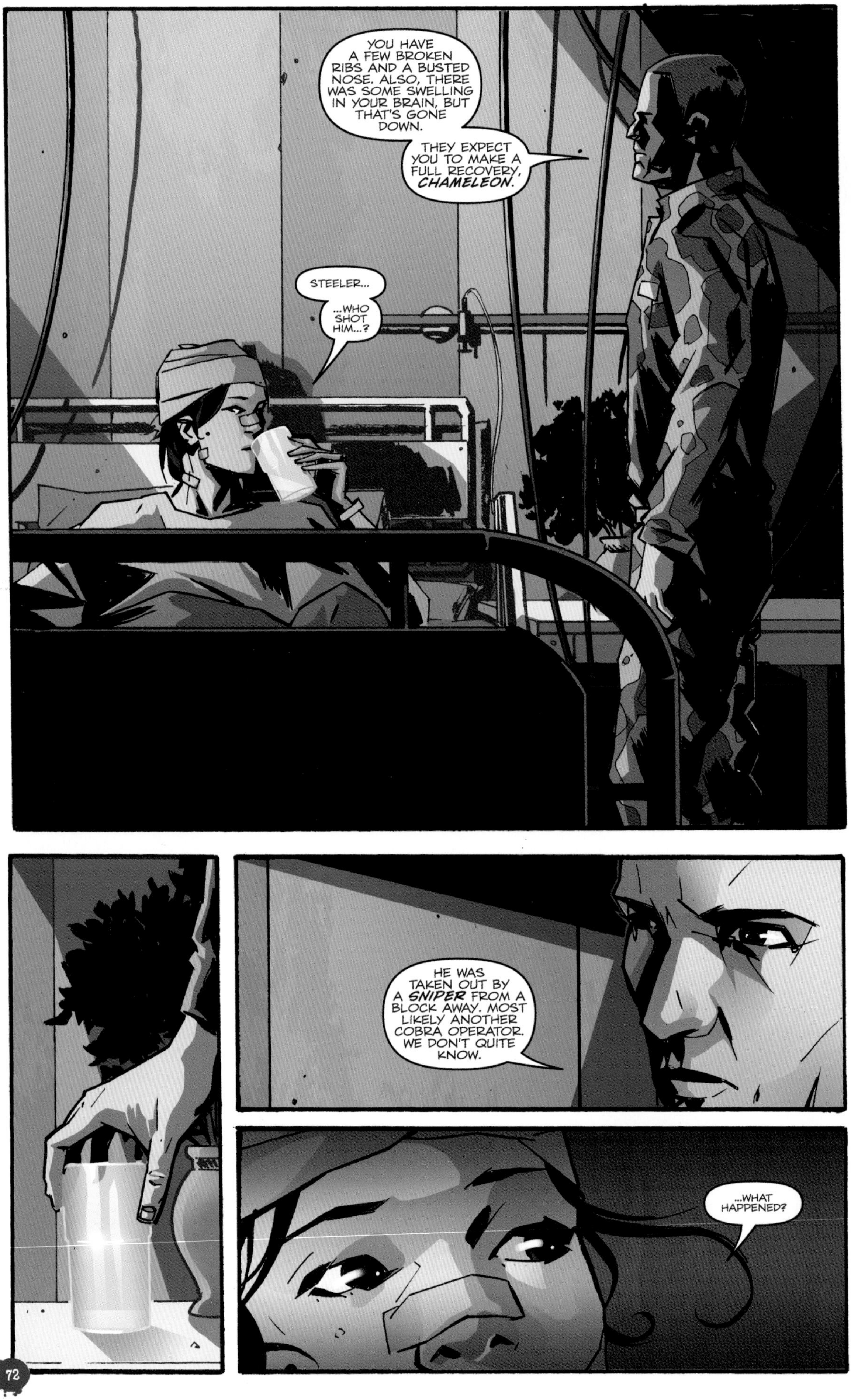
YOU HAVE A FEW BROKEN RIBS AND A BUSTED NOSE. ALSO, THERE WAS SOME SWELLING IN YOUR BRAIN, BUT THAT'S GONE DOWN.
THEY EXPECT YOU TO MAKE A FULL RECOVERY, CHAMELEON.
STEELER...
...WHO SHOT HIM...?
HE WAS TAKEN OUT BY A SNIPER FROM A BLOCK AWAY. MOST LIKELY ANOTHER COBRA OPERATOR. WE DON'T QUITE KNOW.
...WHAT HAPPENED?

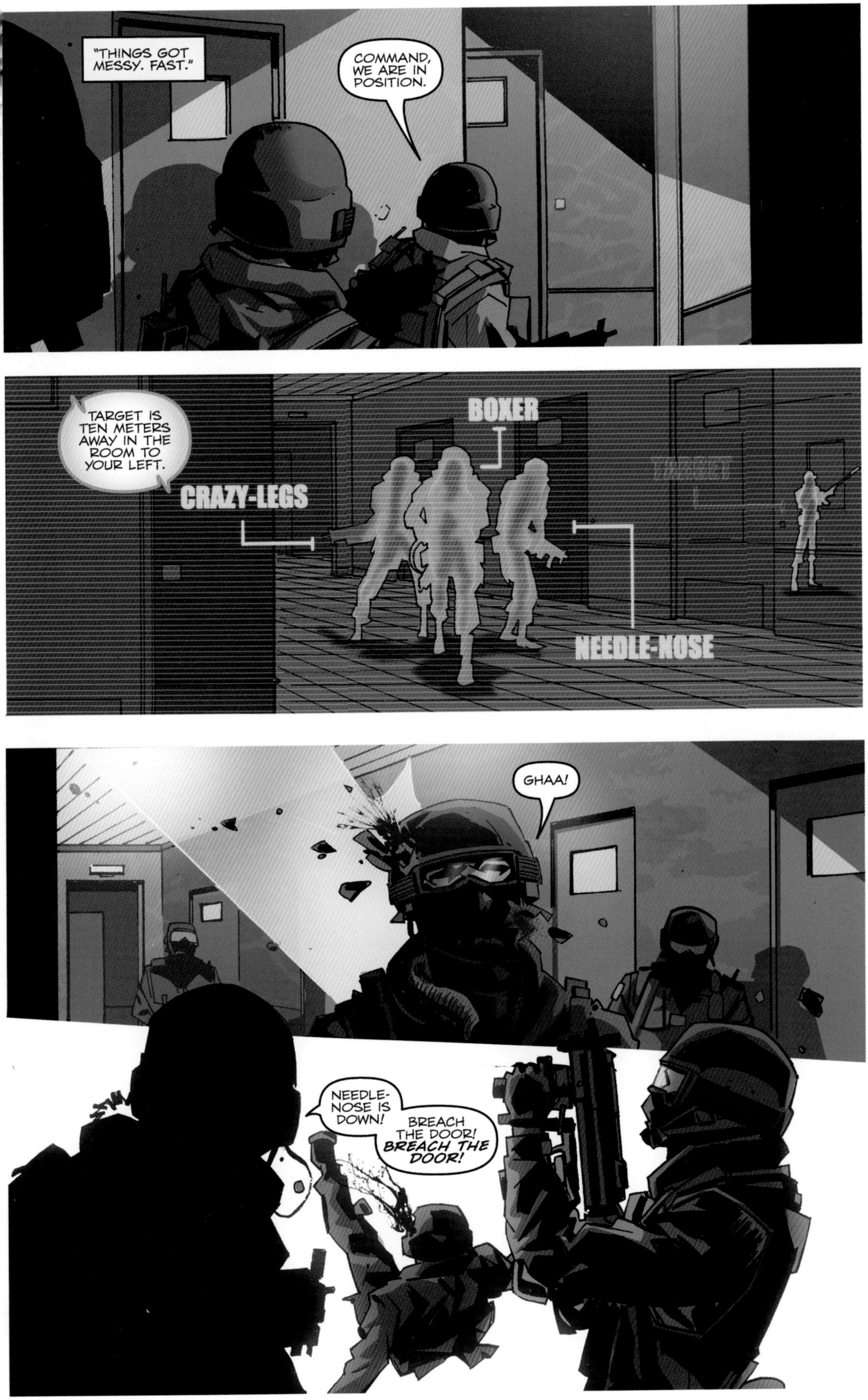
"THINGS GOT MESSY. FAST."
COMMAND, WE ARE IN POSITION.
TARGET IS TEN METERS AWAY IN THE ROOM TO YOUR LEFT.
BOXER
CRAZY-LEGS
TARGET
NEEDLE-NOSE
GHAA!
NEEDLE-NOSE IS DOWN!
BREACH THE DOOR! *BREACH THE DOOR!*

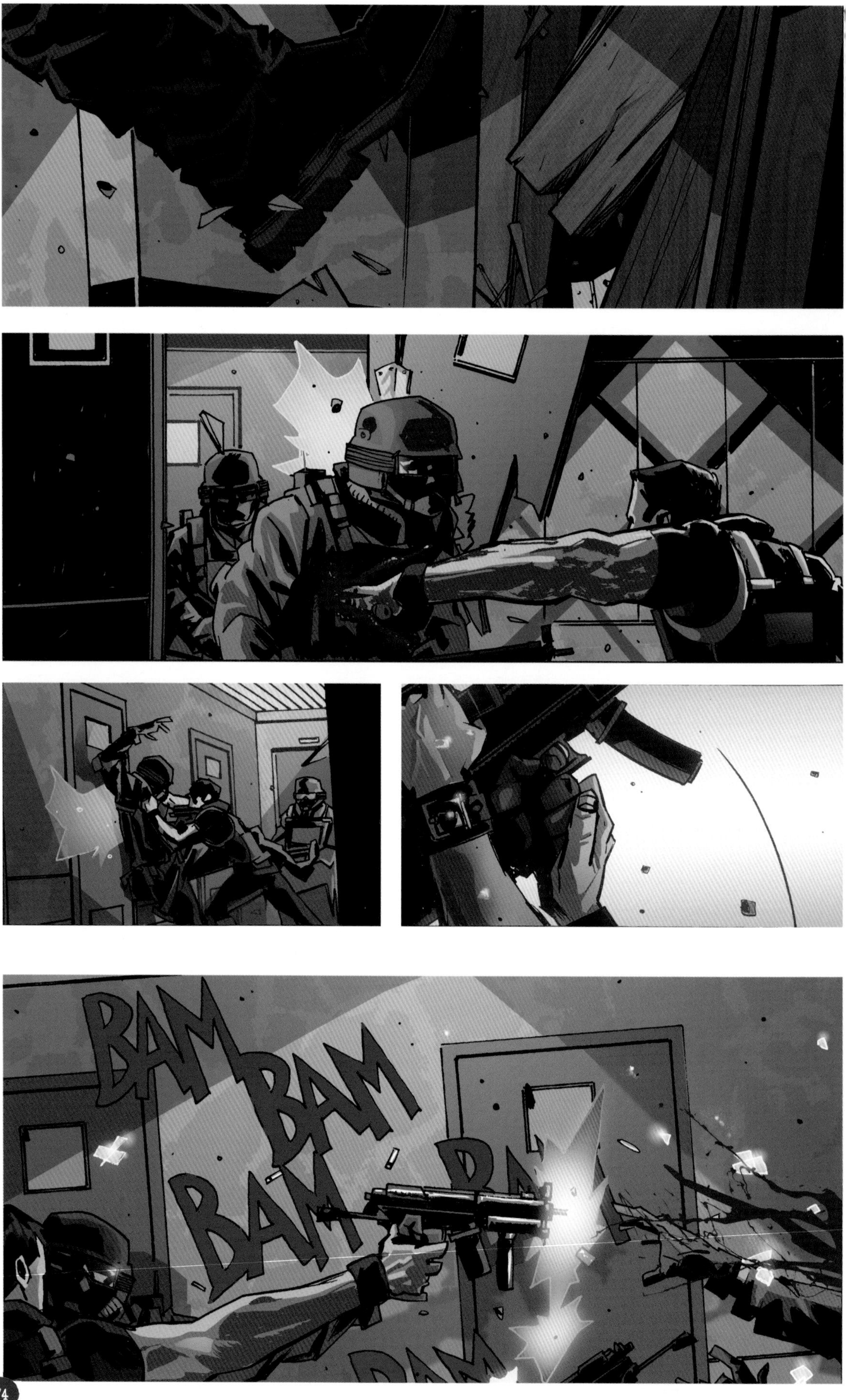
BAM
BAM
BAM

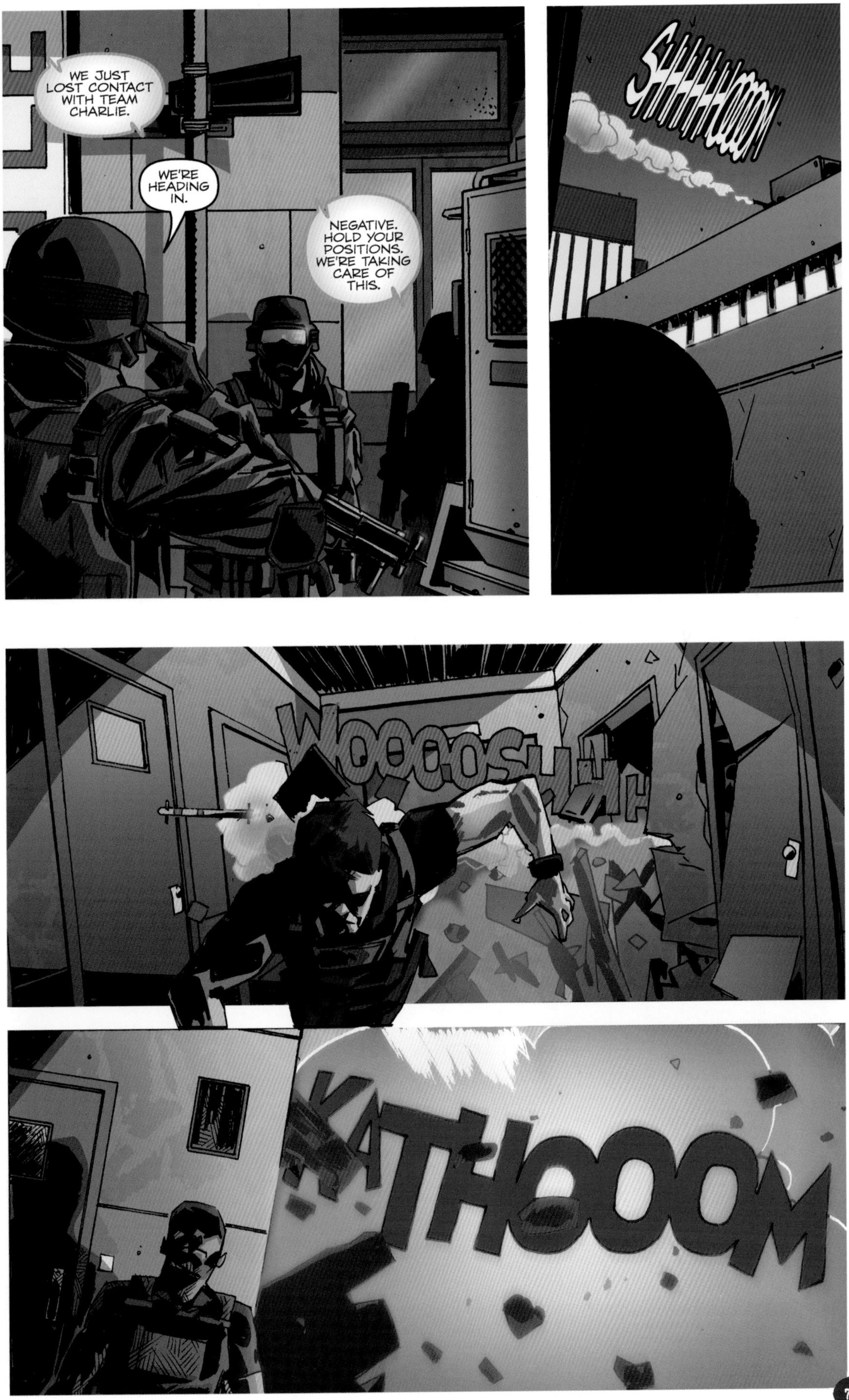
WE JUST LOST CONTACT WITH TEAM CHARLIE.
WE'RE HEADING IN.
NEGATIVE. HOLD YOUR POSITIONS. WE'RE TAKING CARE OF THIS.
SHHHHOOOM
WOOOOSHHH
KATHOOOM

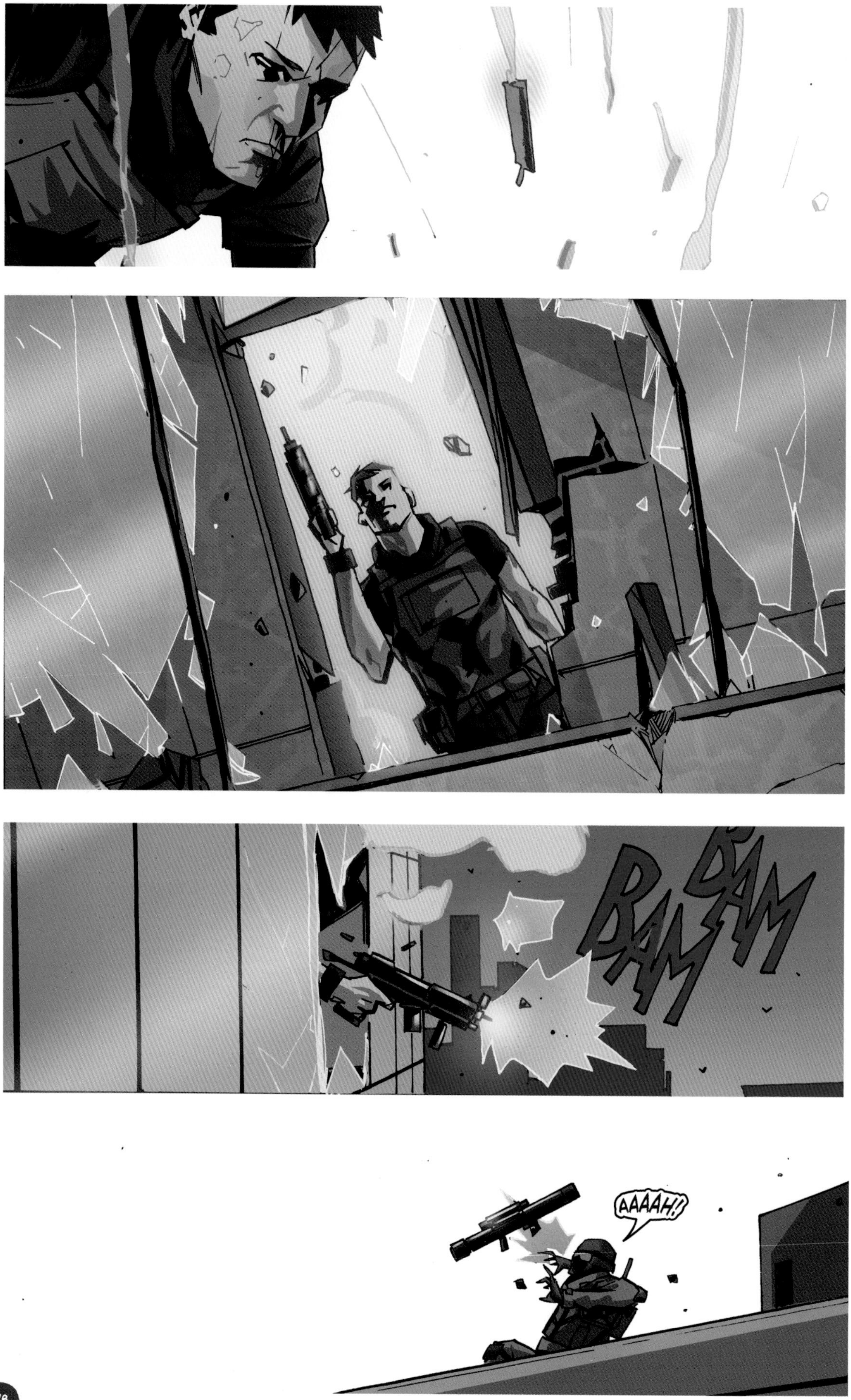
BAM BAM BAM
AAAAH!

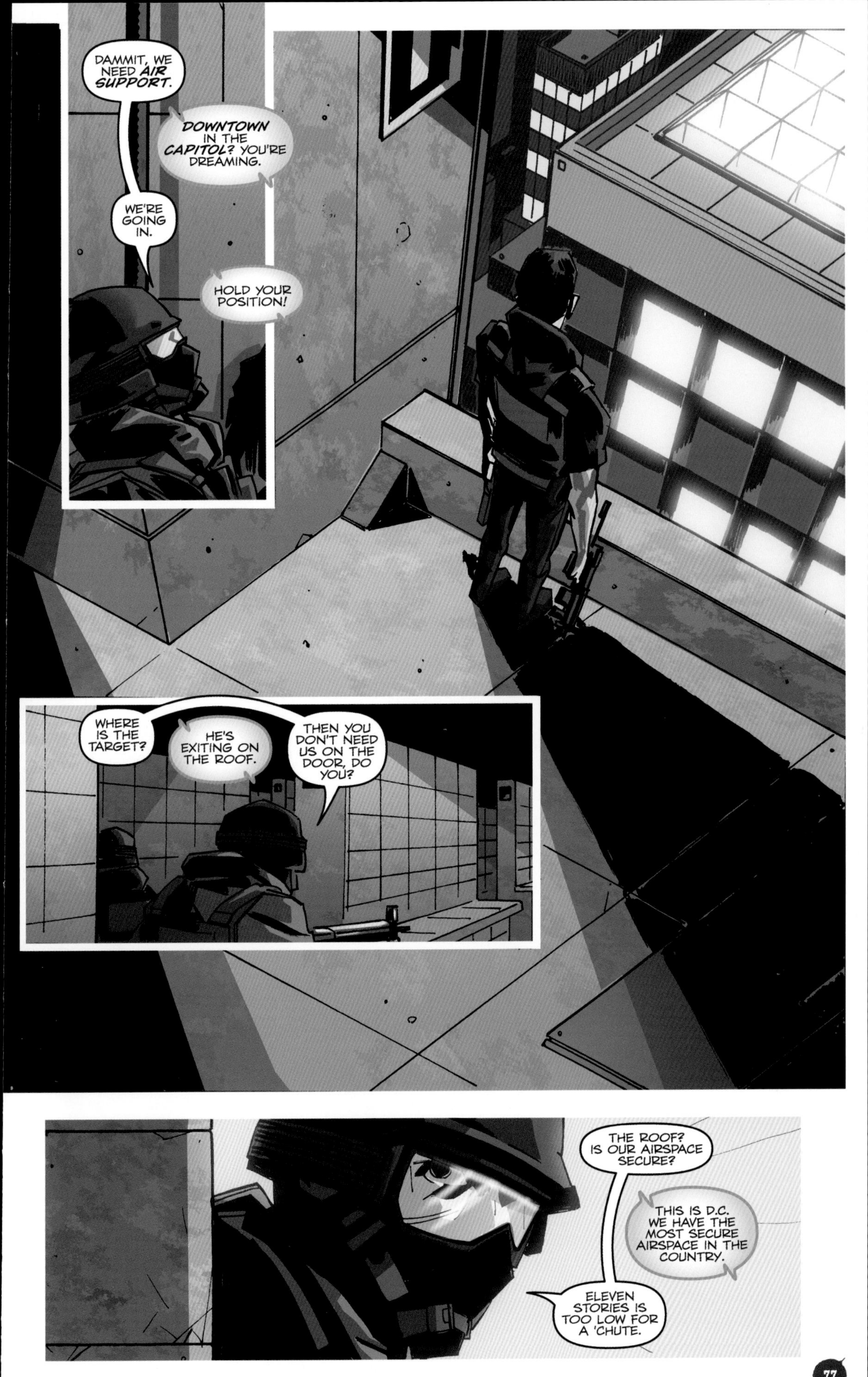
DAMMIT, WE NEED AIR SUPPORT.
DOWNTOWN IN THE CAPITOL? YOU'RE DREAMING.
WE'RE GOING IN.
HOLD YOUR POSITION!
WHERE IS THE TARGET?
HE'S EXITING ON THE ROOF.
THEN YOU DON'T NEED US ON THE DOOR, DO YOU?
THE ROOF? IS OUR AIRSPACE SECURE?
THIS IS D.C. WE HAVE THE MOST SECURE AIRSPACE IN THE COUNTRY.
ELEVEN STORIES IS TOO LOW FOR A 'CHUTE.

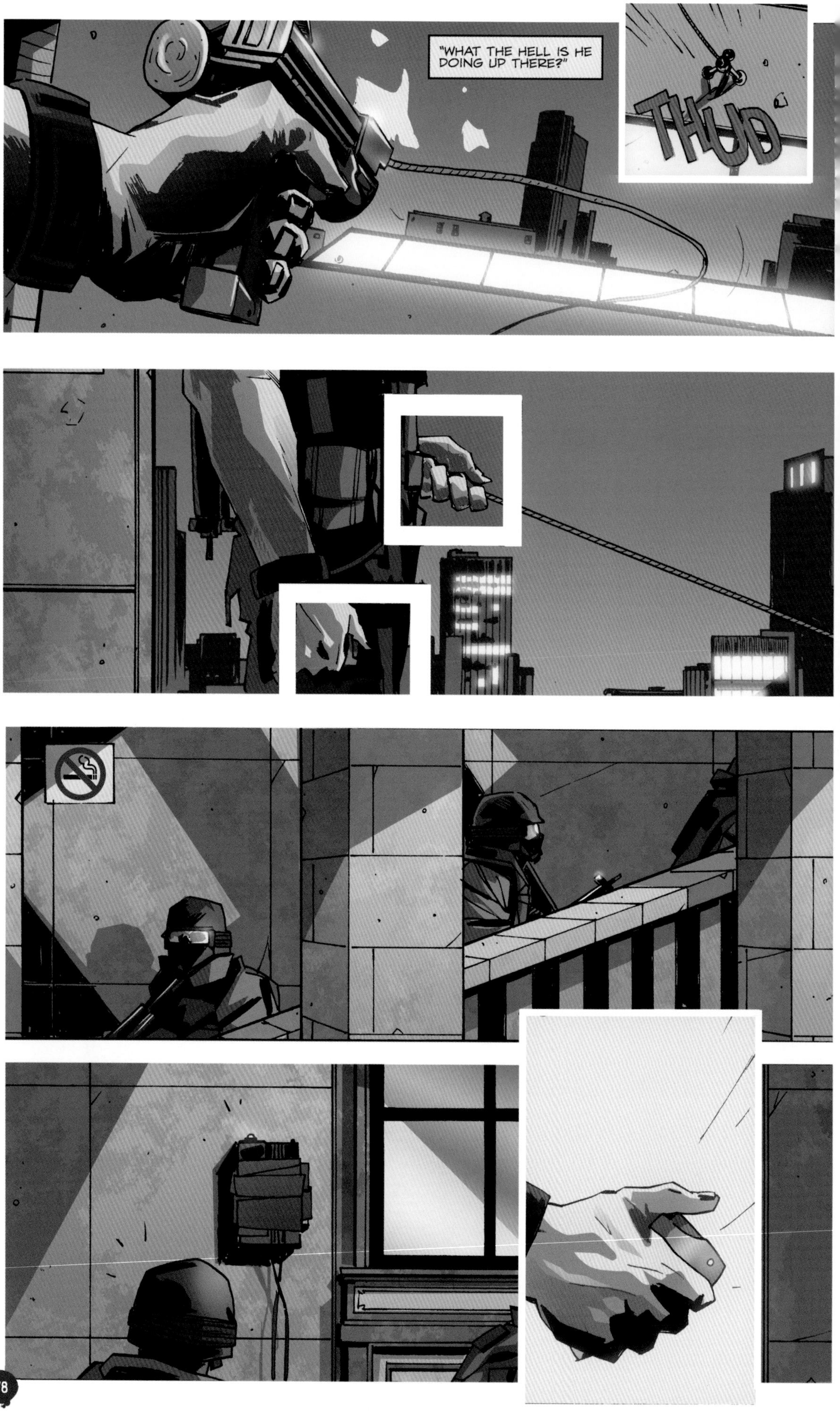
"WHAT THE HELL IS HE DOING UP THERE?"
THUD

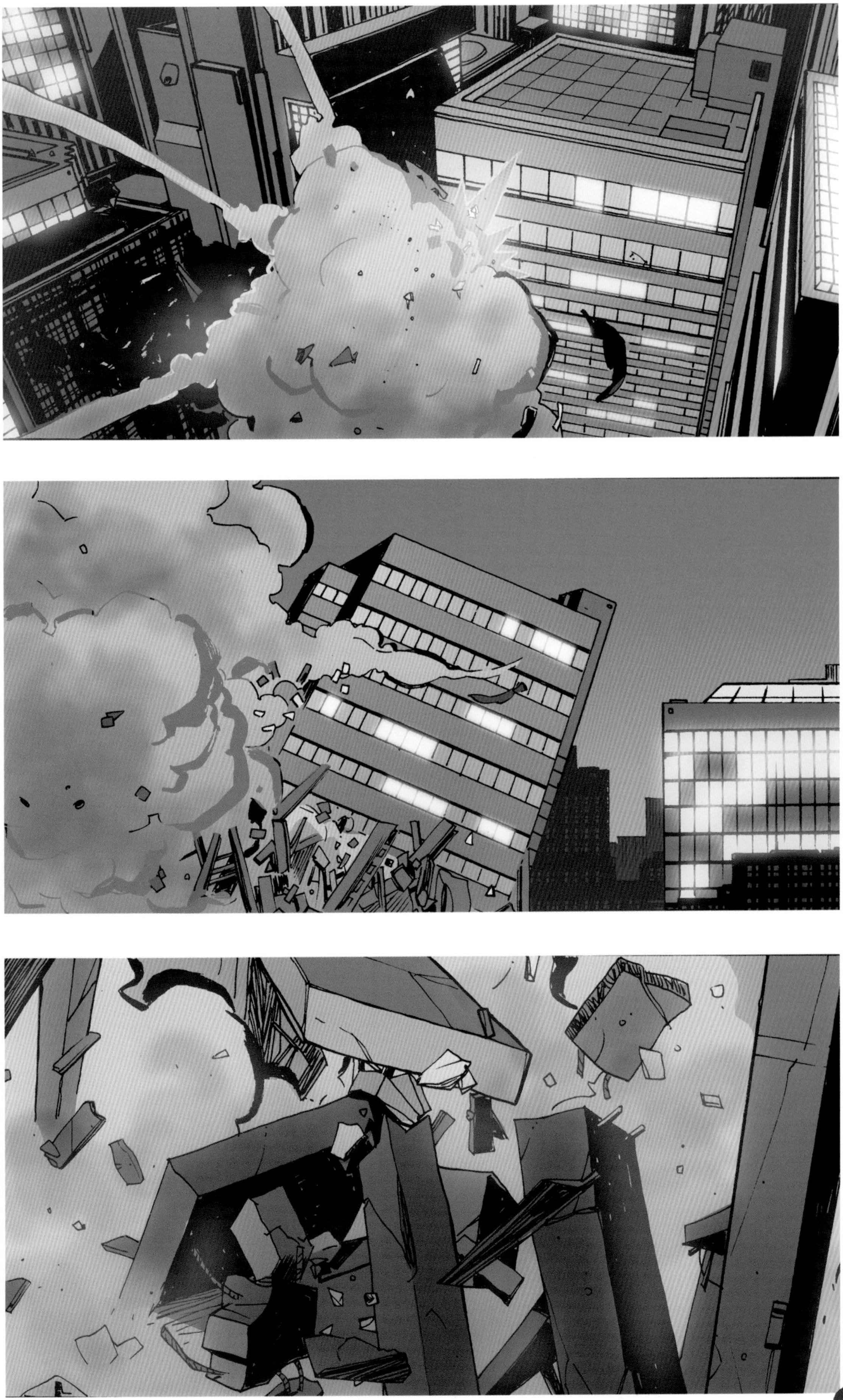

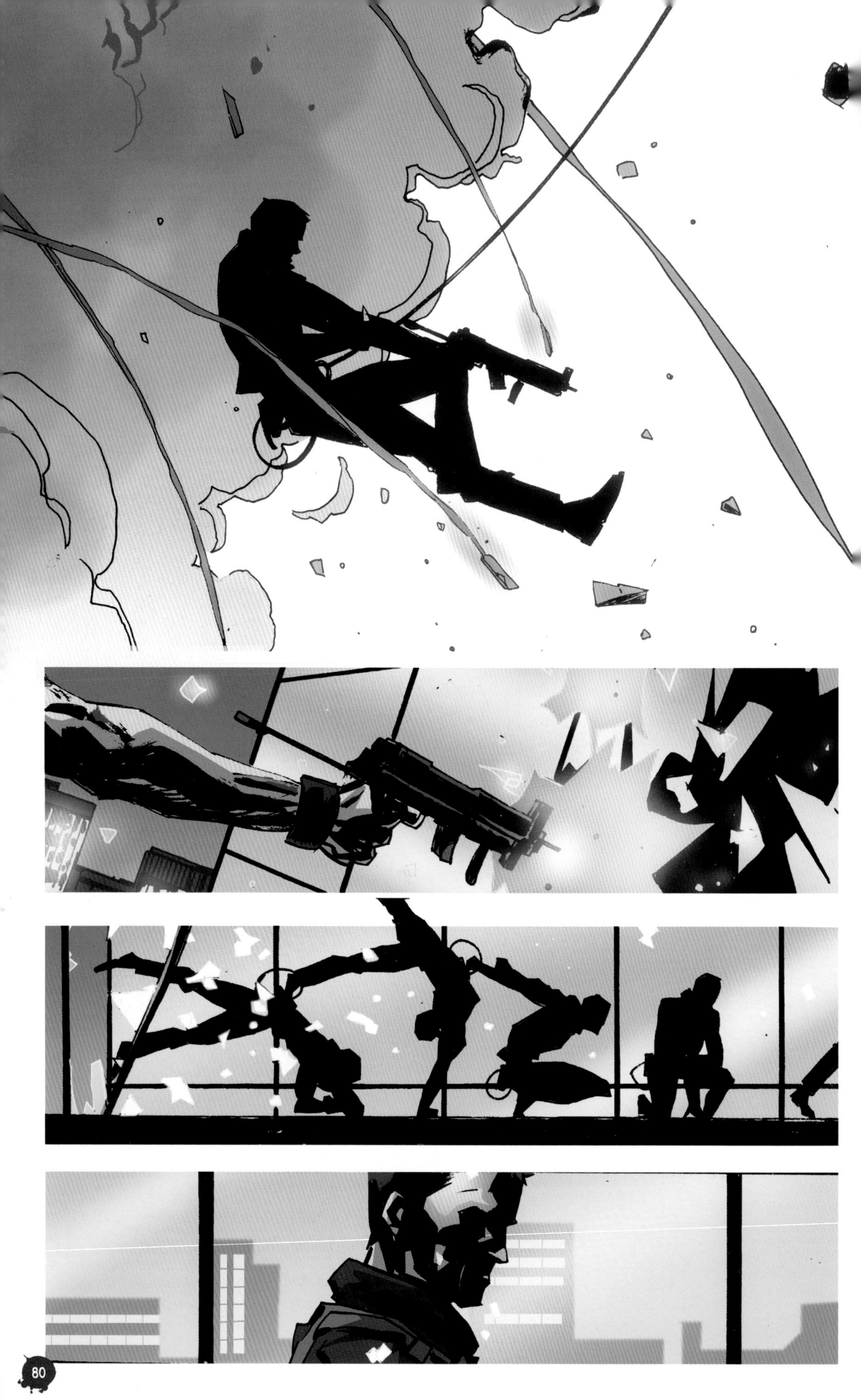

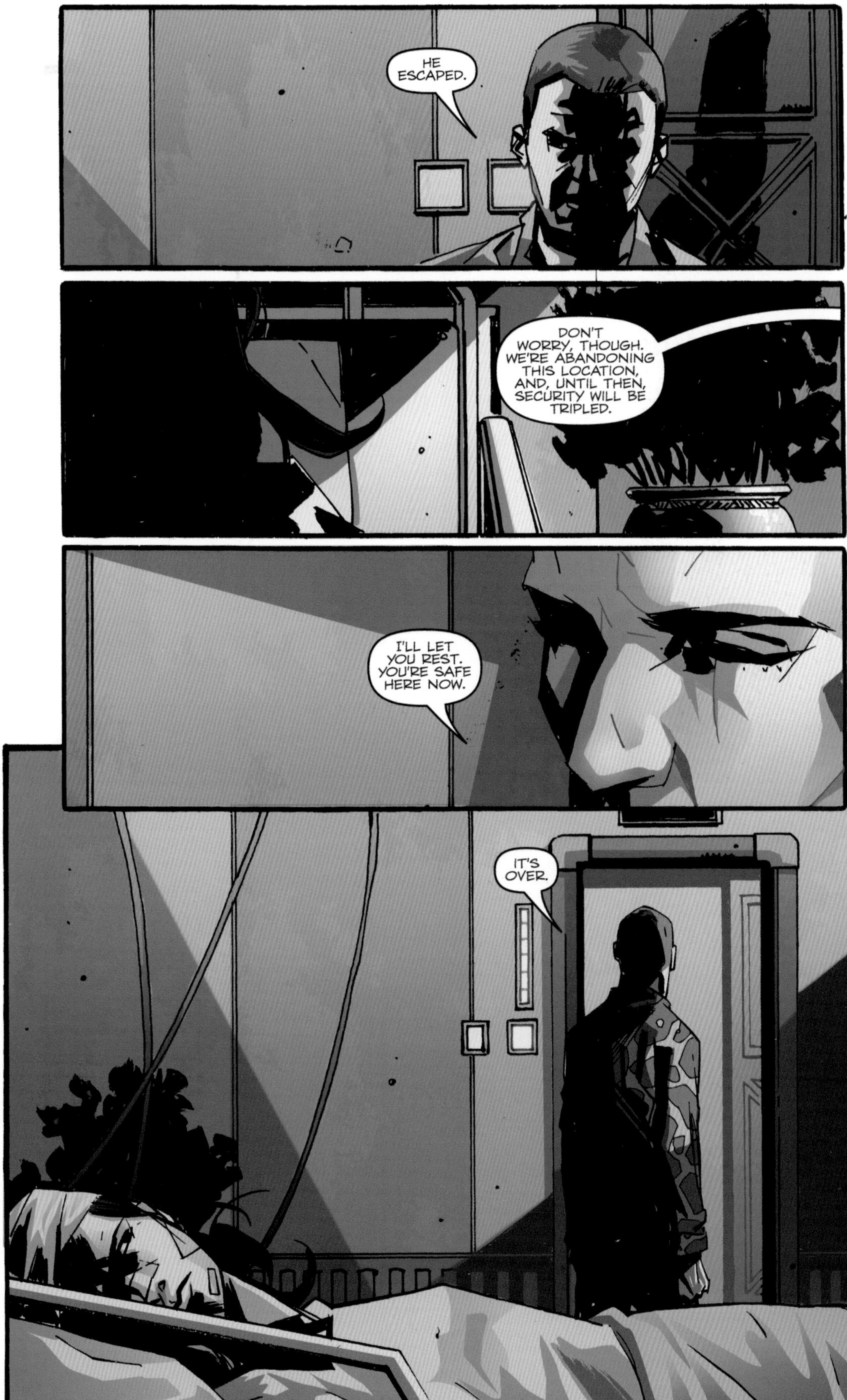
HE ESCAPED.
DON'T WORRY, THOUGH. WE'RE ABANDONING THIS LOCATION, AND, UNTIL THEN, SECURITY WILL BE TRIPLED.
I'LL LET YOU REST. YOU'RE SAFE HERE NOW.
IT'S OVER.

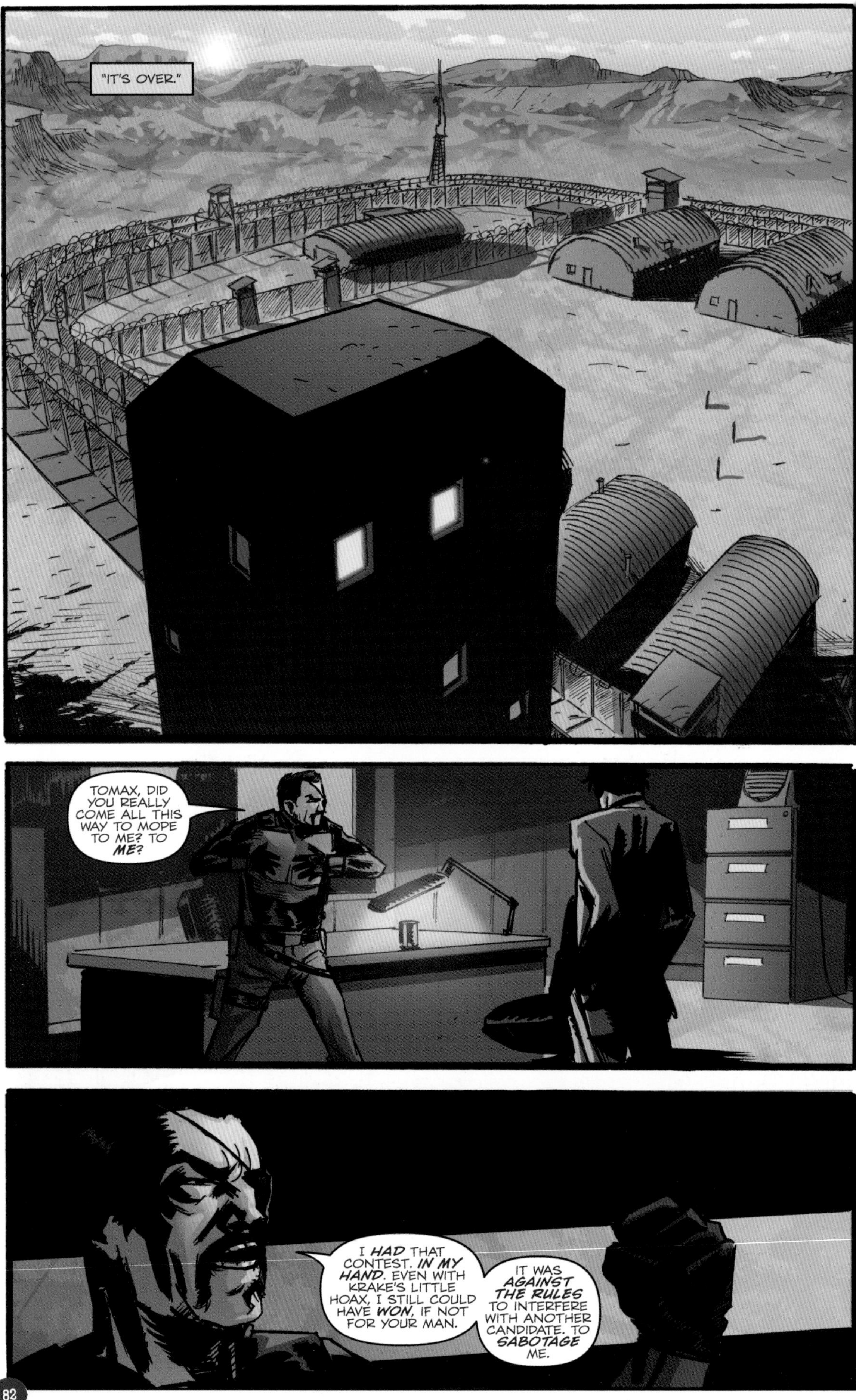
"IT'S OVER."
TOMAX, DID YOU REALLY COME ALL THIS WAY TO MOPE TO ME? TO *ME?*
I *HAD* THAT CONTEST. *IN MY HAND*. EVEN WITH KRAKE'S LITTLE HOAX, I STILL COULD HAVE *WON*, IF NOT FOR YOUR MAN.
IT WAS *AGAINST THE RULES* TO INTERFERE WITH ANOTHER CANDIDATE. TO *SABOTAGE* ME.

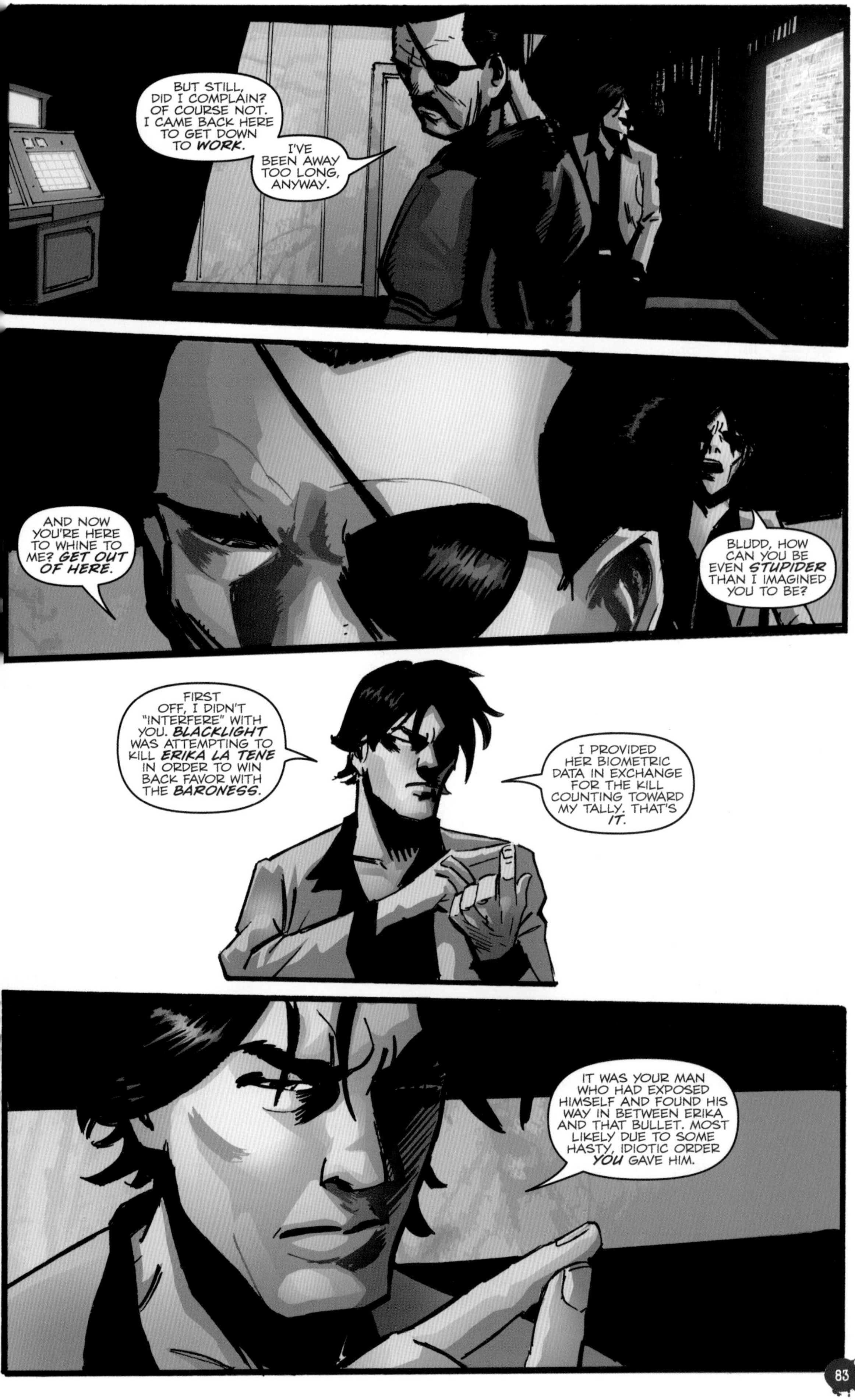
BUT STILL, DID I COMPLAIN? OF COURSE NOT. I CAME BACK HERE TO GET DOWN TO WORK.
I'VE BEEN AWAY TOO LONG, ANYWAY.
AND NOW YOU'RE HERE TO WHINE TO ME? GET OUT OF HERE.
BLUDD, HOW CAN YOU BE EVEN STUPIDER THAN I IMAGINED YOU TO BE?
FIRST OFF, I DIDN'T "INTERFERE" WITH YOU. BLACKLIGHT WAS ATTEMPTING TO KILL ERIKA LA TENE IN ORDER TO WIN BACK FAVOR WITH THE BARONESS.
I PROVIDED HER BIOMETRIC DATA IN EXCHANGE FOR THE KILL COUNTING TOWARD MY TALLY. THAT'S IT.
IT WAS YOUR MAN WHO HAD EXPOSED HIMSELF AND FOUND HIS WAY IN BETWEEN ERIKA AND THAT BULLET. MOST LIKELY DUE TO SOME HASTY, IDIOTIC ORDER YOU GAVE HIM.

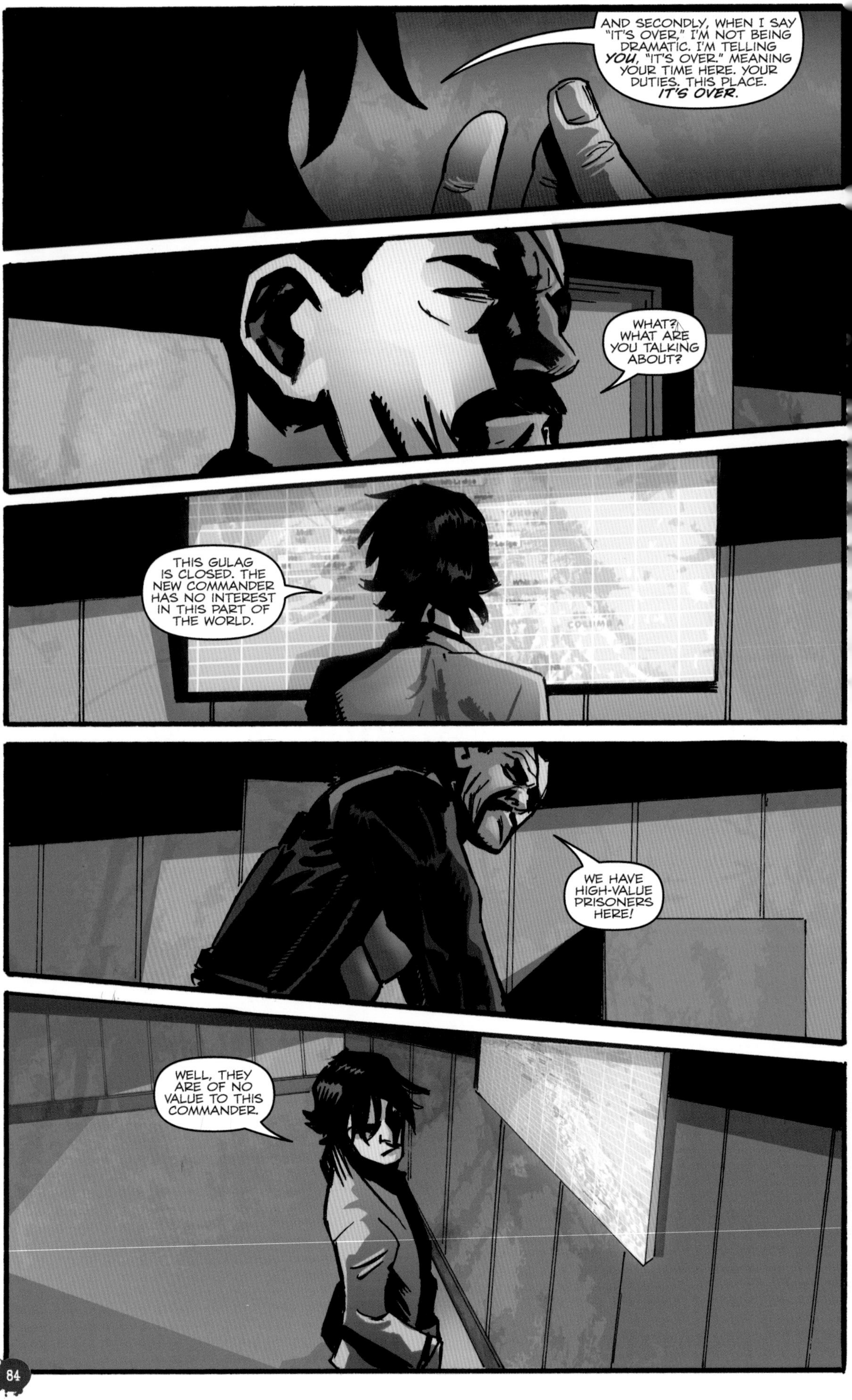
AND SECONDLY, WHEN I SAY "IT'S OVER," I'M NOT BEING DRAMATIC. I'M TELLING ***YOU***, "IT'S OVER." MEANING YOUR TIME HERE. YOUR DUTIES. THIS PLACE. ***IT'S OVER***.
WHAT? WHAT ARE YOU TALKING ABOUT?
THIS GULAG IS CLOSED. THE NEW COMMANDER HAS NO INTEREST IN THIS PART OF THE WORLD.
WE HAVE HIGH-VALUE PRISONERS HERE!
WELL, THEY ARE OF NO VALUE TO THIS COMMANDER.

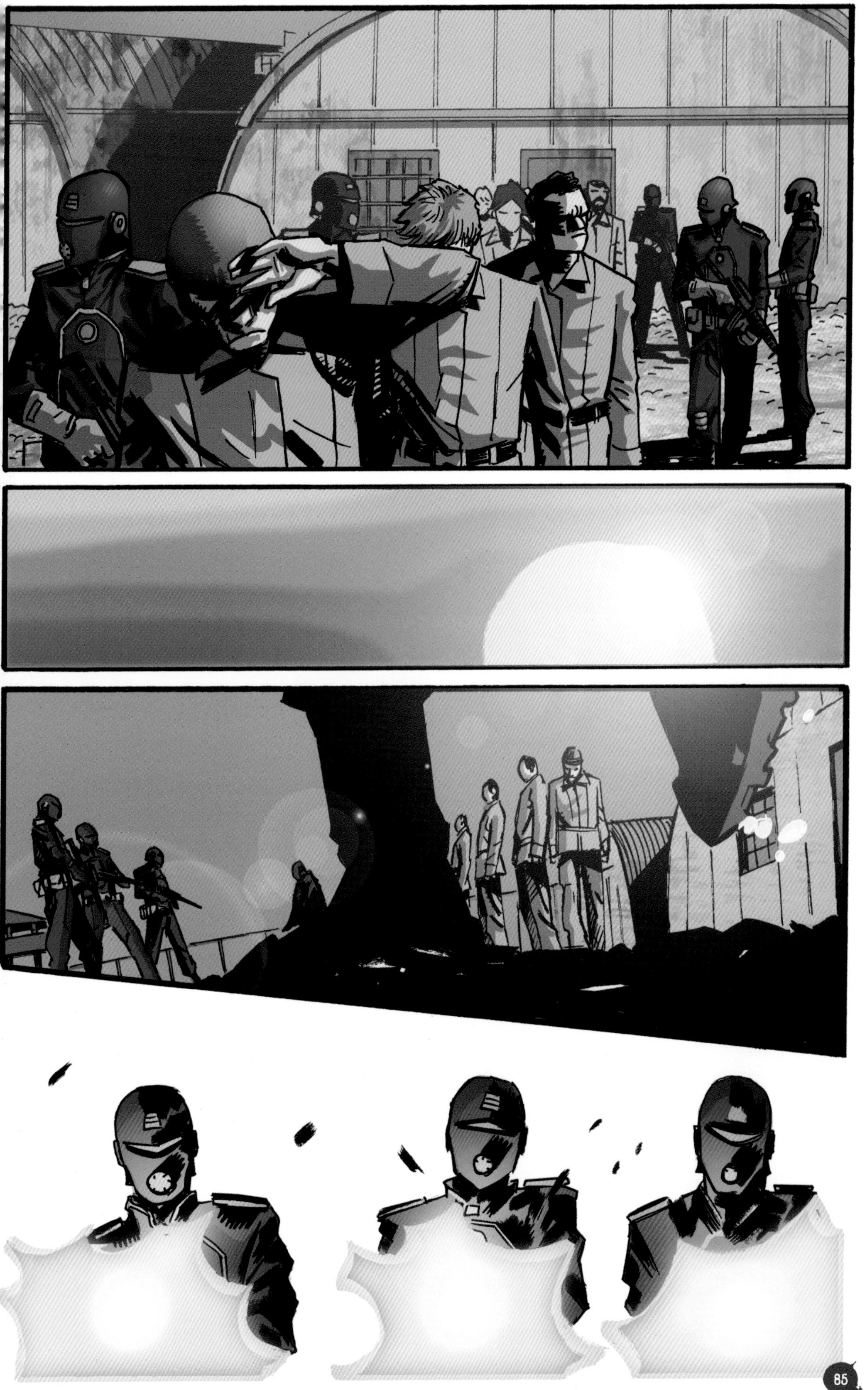

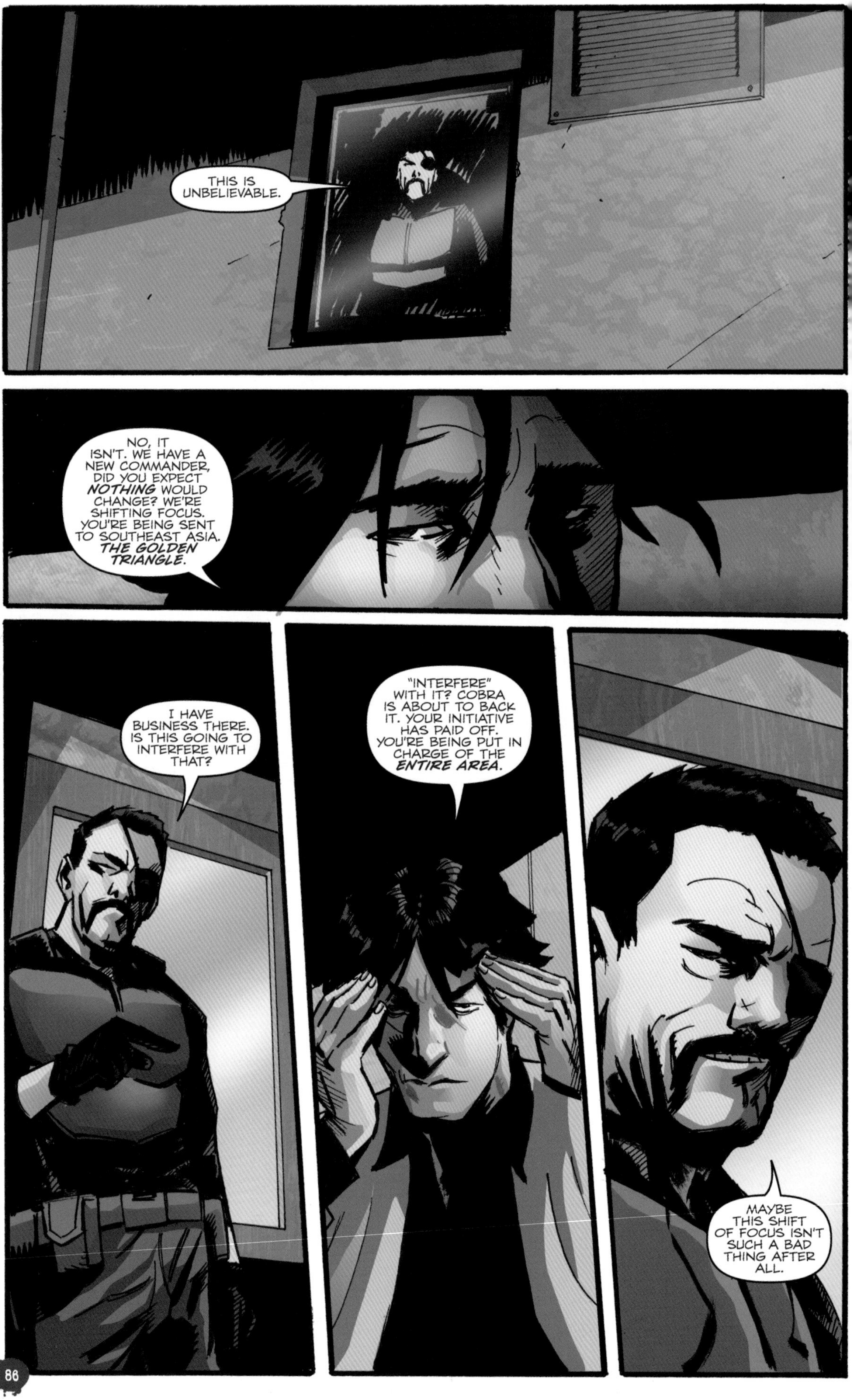
THIS IS UNBELIEVABLE.
NO, IT ISN'T. WE HAVE A NEW COMMANDER, DID YOU EXPECT *NOTHING* WOULD CHANGE? WE'RE SHIFTING FOCUS. YOU'RE BEING SENT TO SOUTHEAST ASIA. *THE GOLDEN TRIANGLE*.
I HAVE BUSINESS THERE. IS THIS GOING TO INTERFERE WITH THAT?
"INTERFERE" WITH IT? COBRA IS ABOUT TO BACK IT. YOUR INITIATIVE HAS PAID OFF. YOU'RE BEING PUT IN CHARGE OF THE *ENTIRE AREA*.
MAYBE THIS SHIFT OF FOCUS ISN'T SUCH A BAD THING AFTER ALL.

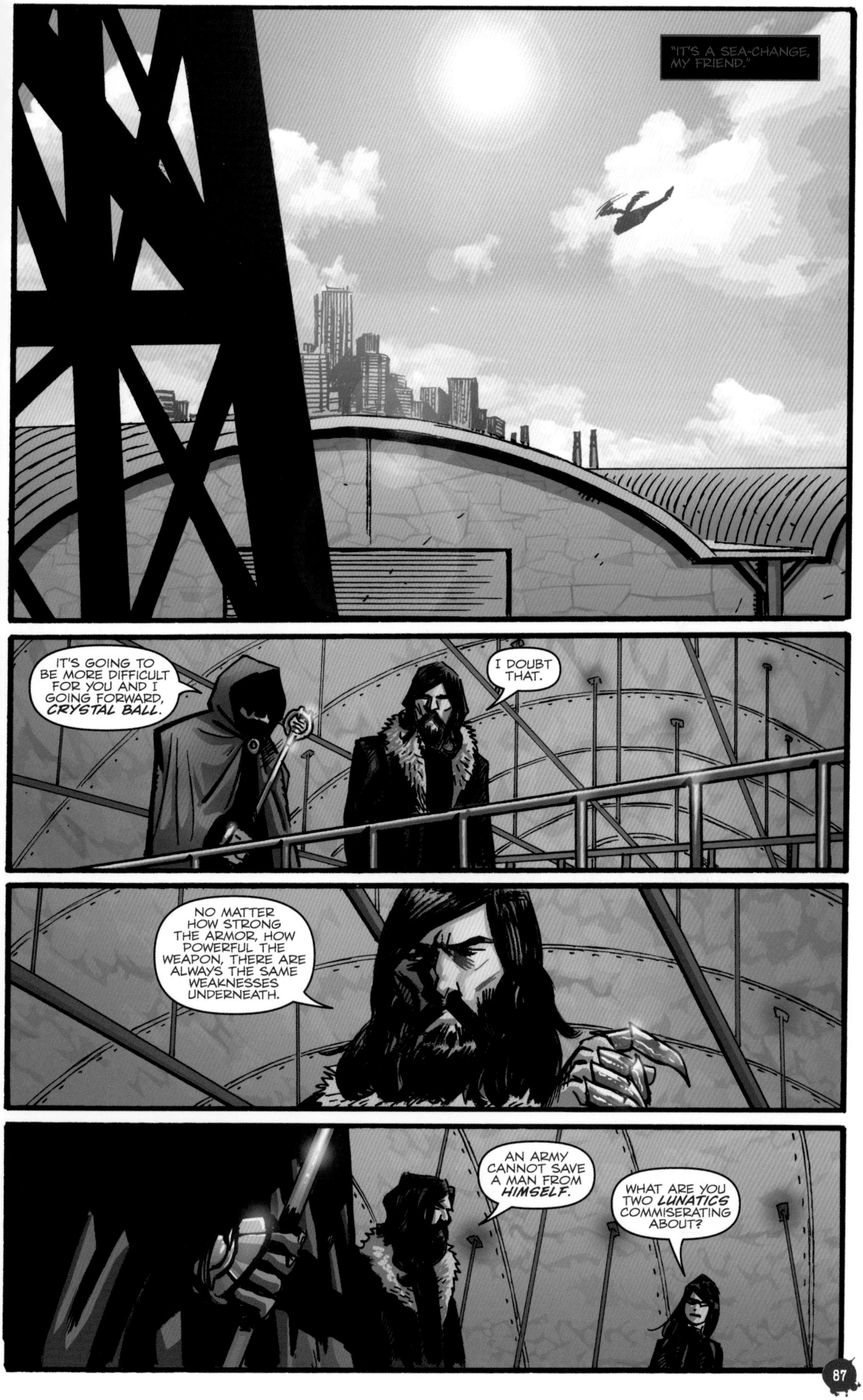
"IT'S A SEA-CHANGE, MY FRIEND."
IT'S GOING TO BE MORE DIFFICULT FOR YOU AND I GOING FORWARD, CRYSTAL BALL.
I DOUBT THAT.
NO MATTER HOW STRONG THE ARMOR, HOW POWERFUL THE WEAPON, THERE ARE ALWAYS THE SAME WEAKNESSES UNDERNEATH.
AN ARMY CANNOT SAVE A MAN FROM HIMSELF.
WHAT ARE YOU TWO LUNATICS COMMISERATING ABOUT?

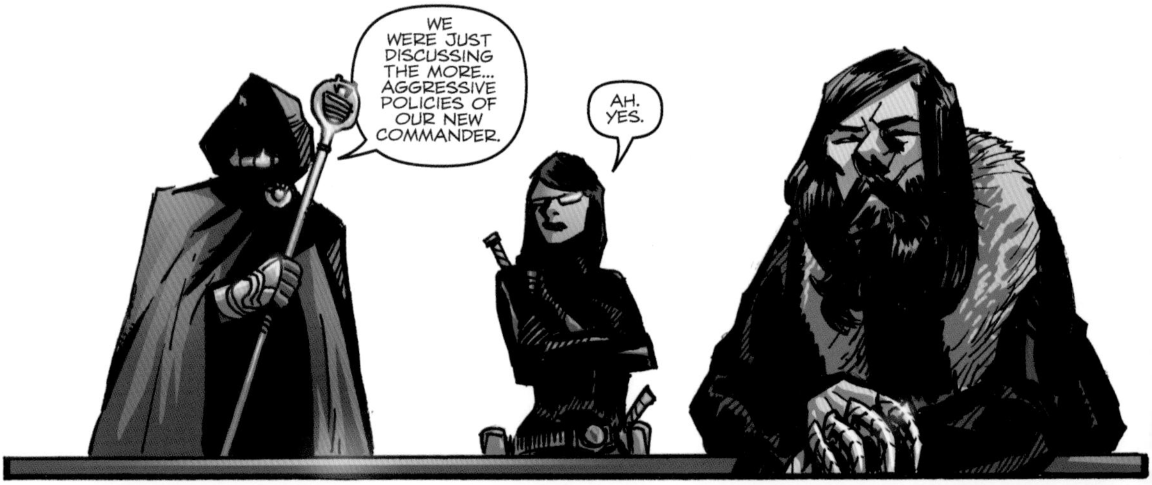
WE WERE JUST DISCUSSING THE MORE... AGGRESSIVE POLICIES OF OUR NEW COMMANDER.
AH. YES.

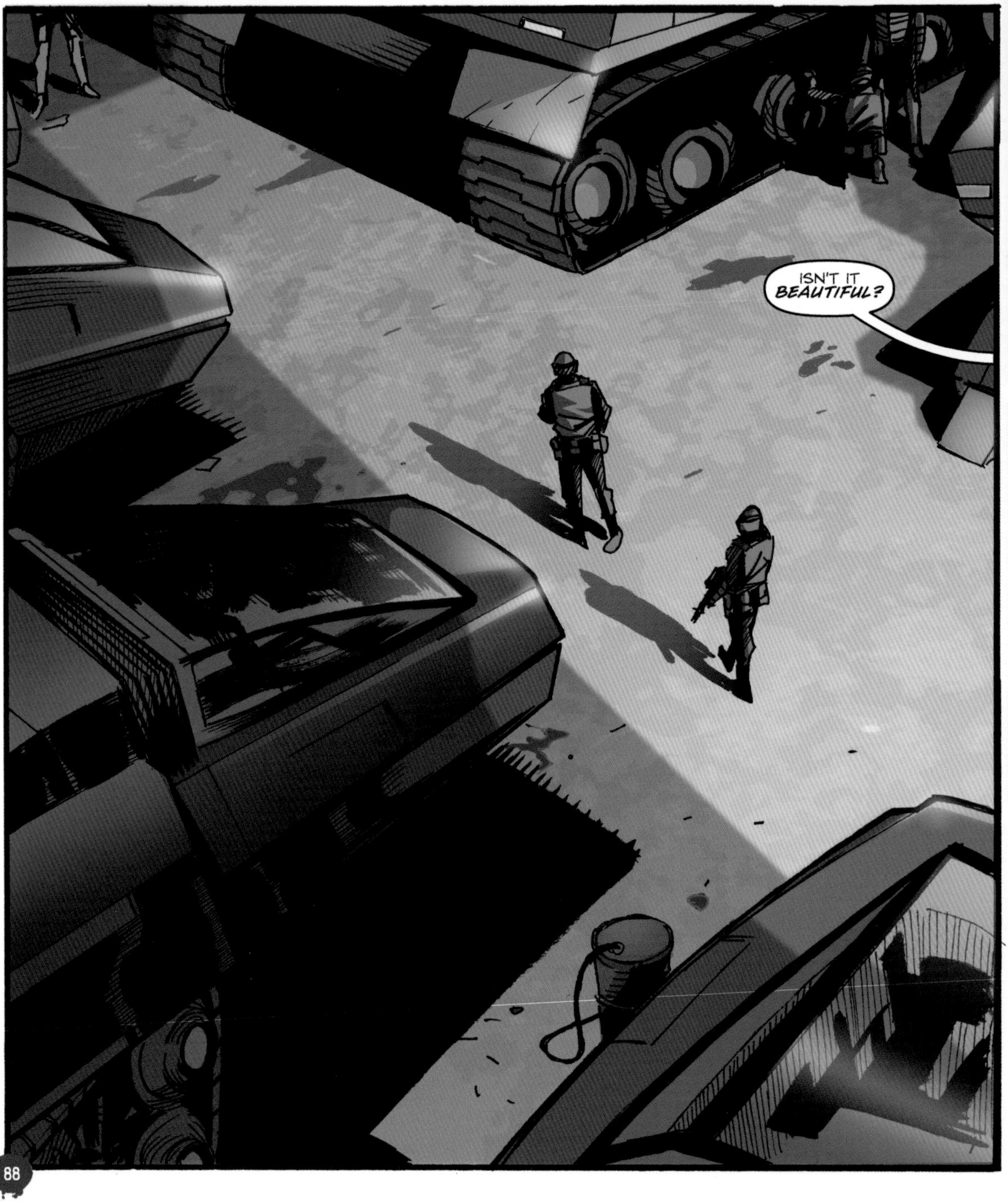
ISN'T IT *BEAUTIFUL?*

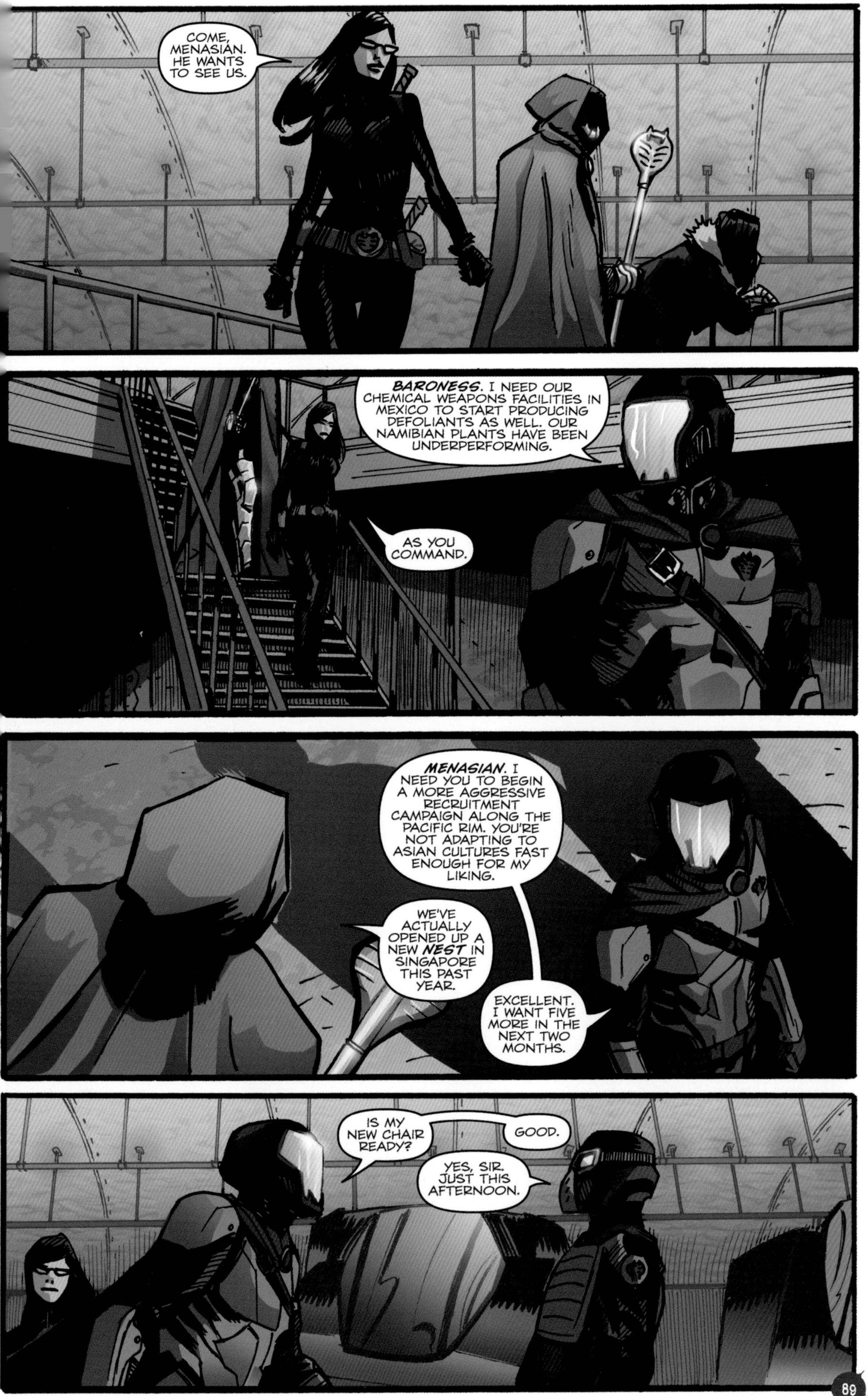
COME, MENASIAN. HE WANTS TO SEE US.
BARONESS. I NEED OUR CHEMICAL WEAPONS FACILITIES IN MEXICO TO START PRODUCING DEFOLIANTS AS WELL. OUR NAMIBIAN PLANTS HAVE BEEN UNDERPERFORMING.
AS YOU COMMAND.
MENASIAN. I NEED YOU TO BEGIN A MORE AGGRESSIVE RECRUITMENT CAMPAIGN ALONG THE PACIFIC RIM. YOU'RE NOT ADAPTING TO ASIAN CULTURES FAST ENOUGH FOR MY LIKING.
WE'VE ACTUALLY OPENED UP A NEW NEST IN SINGAPORE THIS PAST YEAR.
EXCELLENT. I WANT FIVE MORE IN THE NEXT TWO MONTHS.
IS MY NEW CHAIR READY?
YES, SIR. JUST THIS AFTERNOON.
GOOD.

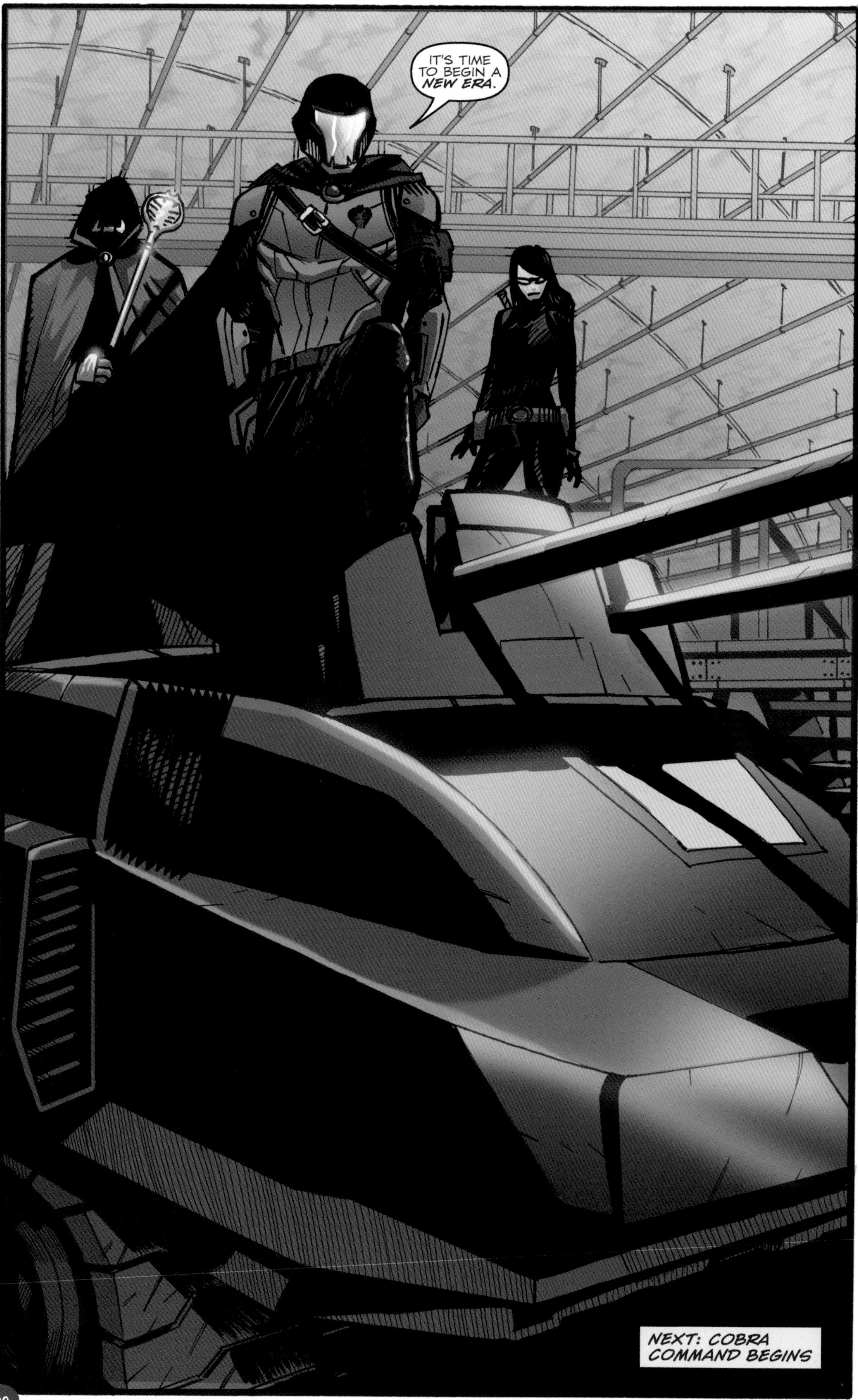
IT'S TIME TO BEGIN A NEW ERA.
NEXT: COBRA COMMAND BEGINS

ART GALLERY

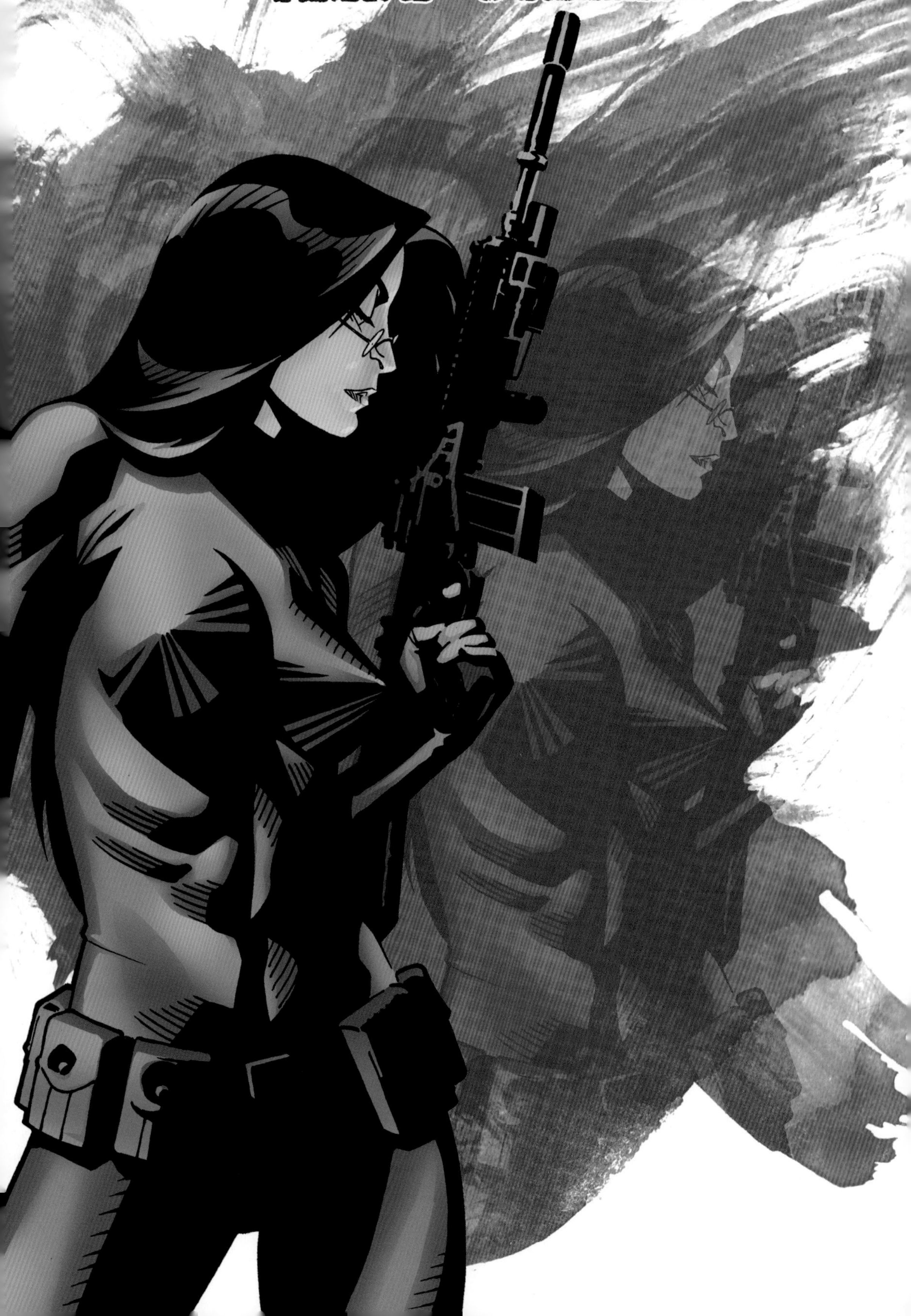

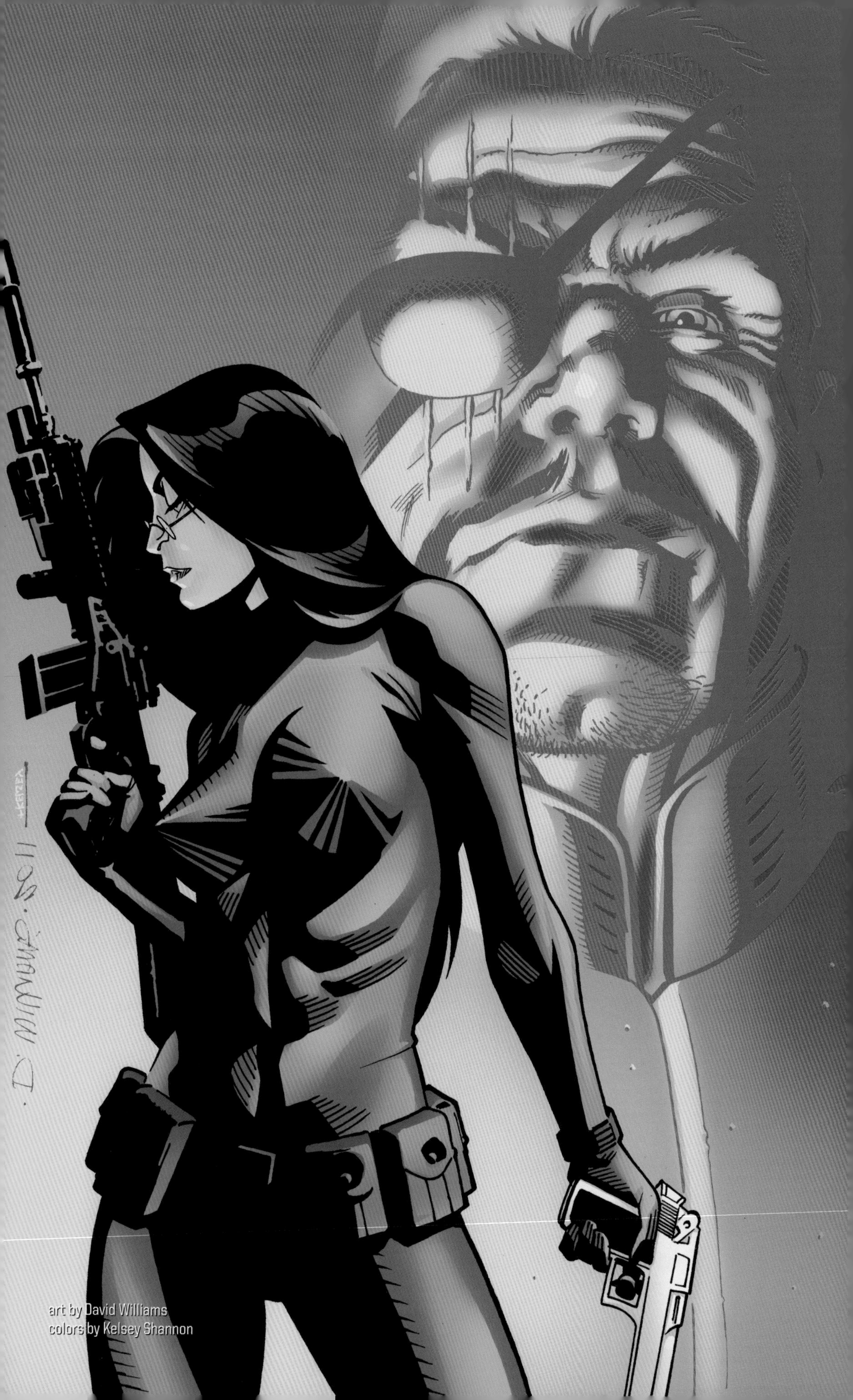

art by David Williams
colors by Kelsey Shannon

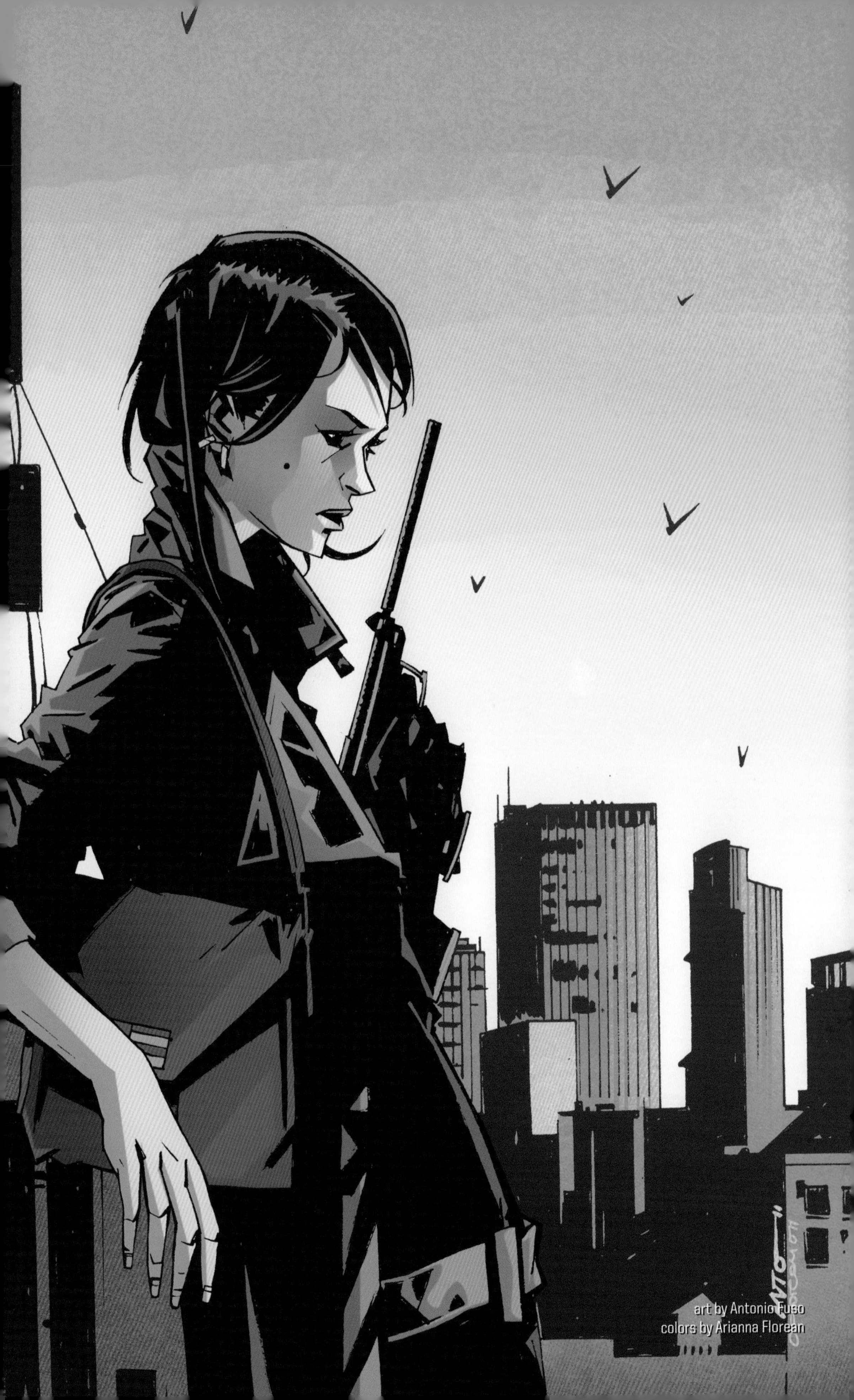

art by Antonio Fuso
colors by Arianna Florean

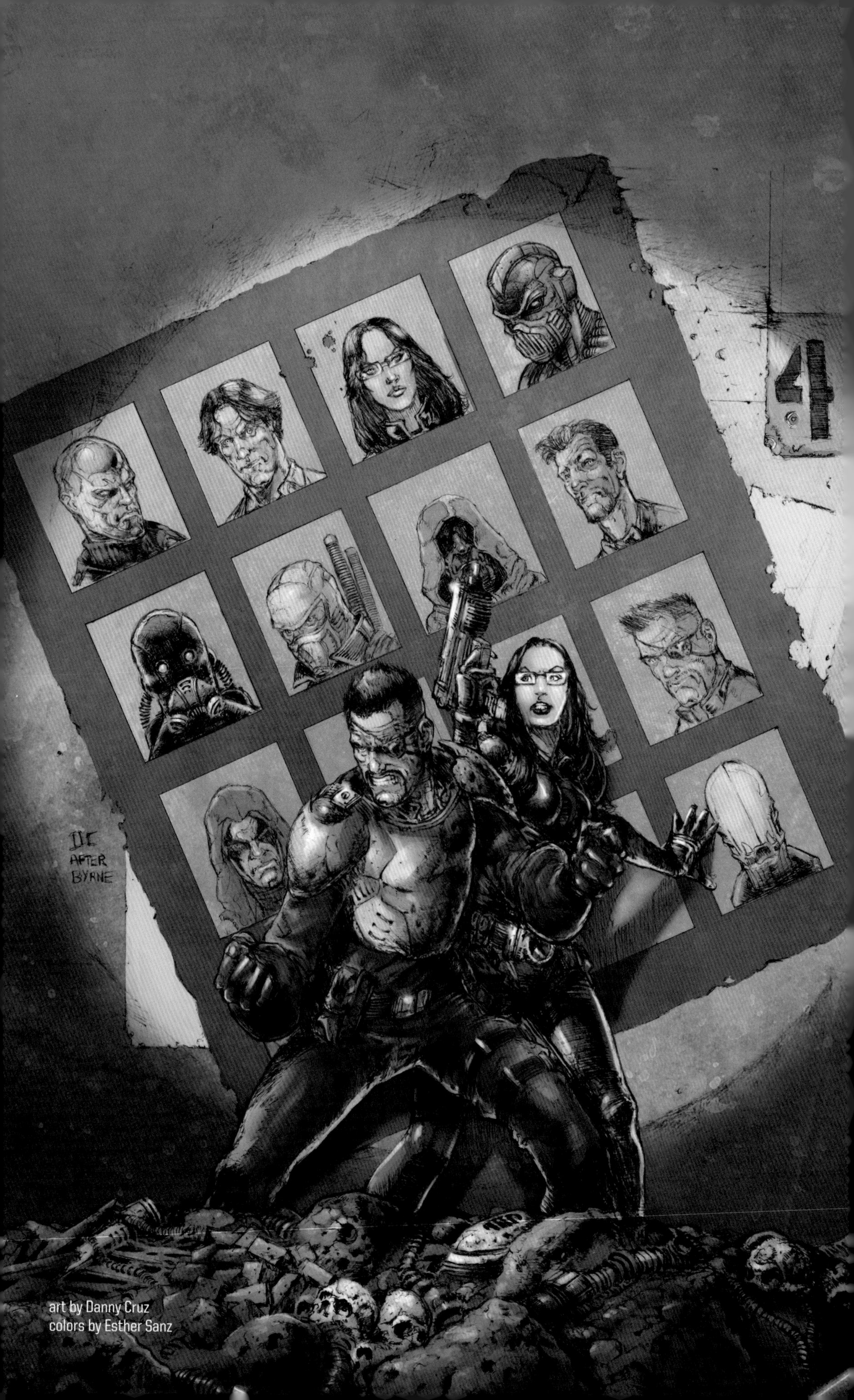
4

art by Danny Cruz
colors by Esther Sanz

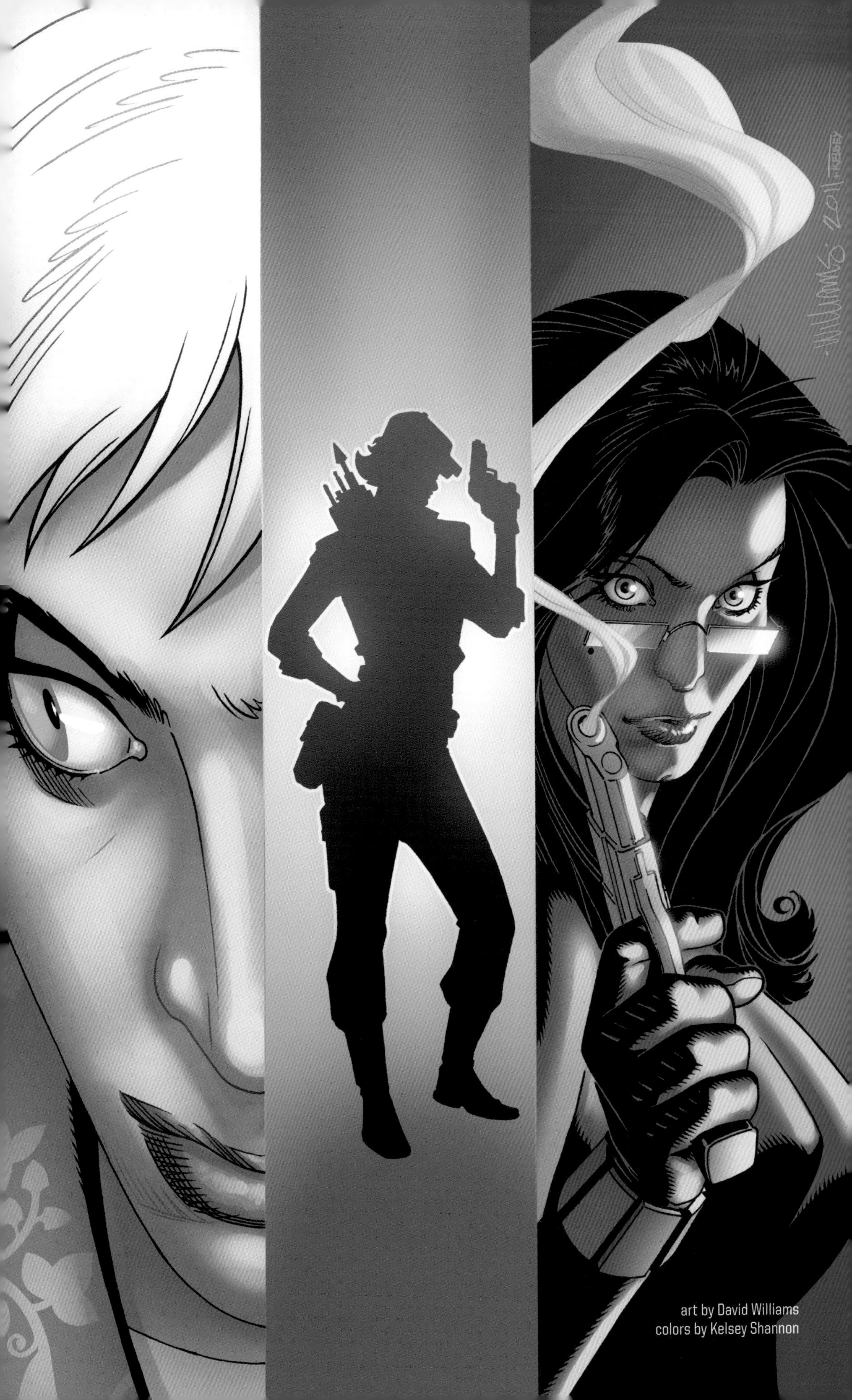

art by David Williams
colors by Kelsey Shannon

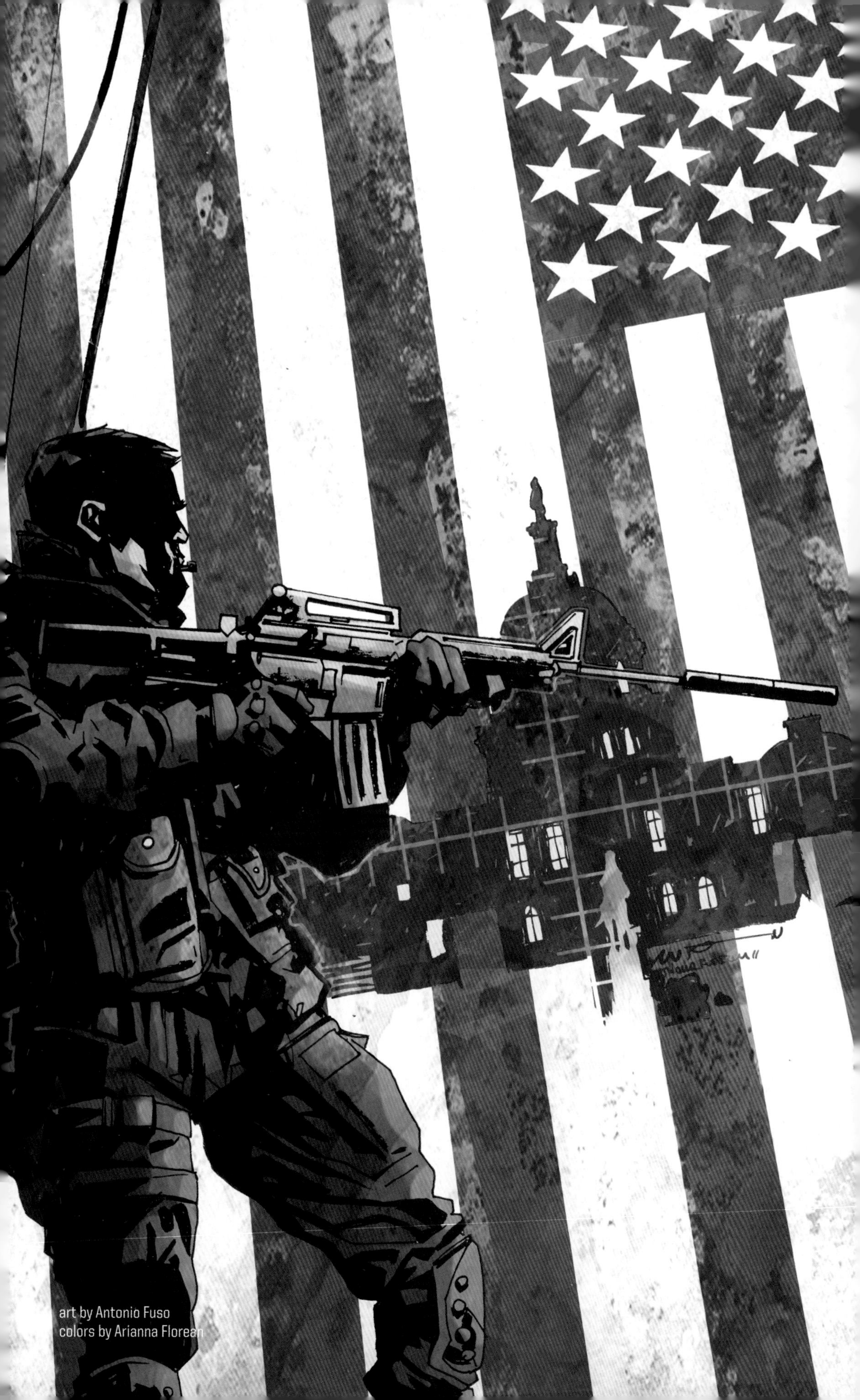

art by Antonio Fuso
colors by Arianna Florean

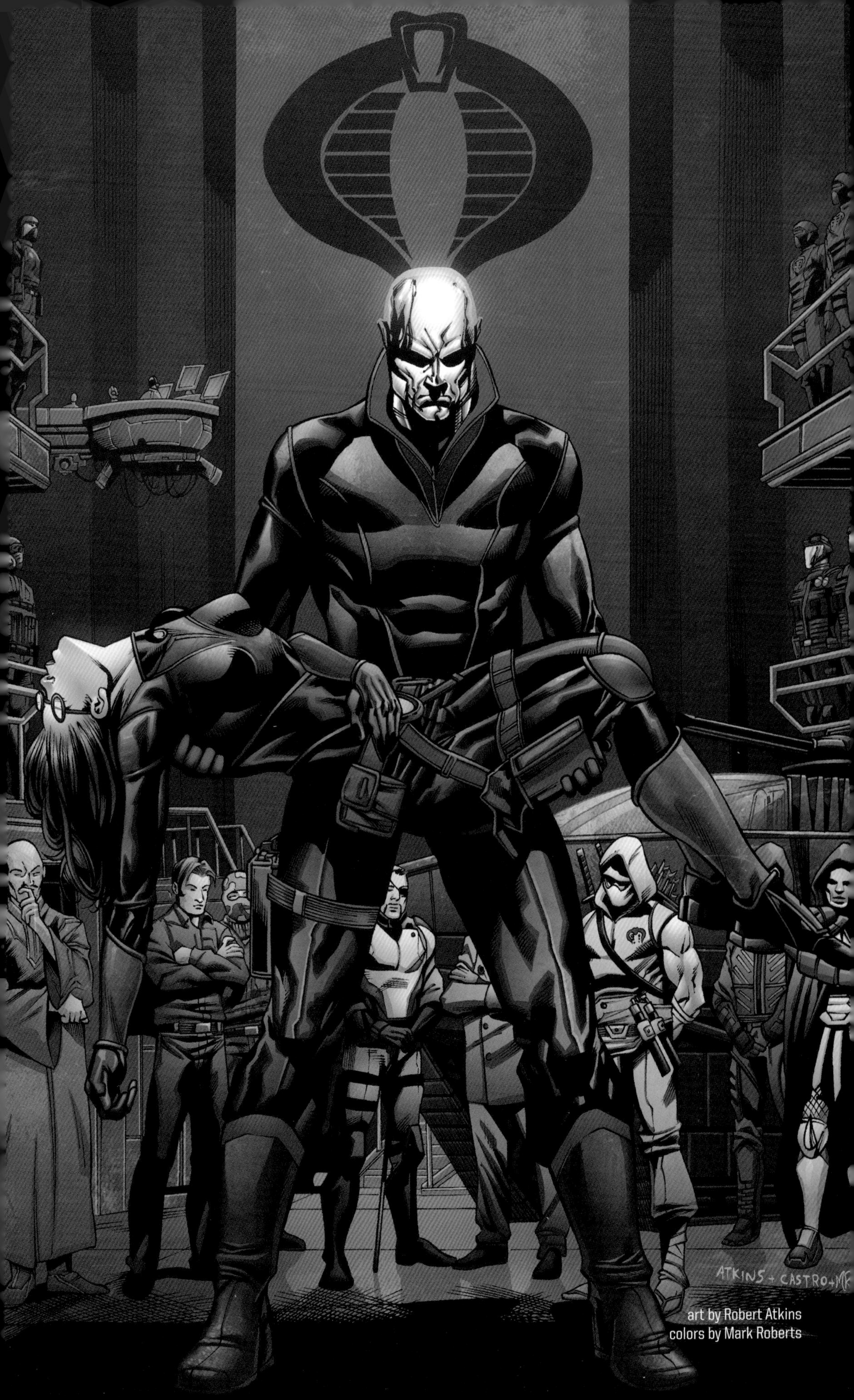
ATKINS + CASTRO + MK

art by Robert Atkins
colors by Mark Roberts

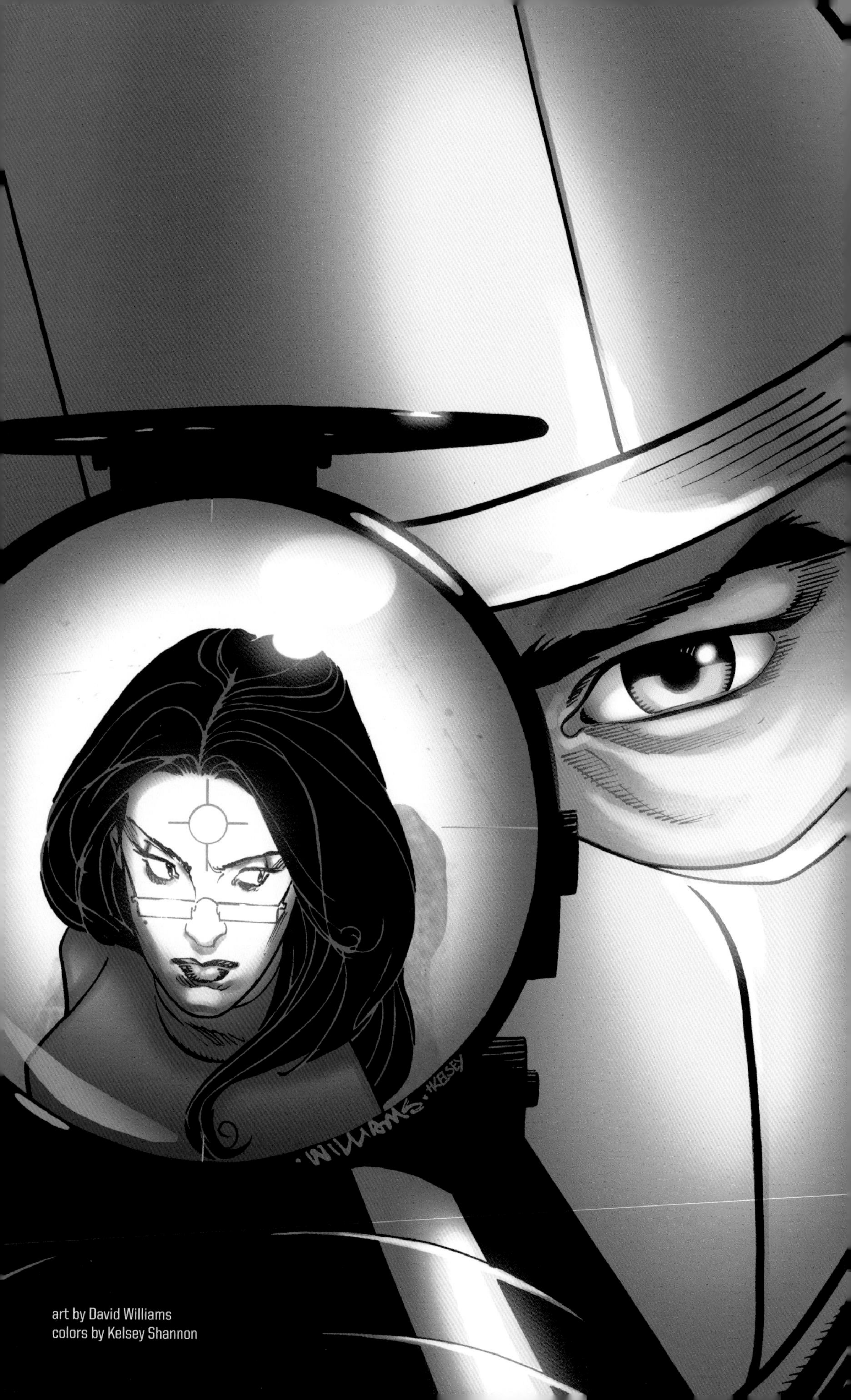
WILLIAMS · KELSEY

art by David Williams
colors by Kelsey Shannon

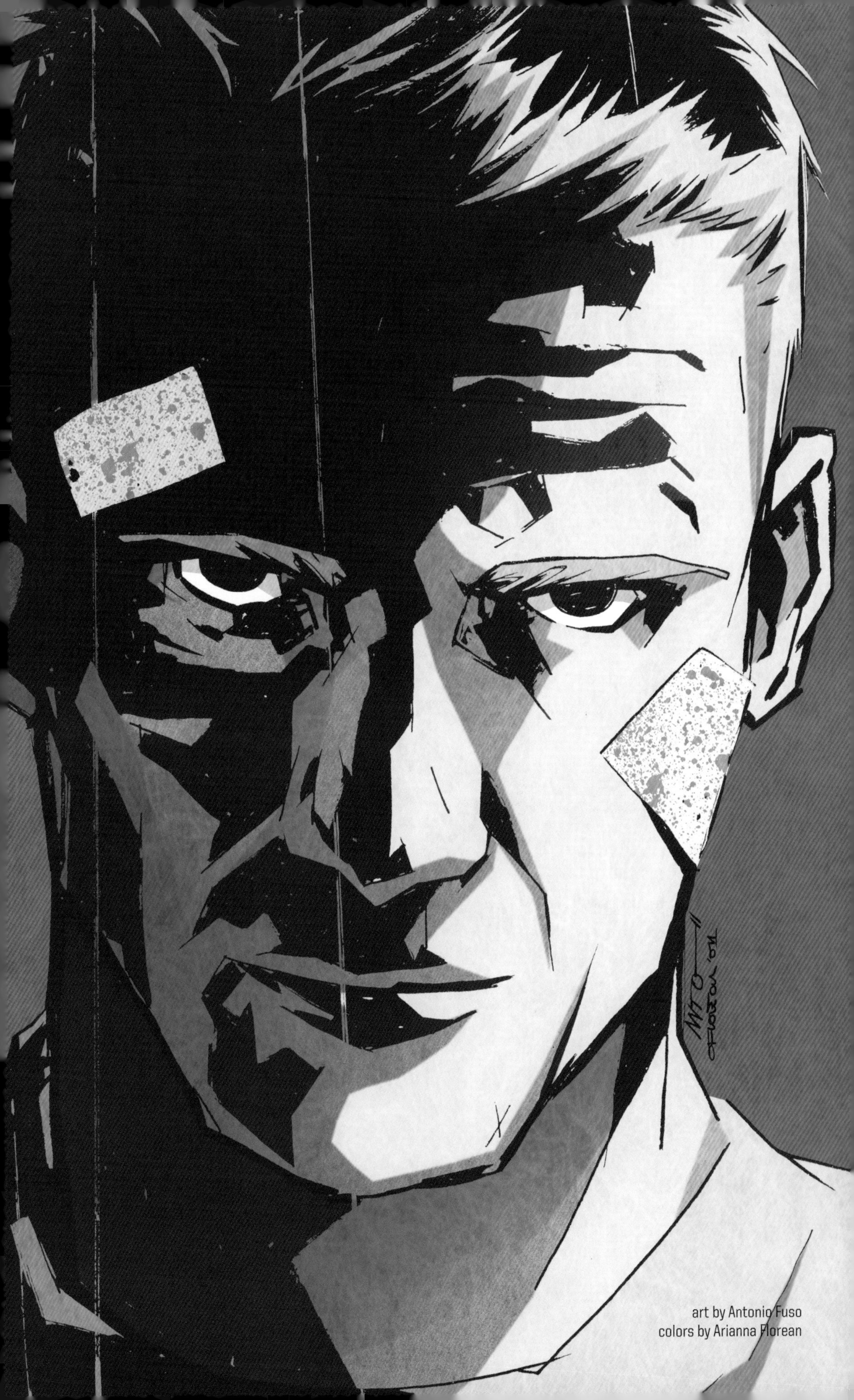

art by Antonio Fuso
colors by Arianna Florean

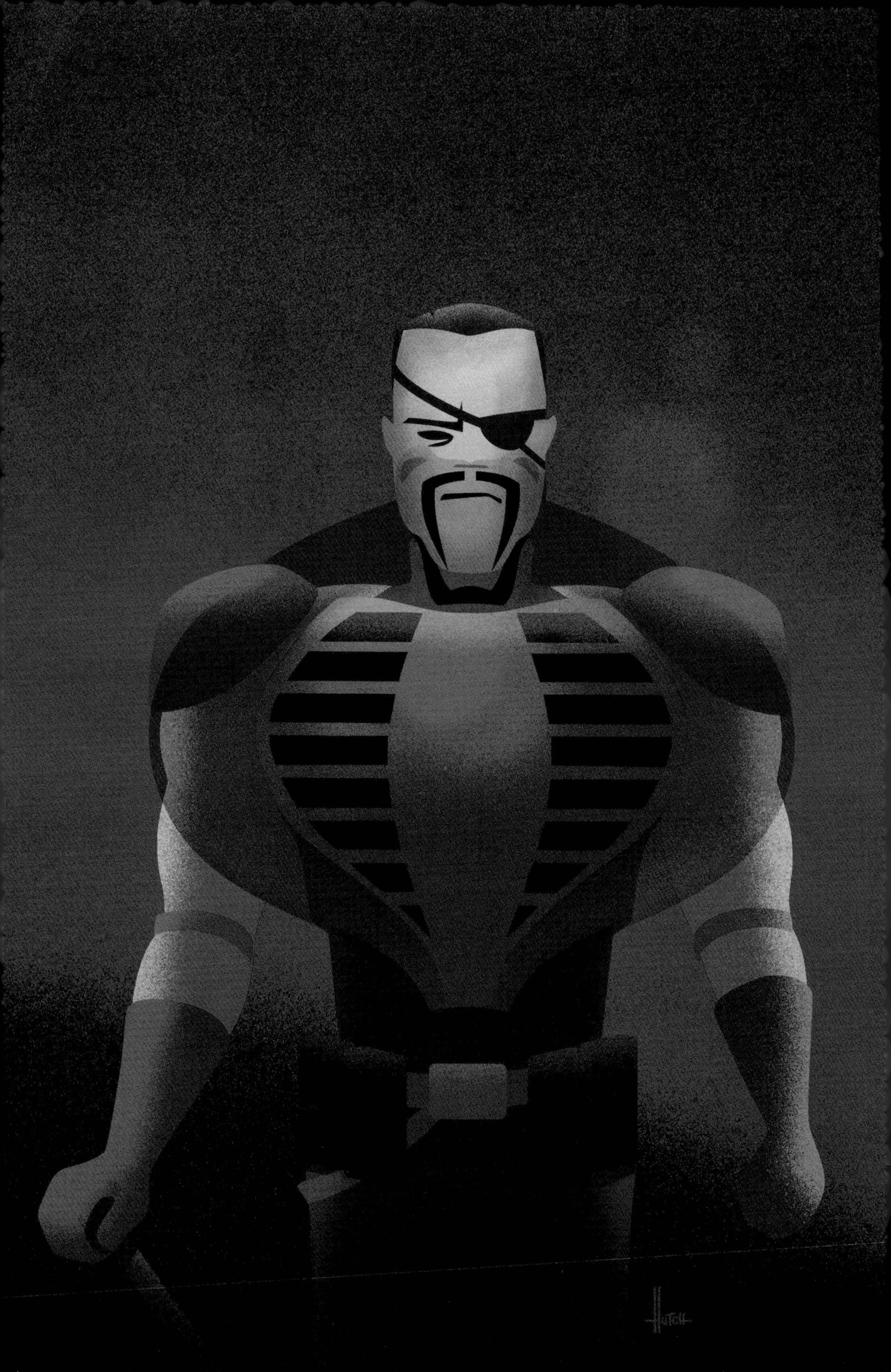
HUTCH

art by Trevor Hutchison

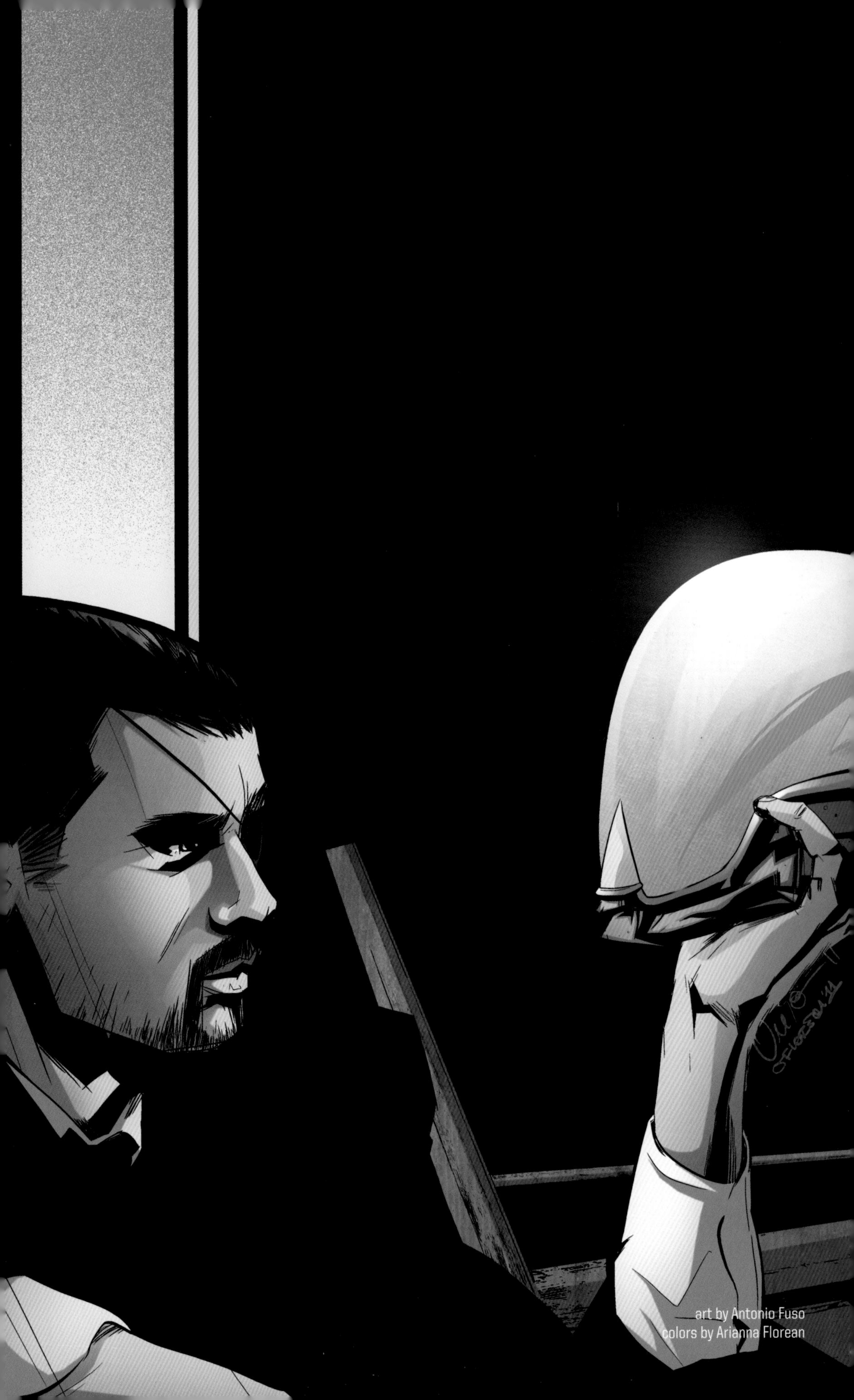
art by Antonio Fuso
colors by Arianna Florean

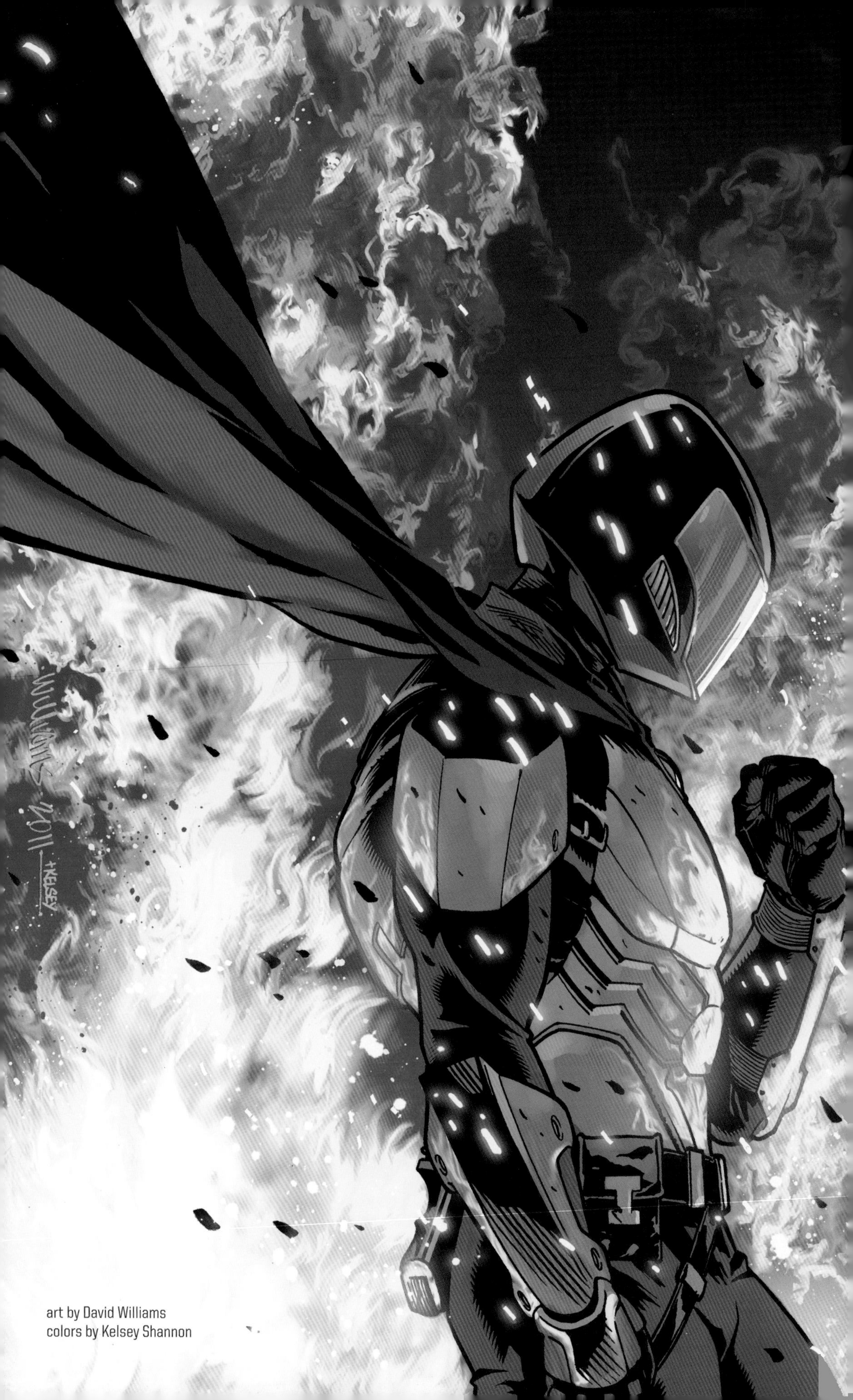

art by David Williams
colors by Kelsey Shannon

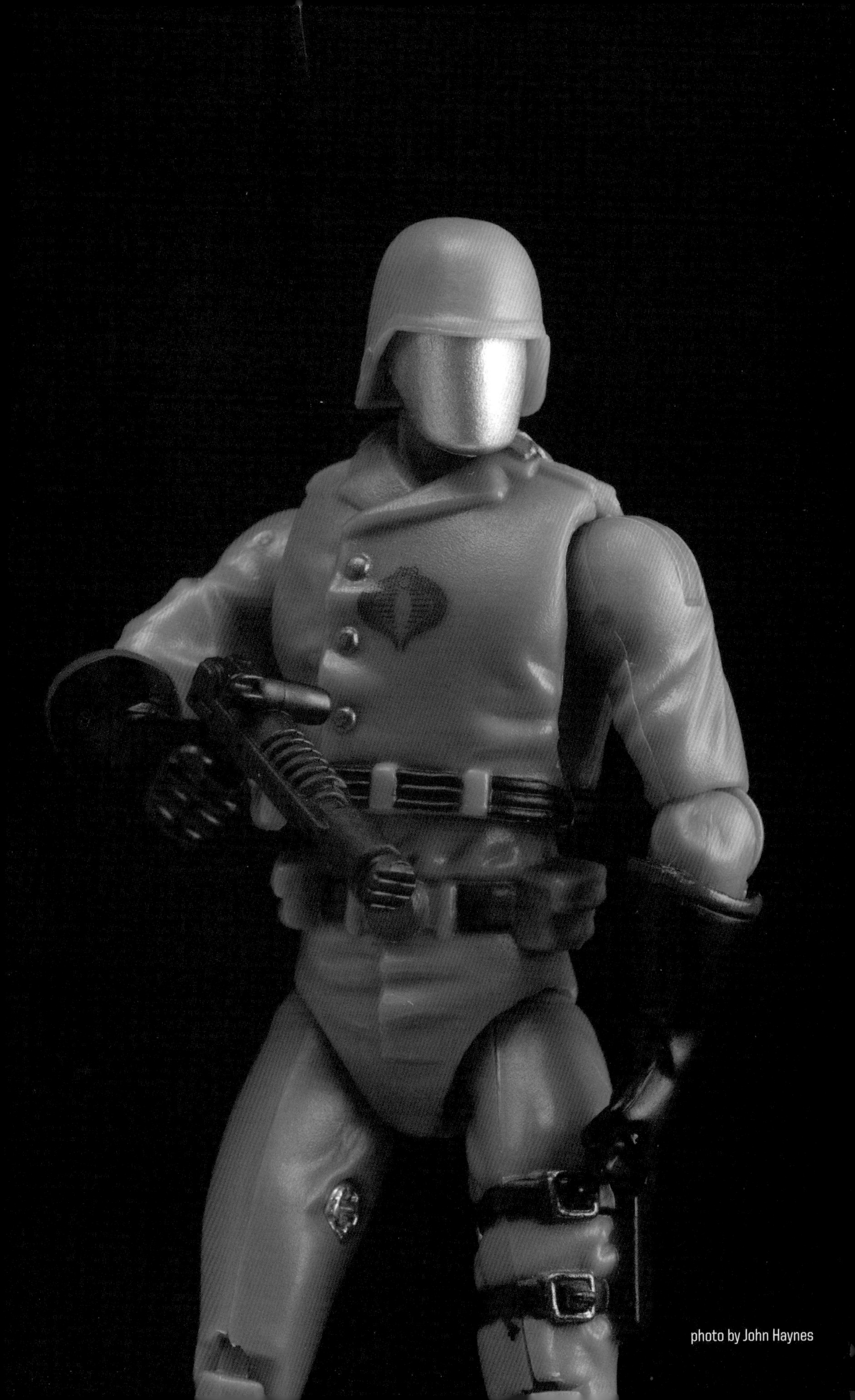

photo by John Haynes

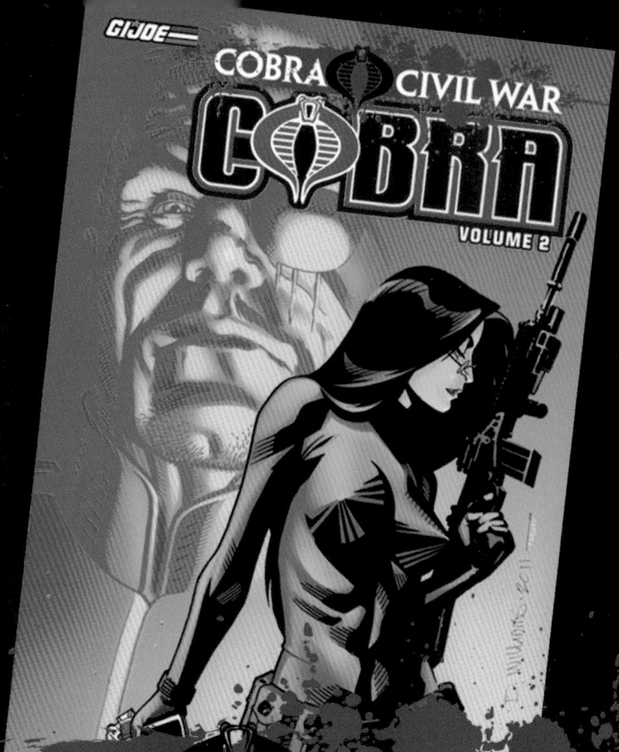
G.I. JOE
COBRA CIVIL WAR
COBRA
VOLUME 2

COBRA CIVIL WAR

NOW AVAILABLE

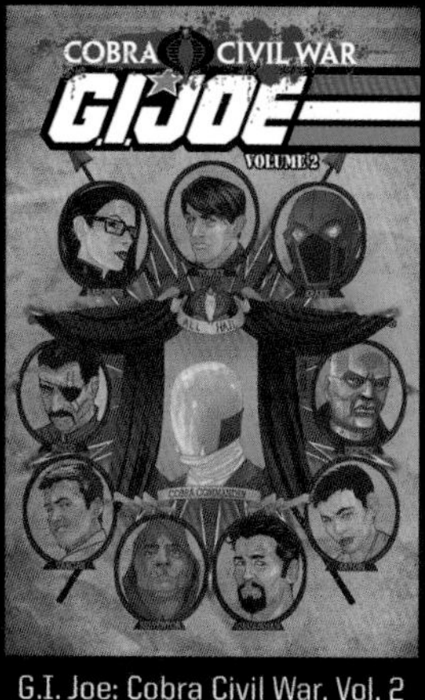
COBRA CIVIL WAR
G.I. JOE
VOLUME 2

G.I. Joe: Cobra Civil War, Vol. 2
ISBN: 978-1-61377-132-7

NOW AVAILABLE

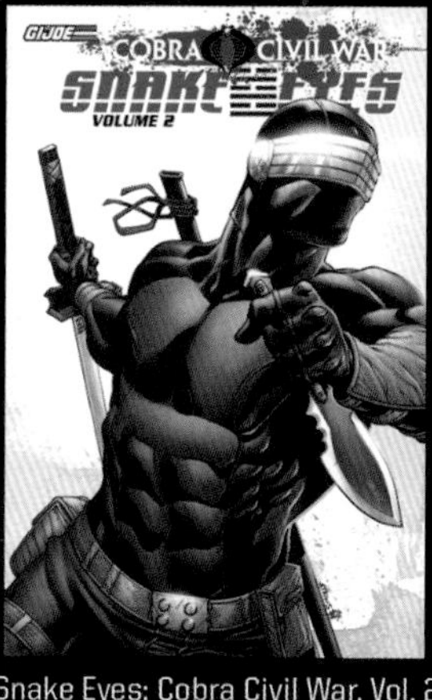
G.I. JOE
COBRA CIVIL WAR
VOLUME 2

Snake Eyes: Cobra Civil War, Vol. 2
ISBN: 978-1-61377-159-4

NOW AVAILABLE

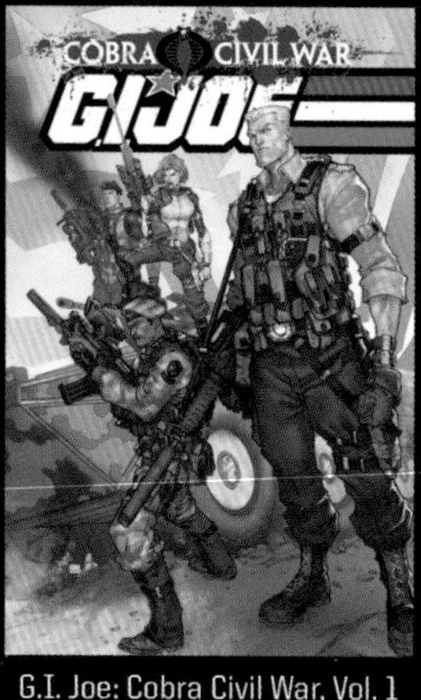
COBRA CIVIL WAR

G.I. Joe: Cobra Civil War, Vol. 1
ISBN: 978-1-61377-023-8

NOW AVAILABLE

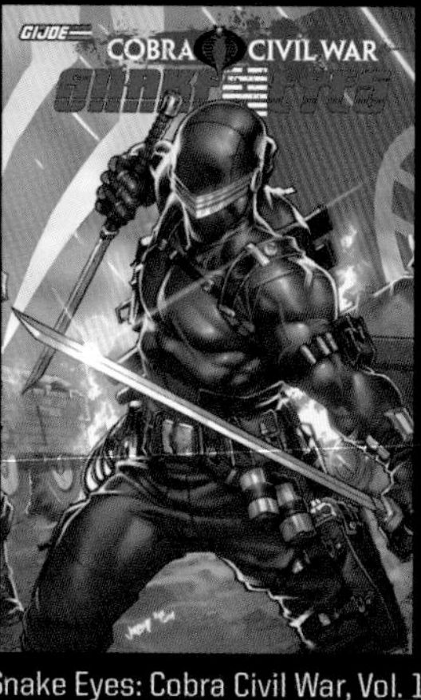
G.I. JOE
COBRA CIVIL WAR

Snake Eyes: Cobra Civil War, Vol. 1
ISBN: 978-1-61377-032-0

NOW AVAILABLE

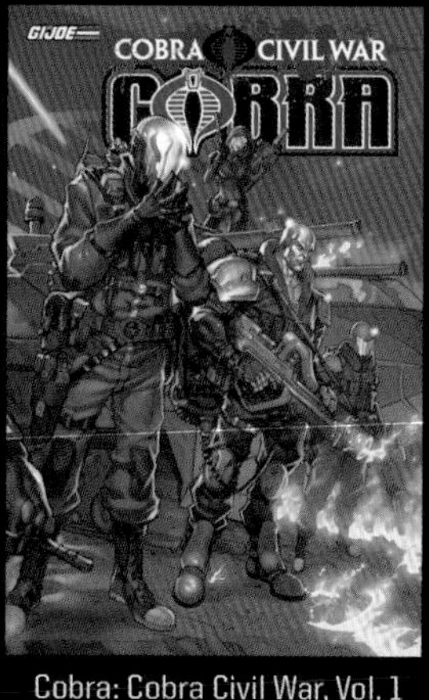
G.I. JOE
COBRA CIVIL WAR
COBRA

Cobra: Cobra Civil War, Vol. 1
ISBN: 978-1-61377-036-8